D0840271

Belief and Truth

Belief and Truth

A Skeptic Reading of Plato

Katja Maria Vogt

Bryan゙ ゙ ゙ ゙ ゙゙ *゙゙*゙゙n
College .
Virginia Beac゙.

OXFORD
UNIVERSITY PRESS

OXFORD
UNIVERSITY PRESS

Oxford University Press is a department of the University of Oxford.
It furthers the University's objective of excellence in research, scholarship,
and education by publishing worldwide.

Oxford   New York
Auckland   Cape Town   Dar es Salaam   Hong Kong   Karachi
Kuala Lumpur   Madrid   Melbourne   Mexico City   Nairobi
New Delhi   Shanghai   Taipei   Toronto

With offices in
Argentina   Austria   Brazil   Chile   Czech Republic   France   Greece
Guatemala   Hungary   Italy   Japan   Poland   Portugal   Singapore
South Korea   Switzerland   Thailand   Turkey   Ukraine   Vietnam

Oxford is a registered trade mark of Oxford University Press
in the UK and certain other countries.

Published in the United States of America by
Oxford University Press
198 Madison Avenue, New York, NY 10016

© Katja Maria Vogt 2012

Drawing Copyright © 2012 by Jens Haas

First issued as an Oxford University Press paperback, 2015.

All rights reserved. No part of this publication may be reproduced, stored in a
retrieval system, or transmitted, in any form or by any means, without the prior
permission in writing of Oxford University Press, or as expressly permitted by law,
by license, or under terms agreed with the appropriate reproduction rights organization.
Inquiries concerning reproduction outside the scope of the above should be sent to the Rights
Department, Oxford University Press, at the address above.

You must not circulate this work in any other form
and you must impose this same condition on any acquirer.

Library of Congress Cataloging-in-Publication Data
Vogt, Katja Maria, 1968–
Belief and Truth : A Skeptic Reading of Plato / Katja Maria Vogt.
p.   cm.
Includes bibliographical references and index.
ISBN 978-0-19-991681-8 (hardcover); ISBN 978-0-19-027719-2 (paperback)
1. Plato.   2. Knowledge, Theory of.   3. Skepticism.
4. Belief.   5. Truth.   6. Ignorance.   7. Investigation.   8. Relativism.   I. Title.
B395.V637 2012
121'.6—dc23   2012004040

Contents

Acknowledgments

In my 1998 book on skepticism, *Skepsis und Lebenspraxis*, I argued that Pyrrhonian skeptics do not have beliefs, can make use of nonassertoric language to express themselves, and can defend their philosophy against the charge that they are unable to live and act. These arguments were based on the premise that beliefs as they figure in ancient skepticism are attitudes of accepting some content as true. On this premise, lingering thoughts, impressions, assumptions, and suppositions, for example, do not count as beliefs. Over the years, I became less interested in the question of whether the skeptic *has* beliefs, and more interested in the question of what beliefs actually are. More specifically, I became interested in spelling out how one can think of beliefs as deficient attitudes, as the Socratic and skeptic traditions in ancient philosophy have it, and how such a notion of belief informs ancient skepticism.

I have long been in conversation about these matters with Jens Haas. Jens, trained as a criminal appeals lawyer and in legal and political philosophy, disputed some of my intuitions. In response to my drafts, he came up with examples and distinctions that often led me back to the drawing board. As he saw it—in agreement with quite a few trends in contemporary epistemology—a philosophical notion of belief should accommodate the fact that beliefs are held with different degrees of confidence or commitment, and it should recognize that we might find ourselves with any number of beliefs that we did not actively 'form.' Moreover, we may not care enough to treat every question as equally important. With respect to quite a few things, we may live happily with beliefs that, if they were challenged, we might revise without much turmoil. Indeed, we may not be able to explore all our beliefs even if we wanted to, given how many things figure in our thoughts and lives. The norms of belief-formation might then vary, depending on the attitudes of different cognizers with respect to different domains. Jens's resilience in objecting to some of the ancient intuitions prompted me to refine many of my views and to formulate more precisely what I saw as the strongest arguments of ancient philosophers in the tradition of Socratic epistemology. It also led me to think through a far wider range of contemporary literature than I otherwise would have.

As a result, the shape and ambition of the book was rather altered, to the extent that it is a different book than I would have otherwise written. But the main claims are long-standing preoccupations of mine and the interpretive work is far removed from Jens's interests. Thus I have to take responsibility for the views that are argued for, and in place of finding an adequate term for Jens's role, I shall have to be content to say that his contributions to this book are invaluable. Jens also wrote the first draft of a translation of Vogt (2006). As in other cases, he got stuck on the first page, sending me a number of questions, and initiating a process that led to what is now chapter 6, "Skepticism and Concepts." His drawing of an empty swimming pool in the sun, on the cover and in the concluding remarks, completes this book.

* * *

I presented work relevant to this book at a number of places, and am indebted to the organizers and audiences at Humboldt University Berlin (2004 and 2010), City University of New York (2005 and 2012), Münster (2005), New York University (2007), Princeton (2007), Notre Dame (2010), and the University of Chicago (2010 and 2012). James Allen, Elizabeth Asmis, Rachel Barney, Jonathan Beere, Richard Bett, Charles Brittain, Agnes Callard, John Cooper, Matt Evans, Verity Harte, Jeff Helzner, Joseph Karbowski, Sean Kelsey, Isaac Levi, Alex Long, Wolfgang Mann, Benjamin Morison, Jessica Moss, Calvin Normore, Gretchen Reydams-Schils, Baron Reed, Gabriel Richardson Lear, Ricardo Salles, and John Wynne were among those whose comments helped me think about my arguments or who took time to discuss some of my ideas with me. I was intrigued by conversations with Juan Comesaña, Jim Pryor, Stephen Schiffer, and Ralph Wedgwood at a conference on skepticism at La Pietra/Florence in the summer of 2008. It was partly in light of these conversations that I decided to write this book.

John Cooper, Jim Pryor, and Carol Rovane read my entry "Ancient Skepticism" for the *Stanford Encyclopedia of Philosophy* and gave generous

and helpful feedback. Though this entry was a separate project, it constituted a significant step in thinking through the issues. James Warren read
my entry on "Academic Scepticism" for a volume he is editing with Frisbee Sheffield—again, not included here, but relevant to my thoughts
about the larger picture. I also want to thank the editors and reviewers of
the journals and collections where some of the chapters appeared, partly
in substantially different earlier versions: Dimitri El Murr, Diego Machuca, Christof Rapp, and Tim Wagner. I am grateful to the publishers
for permission to include these papers, or modified versions of them.
"Belief and Investigation in the *Republic*" appeared in *Plato, The Electronic
Journal of the Plato Society*, 9 (2009), 1–24; "The Aims of Skeptical
Investigation" appeared in D. Machuca (ed.), *Pyrrhonism in Ancient,
Modern, and Contemporary Philosophy* (Dordrecht: Springer, 2011),
33–50; in both cases, some editorial changes were made for inclusion into
this book. A German ancestor of "Skepticism and Concepts: Can the
Skeptic Think?" appeared as "Skeptische Suche und das Verstehen von
Begriffen," *Wissen und Bildung in der antiken Philosophie*, Christof Rapp
and Tim Wagner (eds.) (Stuttgart: J.B. Metzler, 2006), 325–339. I also
want to thank the anonymous referee of my paper "Appearances and
Assent," *Classical Quarterly* 62.2 (December 2012)—a paper that I decided not to include in the book, but that relates in important ways to
some of its concerns.

Columbia University has been most supportive of my work during the
past years. I wrote part of the manuscript during a research leave in the
spring of 2010, spent partly in Paris with the help of the Columbia-Alli-
ance program. In the spring of 2009 and in the fall of 2011, I taught semi-
nars on Ancient Epistemology. I am grateful to the students and visiting
scholars in these classes for giving me the chance to try out many of my
arguments. Avery Archer, Andreas Avgousti, Mark Berger, Robbie Kubala,
Gavin McGown, Christiana Olfert, Ariadna Pop, Nandi Theunissen, and
Justin Vlasits read parts of the manuscript and provided comments that
helped me advance the book.

Peter Ohlin, editor at Oxford University Press, has shown interest in
this project from its early stages. I could not be more grateful for the role
he played throughout. The anonymous referees provided many insightful
suggestions and much valued encouragement from the perspectives of
both ancient and contemporary philosophy. Their notes and comments
were more helpful than I could have hoped.

Belief and Truth

Introduction

The kind of skepticism that interests me in this book is not the skepticism that asks whether or not I know that *this is my hand*, or that *you are not a zombie*. Instead, it is part of an approach to epistemology that thinks of questions about knowledge, belief, and truth as being immediately tied to normative and evaluative questions. Much of the inspiration for this kind of skepticism derives from Socrates, or rather the Socrates of Plato's dialogues. In a famous line of the *Apology*, Socrates says that the unexamined life is not worth living for a human being (38a5–6). Ancient skepticism inherits this spirit. It is centrally about stepping back from belief-formation and counteracting one's tendencies to be quick to judge. Closely related, it is concerned with the ways in which one can fail to understand one's own thoughts, and fail to examine thoughts because one likes or dislikes them, or because one prefers to hold a view as opposed to holding no view. These psychological phenomena are taken to differ importantly from processes of rationally guided belief-formation, in which a cognizer is inclined to accept a thought after careful consideration of whether it is true.

The plan for this book is to think through a range of theories that share intuitions relevant to this kind of normative epistemology. A short way to describe the project is thus to say that I am interested in the Socratic side of ancient epistemology. Somewhat more specifically, I shall discuss Plato's engagement with central Socratic ideas about an examined life, as well as versions of what I call Socratic epistemology, found in ancient skeptical philosophies and in Stoic epistemology.[1]

---

[1] A minimal historical orientation would begin with the initial successors of Plato (429–347 BCE), who focused on Platonic theories: Speusippus (347–339), Xenocrates (339–314), and Polemon (314–269). The founder of Stoicism, Zeno (334–262), studied and philosophized in the Academy for a long time, perhaps as early as under Xenocrates' leadership,

The Socratic side of Plato—and to some extent, even of Aristotle—has historically faced major obstacles.[2] With the onset of monotheistic pre-occupations, such things as essences, souls, contemplation, and so on, received much appreciation in the history of thought. Such things as hypothetical investigation, questions left open, and a mind-set that considers several explanations possible fared considerably worse. And yet this Socratic side of ancient epistemology is a rather robust movement. Some of it even survives in Augustine, though most of it was cast aside as soon as theological premises came to frame philosophical questions. More than that, the Socratic side of ancient epistemology is closely related to many of our concerns and questions today. Philosophers in the Socratic tradition focus on the nature of belief, the value of truth, and the role of concepts in thought, as well as the normative side of knowledge, belief, and ignorance. The ambition of this book, then, is to show that the theories discussed within the Socratic tradition contain sophisticated proposals on precisely these questions.[3]

---

but certainly during Polemon's time as head of the school. Arcesilaus (316/5–241/0) belonged to the next generation. All in all, the first 'doctrinal' phase, later an inspiration for many thinkers, extended over a period of roughly 80 years. After that, Hellenistic philosophy, that is, Socratically inspired philosophy, gained for a while the upper hand. Cf. John Dillon, *The Heirs of Plato: A Study of the Old Academy (347–274 BC)* (Oxford: Oxford University Press, 2003); Francesca Alesse, *La Stoa e la traditione Socratica* (Naples: Bibliopolis 2000). On the Socratic side of Academic skepticism, cf. John M. Cooper, "Arcesilaus: Socratic and Sceptic," in V. Karasmanis (ed.), *Year of Socrates 2001—Proceedings* (Athens: European Cultural Center of Delphi, 2004), 81–103. Reprinted in Cooper, *Knowledge, Nature, and the Good: Essays on Ancient Philosophy* (Princeton, N.J.: Princeton University Press, 2004).

[2]I am not aiming to reconstruct Socrates' philosophy. My approach to Socrates in this book is close to that found in Paul Vander Waerdt's seminal collection of papers, *The Socratic Movement* (Ithaca: Cornell University Press, 1994). Recent discussions by Hugh H. Benson, Thomas C. Brickhouse and Nicholas Smith, Gareth Matthew, and others, are less relevant to my interests. Cf. Benson, *Socratic Wisdom: The Model of Knowledge in Plato's Early Dialogues* (Oxford: Oxford University Press, 2000); Brickhouse and Smith, *Plato's Socrates* (Oxford: Oxford University Press, 1994); Matthew, *Socratic Perplexity and the Nature of Philosophy* (Oxford: Oxford University Press, 1999); Donald Morrison (ed.), *The Cambridge Companion to Socrates* (Cambridge: Cambridge University Press, 2011), including H. Benson's paper "Socratic Method" in that volume (179–200).

[3]After many centuries of interpretation and adaptation of Plato, it would be naive to think that one can do justice to all arguments that have been raised from different sides. I am self-consciously doing what I assume many in the Academy and elsewhere did—they 'did philosophy *with* Plato': that is, I take it, they considered Plato's dialogues extremely helpful

Socratic commitment to investigation is well recognized as a feature of certain Platonic dialogues.[4] And yet many think of Plato as the proponent of a set of doctrines. Plato presumably put forward the Theory of Recollection and the Theory of Forms, as well as ideas about body and soul that associate the body with perception and hold it in low esteem, while associating the soul with knowledge, Forms, and other lofty affairs. This conception of 'what Plato said' is partly already present in Aristotle, who sometimes writes as if Plato formulated one precise version of, say, the Theory of Recollection.[5] Moreover, it is greatly promoted through Neoplatonism, which develops intuitions relevant to the presumed Platonic doctrines. Early modern and modern thinkers who engage with Plato often fail to distinguish between Plato, the ancient Greek philosopher, and the ideas that the tradition considers 'Platonic.'

A Socratically inspired reader will be inclined to push back. She will argue that, though the dialogues differ in many important and interesting ways from each other, and though Plato formulates a number of theories for his and the reader's consideration, he remains committed to ongoing

---

starting points for thinking about philosophical questions that interested them; in the course of doing so, they came up with views about what Plato said, could have said, how his arguments could be developed further, and so on. Christopher Rowe, who sides with a more doctrinal reading than I do, writes in a helpful sketch of different approaches to Plato: "his chief or ultimate aim was to encourage us to do philosophy, and think things out for ourselves rather than supposing that we can get what we need from others, or from books. The latter is the view most congenial to the skeptics' natural modern successors, interpreters brought up in the analytical tradition." Without claiming that this is the only philosophically interesting way to engage with Plato, I am largely adopting this perspective. Rowe, "Interpreting Plato," in Hugh Benson, *A Companion to Plato* (Malden: Blackwell, 2006), 13–24.

[4]The Sophists also stand for an attitude of calling into question people's views relevant to the leading of their lives, and Socrates arguably shares a number of characteristics and preoccupations with the Sophists. On the Sophists, cf. Rachel Barney, "The Sophistic Movement," in Marie Louise Gill and Pierre Pellegrin (eds.), *A Companion to Ancient Philosophy* (Malden: Blackwell, 2006), 77–100, 79; and Richard Bett, "Is There a Sophistic Ethics?" *Ancient Philosophy* 22 (2002): 235–62. Insofar as Socrates is accused of being a Sophist, he probably is guilty as charged. For a related argument about the charge that Socrates moves away from traditional religion, cf. Myles Burnyeat, "The Impiety of Socrates," *Ancient Philosophy* 17 (1997): 1–12.

[5]As I see it, even Aristotle looks different if read with the skeptical tradition in mind. Aristotle's references to learning as recollection might appear to be ascriptions of doctrine to Plato. Read through the Socratic-skeptical lens, however, Aristotle might be doing something slightly different, namely invoking and to some extent 'sharpening' theories formulated by predecessors, thereby setting out a range of theoretical options for his consideration.

investigation.[6] Plato's dialogues are not treatises in disguise.[7] It is far more compelling to assume that Plato has philosophical reasons for writing dialogues, reasons that relate to Socratic caution: one should not claim or imply that one has knowledge if in fact one does not.[8] In some of the early dialogues, confident and sometimes quite conceited interlocutors are shown to lack the expertise they claim to have. In observing their failure, one should not assume that they are on display for the amusement of readers safe from such embarrassment. Arguably, it would be pointless to write these dialogues if one thought that only others would fail in the relevant ways, while oneself was obviously in a different situation. Instead, if one takes seriously how difficult the questions under discussion are, and how deeply the views one is likely to have on them are interwoven with one's upbringing, culture, and way of life, it should be clear that anyone might fail.[9] Socratic caution involves a deliberate attempt to come up with counterarguments to views one might otherwise be inclined to hold.[10]

Notably, not setting oneself up as an expert is entirely compatible with having certain ideas about the way things could be explained; with viewing certain proposals as worthy of repeated investigation; with thinking that one has formulated a theory that is likely to get some central points right; or with assuming that one has thought carefully through some proposals and found them to be lacking. As a result, the impression naturally

---

[6]Cf. Michael Frede, who argues that, even in a dialogue like the *Sophist*, the form of the dialogue captures a distinctively Socratic intuition—the idea that to hold forth on something presupposes a privileged position of authority. "The only person entitled to do this is one who has sorted things out in such a way that there is no confusion whatever connected in any way whatever with the question at issue." Frede takes it that Plato does not think of himself as inhabiting such a position. Accordingly, even his more positive dialogues retain the spirit of not setting oneself up as 'the one who knows.' "The Literary Form of the *Sophist*," in Christopher Gill and Mary Margaret McCabe (eds.), *Form and Argument in Late Plato* (Oxford: Oxford University Press, 1996), 135–52, 140.

[7]I am borrowing the phrase "treatises in disguise" from Michael Frede, who makes a similar point in "Plato's Arguments and the Dialogue Form," *Oxford Studies in Ancient Philosophy* sup. vol. (1992): 201–19, 219.

[8]On the range of ways in which Plato uses the form of the dialogue, cf. Mary Margaret McCabe, "Form and the Platonic Dialogues," in Benson, *A Companion to Plato*, 39–54.

[9]This is a point Frede makes in "Plato's Arguments," 214–17. Cf. Myles Burnyeat, "Socratic Midwifery, Platonic Inspiration," *Bulletin of the Institute of Classical Studies* 24 (1977): 7–16, 9, on the way in which Socrates often appeals to people's commitments and values.

[10]Cf. Alex Long, *Conversation and Self-Sufficiency in Plato* (Oxford: Oxford University Press, forthcoming) on related issues.

arises that Plato, say, is rather strongly inclined to think that there are Forms—perhaps even that he would not give up on this view though he might be aware of major difficulties in spelling it out. And yet, another impression arises too, namely that Plato is acutely aware of such difficulties, difficulties that, though at times bracketed off, might motivate extended discussions in another dialogue.[11] That is, even where Plato appears most dogmatic—say, talking about the Forms—he is not laying out a theory.[12] In writing dialogues that return to a set of interrelated questions he keeps tackling questions left open, or questions that arise when a certain topic is looked at from another angle.

Plato thus has much to offer for later philosophers with skeptical inclinations.[13] It is likely that those leading figures in the Academy who became the first skeptics and those who formulated Stoic philosophy

[11]To take one example: in *Republic* V, a book that is considered part of the more 'doctrinal' middle period, Plato says that ignorance is concerned with 'what is not' (477a10–b1). This claim remains unaccounted for. As I see it, this doesn't mean that Plato is unaware of its difficulty; rather, he is bracketing it for the time being, as something that deserves separate discussion. Much of the *Sophist* is concerned with asking, "What is not-being?" and with the relationship of not-being and false belief. Such features of the dialogues suggest that, even where Plato appears most doctrinal, he is aware of questions left open.

[12]Plato might be most dogmatic in his theology, including topics that relate to theology. He argues with much fervor against the multitude of morally unconcerned Greek divinities and for the theological claim that God is good. It is easy for us to find Euthyphro, enthusiast for traditional religion, a pompous person with confused views. And yet, as Burnyeat, "The Impiety of Socrates," points out, it is Plato's commitment to a different theology—a theology where divinity is good and single-minded—that motivates some of the moves *he* is often criticized for, such as censorship of poetry in the *Republic*, or the *Laws*' view that those who cannot be cured from impiety, violating 'our' piety, are to suffer the death penalty (10.909a).

[13]Julia Annas argues that, to "show that Plato is a skeptic one would have to show that he never puts forward doctrines," which she takes to be an "implausible position." "Plato the Skeptic," in Paul A. Vander Waerdt (ed.), *The Socratic Movement* (Ithaca: Cornell University Press, 1994), 309–40, 334. Against Annas, and as explained above, I take this to be quite conceivable. Annas also interprets her question—"is Plato a skeptic?"—as the question of whether Arcesilaus puts forward a reading of Plato that can convince us today. However, it is unlikely that anyone today will recognize the philosophy of any philosopher in the Platonic tradition as, entirely, *her* take on Plato. By finding doctrines in Plato, I assume that Annas does not take herself to be committed to endorse the philosophy of any particular 'doctrinal Platonist' from antiquity. At an earlier point in her paper, Annas applies a range of criteria when asking whether Plato might be read as a skeptic, criteria such as whether Socrates always argues ad hominem; whether Plato always argues for two sides of an issue; and so on. It is a widely accepted method today to read the dialogues individually and find different arguments, methods, etc., in them. Accordingly, any such criterion is bound to produce a negative answer.

read Plato with a focus on these ideas.[14] Notably, the Stoics firmly belong in the group of the skeptically inclined.[15] One need not end up embracing skepticism in order to appreciate the force of skeptical concerns, and the Stoics' emphasis on epistemic caution is second to none. They think a state of mind is attainable in which one would indeed only assent as and when one should. But this state of mind is rather hard to achieve.

As far as we know, early skeptics and Stoics thought their way through a given Platonic dialogue or sections thereof in order to see whether a given theoretical route might work, or whether one would have to modify it to make sense of a given intuition.[16] Perhaps they did pretty much what we do today, when, say, in a seminar on the *Theaetetus*, we ask such questions as "What is compelling about the Cold Wind Example?" As a group of interlocutors, these philosophers took different perspectives. Some of them pushed the open-mindedness in Plato further, cultivating methods of argument that keep one from assenting to any given claim.[17] These are the Academic skeptics. Others thought it important to insist that knowledge, though hard to achieve, is possible. In conversation with the skeptics, these philosophers—the early

---

[14]This is compatible with the Stoics taking Plato to 'stand for' particular theories, such as the Theory of Forms. For an influential account of how the Stoics might have engaged with what they saw as Socratic ethical views in Plato's dialogues, cf. Gisela Striker, "Plato's Socrates and the Stoics," in Paul Vander Waerdt (ed.), *The Socratic Movement* (Ithaca: Cornell University Press, 1994), 241–71.

[15]Cf. Michael Frede, "The Sceptic's Two Kinds of Assent and the Question of the Possibility of Knowledge," in R. Rorty, J. B. Schneewind, and Q. Skinner (eds.), *Philosophy in History* (Cambridge: Cambridge University Press, 1982), 255–78; and his "Stoics and Sceptics on Clear and Distinct impressions," in Myles Burnyeat (ed.), *The Sceptical Tradition* (Berkeley: University of California Press, 1983), 65–94.

[16]As David Sedley argues, it is likely that these ancient thinkers had favorite dialogues—ones they saw as expressing ideas about knowledge that they themselves considered central—and then read other dialogues from that point of view. "Three Ancient Interpretations of the *Theaetetus*," in Gill and McCabe, *Form and Argument*, 79–104, 86.

[17]In engaging with Plato and Plato's Socrates, ancient readers might have attempted a distinction between the historical Socrates and Plato's Socrates. In thinking in terms of "Plato's Socrates," one recognizes that, though the Socrates of some dialogues might be closer to the historical Socrates than the Socrates of other dialogues, the dialogues are at every point Plato's philosophical work. This point is made, for example, by Charles H. Kahn, *Plato and the Socratic Dialogue: The Philosophical Use of a Literary Form* (Cambridge: Cambridge University Press, 1996). Kahn aims to revive a version of the so-called unitarian reading of Plato, a view that I do not share, but that I shall not address.

Stoics—tried to formulate ever more sophisticated criteria, criteria that would make sure that a given truth-claim indeed qualified as knowledge. Yet another development leads toward the kind of skepticism that much of this book shall explore, Pyrrhonian skepticism. Aenesidemus left the Academy, aiming to formulate a version of skepticism that draws not only on Socratic commitment to investigation, but also on pre-Socratic discussions about appearances. The following chapters take their content and their method from the debates between these groups of philosophers. They are a series of attempts to think through, and then to rethink, a set of Socratic intuitions. The upshot is of a skeptical nature: I shall leave open which, if any, of the various approaches 'wins.'[18]

In other words, I shall discuss epistemological questions that are particularly salient for those ancient philosophers who devote themselves to ongoing investigation. What is their attitude toward belief? Do they take themselves to attain truths? How do they see the distinction between belief and knowledge? What kind of thought is involved in investigation? The central intuition is that the kind of truth-claim we ordinarily make is prone to be deficient: it is too quick, too strongly attached to what we would like to be the case, too much subject to a desire to be right, too changeable, and so on. This kind of truth-claim is called *doxa*.

Doxa, then, is a deficient cognitive attitude. This idea is to be found in Plato, but also in ancient skepticism and in Stoic epistemology, both of which pick up on the proposals in Plato that interest me here. Chapters 1, 2, and 3 engage immediately with the *Apology*, *Ion*, and *Philebus*, discussing Socratic views on ignorance; with the *Republic* on belief and investigation; and with the *Theaetetus* on the distinction between true and false beliefs. Chapter 4 stays with the *Theaetetus*, aiming to explain how skeptical responses to conflicting appearances improve upon metaphysical responses. Here and in the chapters that follow, I refer to Pyrrhonian skepticism when I speak of skepticism. Pyrrhonian skeptics pick up on long-standing discussions about appearances and reality. It is their skepticism—a skepticism that reflects on a range of epistemological and

---

[18]I do not mean to imply that there is a consistent Socrates character throughout the dialogues; on the contrary, the skeptical bent of my interpretation means that I do not imply that there is *one* Socratic epistemology. Instead, I am interested in epistemological discussions that develop, in different ways, some core Socratic intuitions.

metaphysical questions—that interests me.[19] Chapter 5 addresses the question whether Pyrrhonian investigation is genuine investigation, that is, whether it is adequately responsive to the value of truth. Chapter 6 discusses what I take to be the greatest threat to Pyrrhonian skepticism: the objection that without forming beliefs, the skeptic cannot even *think*. In siding with the skeptical project, I take it that I need a response on the skeptic's behalf to this potentially fatal objection. Chapter 7 returns to the question of whether beliefs are adequately characterized as true or false. The Stoics take the bleakest view of *doxa*: it is such a lowly state that it does not even merit evaluation as true. In my concluding remarks, I return to the starting point of this book, restating why the lines of thought that motivate skepticism—as conceived of by ancient thinkers— deserve to be taken seriously today.

Many of the ideas about belief that are the topic of this book are hidden and easily overlooked, because the Greek term for belief, *doxa*, is often translated as opinion. This translation, though tempting because it captures the derogative sense of *doxa*, is misleading. It suggests that there is a broader category, belief, of which opinions are a subclass. Other subclasses, presumably, would not share the deficiencies of mere opinion. But there is no such broader category.[20] In the range of theories I refer to as Socratic epistemology, there is no terminological noun for belief other than *doxa*. There are related attitudes such as hypotheses, suppositions, or assumptions: one asks what would follow if something were true; or one entertains the idea that it is true; and so on. These attitudes count as distinct from holding something to be true or from what I call truth-claims. *Doxa* is the technical term for 'belief,' understood—minimally— as holding to be true.[21] *Doxai* (the plural of *doxa*) are not in every way like beliefs in today's sense. Instead, they are truth-claims or acceptances of

---

[19]I am not discussing Academic skepticism separately, though many discussions throughout the book touch on issues relevant to Academic skepticism. This choice reflects my assessment that the questions crucial to my project—how a skeptic can think and investigate and how questions about belief relate to questions about appearances—are more explicitly the subject of Pyrrhonian philosophy.

[20]As will be discussed in chapter 7, there is one passage where the Stoics use *hupolēpsis* (assumption, supposition) to cover the domain of all truth-claims. However, *hupolēpsis* is not a technical term in their epistemology or any other Socratically inspired epistemology. Aristotle has a specific use for the term, but to discuss this would go beyond the topic of this book.

[21]In the simile of the Line in *Republic* VI, Plato refers to subclasses of *doxa* as *pistis* and *eikasia*; both are kinds of *doxa* and share the general characteristics of *doxa*.

content that fall short of knowledge.[22] In forming a belief, one makes a truth-claim, and this might be taken to imply that one considers oneself entitled to say 'how things are.' But one only has a belief, and it is shameful, as Socrates puts this in the *Theaetetus*, to speak as if one knew something when in fact one does not (196d).[23]

This shortcoming—that *doxai* fall short of knowledge and at the same time are truth-claims—is the most general reason for the derogative sense of the notion. It marks a difference between Socratic and contemporary ideas about belief. According to the former, belief and knowledge are two *kinds* of attitudes that involve a truth-claim. The truth-claim of belief, however, is inferior and in various ways (depending on the particular theory under consideration) different from the truth-claim of knowledge. The attitude of knowledge thus does not involve the attitude of belief, or rather, it does not involve belief in the sense in which today it is standardly assumed that a cognizer who knows that p also believes that p. The relevant ideas are not wholly foreign to contemporary epistemology. And yet even epistemologists who explore the idea that one should only assert something if one knows it tend to phrase this as the norm that one should not *believe without knowing*.[24] That is, they assume that knowing involves holding a belief. Contrary to this assumption, Socratic epistemology explores the idea that, in coming to know something, knowledge that p *transforms* and *replaces* belief that p.

For the remainder of this introduction, I shall sketch some of the relevant intuitions about *doxa*, in the hopes of making comprehensible the proposal that *doxa* is inherently deficient. To this end, it is helpful to recall the closeness of the Greek *doxa* with notions of seeming, appearance, and reputation. The verb *dokein* means 'to appear,' and *doxa* thus

---

[22]The idea that knowledge is better than true belief is not absent from contemporary discussions. For critical discussion, cf. Ernest Sosa, "Value Matters in Epistemology," *Journal of Philosophy* 107.4 (2010): 167–90. However, the idea that knowledge is better than true belief is different from the idea that beliefs are inherently deficient.

[23]Timothy Williamson's knowledge rule for assertion, namely that one should assert that p only if one knows that p, captures a similar intuition (*Knowledge and Its Limits* [Oxford: Oxford University Press, 2000], chapter 11).

[24]Timothy Williamson writes about the relevant ideas: "It is plausible, nevertheless, that occurrently believing p stands to asserting p as the inner stands to the outer. If so, the knowledge rule for assertion corresponds to the norm that one should believe p only if one knows p. Given that norm, it is not reasonable to believe p when one knows that one does not know p." *Knowledge and Its Limits*, 255–56.

often denotes something in the domain of appearances. *Doxa* can refer to appearances in a nonphilosophical sense: one's reputation among other people. For example, Socrates says in the *Euthyphro* that shame accompanies fearing the reputation—*doxa*—of badness (12b9–c1). Similarly, the well-known discussion in *Republic* I, on whether it is enough to *appear* just or whether one should *be* just, is phrased in terms of *doxa*. To have the *doxa* of justice is to have a reputation for justice. Later on in the *Republic*, *doxa* is discussed in epistemological and metaphysical terms: as a cognitive attitude that has its own kind of object.[25] If the *Republic* is read in Greek rather than translation, Book I is strikingly continuous with the metaphysics of the middle books: *doxa* is associated with the domain of appearance and perception, and contrasted with the domain of being.[26]

Consider the following range of formulations. Someone might say "*Dokei moi* that p": "It seems to me that p." In some cases (though perhaps not all cases), this cognizer might be said to have engaged in the cognitive activity that the verb *doxazein* picks out: to form a belief, make a judgment, or perhaps, to think of something in a certain way, with thinking envisaged as inner assertoric speech.[27] And now she might be said to have a *doxa*. Does this final formulation still carry the implication of seeming or mere appearance? The answer must be "It depends": the word is used differently in different contexts, and philosophers theorize

[25]As Sedley points out, the idea that *doxa* and *epistēmē* each has its own kind of objects is mentioned in as early a dialogue as the *Charmides* (168a3–9), where the object of knowledge is a *mathēma*, a field of learning or a discipline. D. Sedley, *The Midwife of Platonism: Text and Subtext in Plato's Theaetetus* (Oxford: Oxford University Press, 2004), 178.

[26]This metaphysical dimension of *doxa*'s inferiority does not survive in Hellenistic epistemology. Skeptics and Stoics do not adopt it—the skeptics, because they do not adopt any theories, and the Stoics, because they basically disagree with Platonic metaphysics. Where Plato thinks that *doxa* is inferior insofar as it deals with the world of becoming, the Stoics consider *doxa* as a state that, itself, is in change: the person with mere *doxa* is the person who is likely to change her mind.

[27]This is a conception of thought famously developed in Plato's *Theaetetus* 189e–190a and of great influence in ancient epistemology. Thinking is "speech which the mind itself goes through with itself about whatever it's considering. [...] when the mind is thinking, it's simply carrying on a discussion, asking itself questions and answering them, and making assertions and denials. And when it has come to a decision, either slowly or in a sudden rush, and it's no longer divided, but says one single thing, we call this its *doxa*. So what I call *doxazein* is speaking (*legein*) and what I call *doxa* is speech (*logos*); but speech spoken, not aloud to someone else, but silently to oneself." Tr. McDowell/Levett with changes.

doxa in different ways. For current purposes it is important that, notwithstanding these differences, the ancient philosophers have the connotations of seeming-ness and appearance in mind, even if only in the back of their minds, when they discuss *doxa*.[28]

Indeed, *doxa* can be seen in such a negative light that it clearly falls into the domain of ignorance. In some sense, today's philosophers might share the intuition that, where one does not have knowledge, one is ignorant. The early Greek association of *doxa* and ignorance runs deeper. For example, in Parmenides' poem there are but two spheres: the sphere of knowledge on the one hand, and the sphere of belief-or-ignorance on the other. Indeed, in early Platonic dialogues it appears that there are only these two conditions: knowledge or ignorance.[29] The badness of *doxa* is thus, at least in some ways and in some contexts, the badness of ignorance.

In the *Meno*, and more explicitly in the *Republic*, Plato begins to work with a tripartite distinction between ignorance, *doxa*, and knowledge. Though it is still true that some of *doxa*'s deficiency lies in the fact that it falls short of knowledge, more needs to be said. In particular, *doxa* needs to be looked at more closely because, if one wants to achieve knowledge, one must start somewhere. And where else to start than from ideas one already has? If one were to endorse one's ideas as truth-claims, one would hold *doxai*. If, on the other hand, one were to hypothesize them, one could use them in investigation without tainting one's state of mind with an inferior kind of cognitive attitude. Before one begins to investigate, however, one is likely to hold beliefs. Acquisition of knowledge, then,

---

[28]When I speak of 'ancient philosophers' here, I mean to include the majority of philosophers between, say, Parmenides, and the Stoics. The history of skepticism is rather disjoint: Sextus Empiricus, an important figure, writes much later than his predecessors (second century CE), and we know little about his context. I'm including him, but as an outlier; he responds to arguments (and includes or adapts arguments) that are largely formulated in the Hellenistic era and prior to it. Aristotle is a special and complicated case; his views on *doxa* are not the subject of my investigation.

[29]I am not here addressing long-standing issues about the notions of knowledge, expertise, and wisdom in early Socratic dialogues. Cf. Benson, *Socratic Wisdom*. I share some of Benson's main ideas, in particular the view that Socrates is not to be viewed as exclusively concerned with "ethics." What we today call normative epistemology is crucial for the way in which Socrates thinks about questions of how to lead a good life; this leads quickly to issues about investigation, method, and so on. Unlike Benson, however, I am not going to base any of my argument on Aristotle's depiction of Socrates; as I see it, this involves a host of difficulties, many of them relating to the interpretation of Aristotle's writings.

would seem to involve moving from having beliefs—states to be gotten rid of—to having knowledge.

In order to see more clearly the idea that knowledge *replaces* belief, recall a well-known passage from the *Meno*. Socrates teaches a young slave, who had no previous training, some geometry; eventually the boy arrives at the right answer to a geometrical problem. As Socrates puts it, the slave boy now formulated a correct belief. For the belief to become a piece of knowledge, he would have to repeat this and similar exercises. Eventually, the belief would settle down in his mind. It would become a piece of knowledge. That is, contrary to the long-standing idea that something must be *added* to true belief for it to become knowledge—say, a justification—this line of thought suggests that, once the true belief has become stable (which might involve that the relevant reasoning is in place), a piece of knowledge *replaces* what was earlier a true belief.[30] This stable attitude, so the proposal goes, is genuinely different. That is, it is not the case that an attitude gets changed in one of its properties, becoming stable. Instead, through stabilization a new attitude—knowledge—is generated.

The passage in the *Meno* is short, and its interpretation is controversial. For present purposes, it suffices that the passage can be interpreted in this fashion. It is possible to read the text as suggesting that the formerly held belief comes to be *replaced* by a piece of knowledge. This idea is central to the tradition of Socratic epistemology: belief is an inherently deficient attitude. In moving from belief to knowledge, one does not add something to an attitude that one otherwise keeps in place—rather, one comes to have a different attitude altogether.

The traditional, Neoplatonically inspired, story about Plato focuses elsewhere in the *Meno*. Plato, it is argued, holds the Theory of Recollection. Investigation and learning are possible, it is said, because knowledge is latently present in the soul. The soul 'saw all things' prior to its birth in

---

[30]Cf. David Sedley, who argues that the *Meno* does not compel us to consider knowledge a species of *doxa*: *doxa* 'becoming' *epistēmē* could mean 'being replaced by'—a child becomes an adult, but an adult is not a species of a child. Sedley points out, in my view rightly, that the cave image of the *Republic* describes just this kind of progression from *doxa* to *epistēmē* ("Three Ancient Interpretations," 93). For objections to this line of argument, cf. Gail Fine, "Knowledge and True Belief in the *Meno*," *Oxford Studies in Ancient Philosophy* 27 (2004): 41–81. Few commentators pursue the idea that belief is weak and knowledge firm. For brief discussion, cf. Gail Fine, "Nozick's Socrates," *Phronesis* (1996): 233–44.

a human body. The slave boy can formulate the correct answer because knowledge is already present in his soul. Learning is recollecting: it can be hard to access latent knowledge, because it is buried under false conceptions, which first need to be cleared away. This is a forceful story, and it merits being retold.[31] Notably, however—and this is what any skeptical or Stoic reader would emphasize—it is not presented as a theory, supported by arguments. It is something priests and priestesses say. Presumably, if people who are close to divinity put forward an idea, we should take it seriously. But it is one thing to take it seriously and another thing for it to be literally true.[32] Reference to the views of priests is a cousin of the use of similes in philosophical investigation: a certain view can be considered, and yet it is not claimed that it can be accounted for and presented as knowledge.

In the *Meno*, three solutions to the puzzle of how investigation is possible are on offer. First, recollection: it is possible to investigate a matter because we know and do not know it at the same time when we begin to investigate; we know it latently, but not overtly (81a–d). Second comes a distinctively Socratic idea, namely that, even though we do not know whether recollection is true, we should continue to investigate, because otherwise we would become lazy people (81d–e). Third, and after the geometry example (81e–85b), comes the proposal that we need a distinction between true belief and knowledge. It is possible to investigate because the dichotomy of either knowing or not knowing something, which was a premise of the Meno Problem, is compatible with a tripartite distinction between ignorance, belief, and knowledge. It is possible to have beliefs about things that one does not know.

In fairness to those interpreters who focus on Recollection rather than this last move, it must be admitted that the threefold distinction between ignorance, *doxa*, and knowledge is not explicitly argued for. Instead, *doxa* sneaks in via the route I sketched above—through formulations that employ

---

[31]I am not claiming here that some recent scholar sees precisely this line of thought in the *Meno*; instead, this is a sketch of the ideas that were historically influential.

[32]David Sedley and Alex Long divide the text up such that only 81a–c is attributed to priests and priestesses, and 81c–e appears as "epistemological doctrine" put forward in Socrates' own voice. Plato, *Meno and Phaedo*, ed. and trans. Sedley and Long (Cambridge: Cambridge University Press, 2011), xvii. From the perspective of the skeptic reading I put forward, there is no such transition; 81c–e continues to talk about Hades, the soul, and so forth. Indeed, Sedley and Long admit that "the only conclusion Socrates will absolutely insist on" is that one should seek, because to give up based on the Meno Problem is to be lazy.

the verb *dokein*. In a famous line, Socrates formulates a principle for question and answer: say what you think. You, Socrates says to the slave boy, should respond by saying what seems to you (*soi dokoun*) (83d4). He goes on to tell Meno that he will only want to hear the boy's *doxai* (84d3) and eventually states that the boy formulated no *doxa* that was not his own (85b12). The *doxai* he came up with were in him (c4). The person who is ignorant still has correct *doxai* (c6–7). For current purposes, we can break off here. The point has been made that, though someone is ignorant of something, she is not entirely ignorant in such a way as to have no views on the matter. And that was the initial assumption in the Meno Problem, that one either is ignorant in such a way as to have no starting point for thinking about something, or one already has knowledge. The problem, it turns out, was formulated in a misleading way. The ignorant person has something at her disposal that allows her to start thinking about things.

A deflationary reading of the *Meno* focuses on this: investigation is possible because we have beliefs about the things that we do not know. As unendorsed hypotheses, these attitudes are respectable starting points for investigation. This is how skeptics, who want to investigate without *doxai*, are likely to read the *Meno*.[33] Right after discussion of the Meno Problem, Socrates introduces a so-called hypothetical method. That is, he introduces something of enormous interest to skeptics: a method that steers clear of truth-claims and that nevertheless allows an investigator to engage with her thoughts and the thoughts of others.

And yet one may want to defend Recollection. Recollection aims to capture, apart from explaining how investigation is possible, the following phenomenon: a learner might, in a certain sense, already have available to herself the content that she is in the process of learning. As part of the deflationary reading, this phenomenon gets reexplained, without reference to an earlier life of the mind. As Hellenistic philosophers suggest, a reasoner has content available through the concepts that were acquired early on in *this* life. The having of these concepts, called preconceptions, actually *makes* her a reasoner.[34] Hellenistic readers of the *Meno* are likely

[33]This suggestion was first made by Gisela Striker, "Sceptical Strategies," in M. Schofield, M. Burnyeat, and J. Barnes (eds.), *Doubt and Dogmatism: Studies in Hellenistic Epistemology* (Oxford: Oxford University Press, 1980), 54–83. Reprinted in Striker, *Essays on Hellenistic Epistemology and Ethics* (Cambridge: Cambridge University Press, 1996) 92–115, 112.

[34]On the history of different readings of recollection, cf. Dominic Scott, *Recollection and Experience: Plato's Theory of Learning and its Successors* (Cambridge: Cambridge University Press, 1995).

to point out that Socrates first of all asks whether the slave boy knows Greek. As a knower of Greek, the slave boy has some kind of understanding of what Socrates says when he says, "Let's draw a square." In the terms of Hellenistic philosophers, he has a preconception—some preliminary notion of what squares are. Preconceptions may need to be made explicit in investigation, and they may need to be developed further. Still, there is a sense in which coming to understand something involves realizing that the answer fits the preconception one already had. A knowledge-belief distinction on the one hand, and the theory of preconceptions on the other, thus aim to address the questions that the *Meno* raises.

Doxa, so far, appears as a lowly cognitive attitude related to ignorance, mere appearance, and so forth. It can be utilized in investigation only by being turned into a different attitude: hypothesis. Otherwise it is such that the Socratically inspired thinker aims to stay away from it. This—though it is a mere sketch that would need much filling in—is a set of ideas that skeptically inclined Hellenistic philosophers engage with. Against them, one might argue that they neglect the difference between true and false beliefs. They evaluate all *doxa* as deficient. Doing so, do they not miss out on something important, namely that true belief is better than false belief? This idea is expressed in the *Symposium* (202a): "what is unreasoned" cannot count as knowledge, and "what hits the truth" cannot be ignorance. Hence, true belief might be its own category, situated between knowledge and ignorance.

One might push even further. Why should a true belief not count as the best kind of judgment, and thus as knowledge?[35] Part II of the *Theaetetus* explores precisely this proposal, that knowledge is true belief. Plato takes this proposal rather seriously, and rightly so. If truth is what we are after, then true belief should qualify as knowledge.[36] If, on the

---

[35]These questions are rarely discussed in Plato scholarship. An interesting exception is Robert Nozick, "Socratic Puzzles," *Phronesis* 40 (1995): 143–55. Nozick recognizes the problem and thinks through the following potential solution: someone who forms a true belief might not 'have' the truth, because beliefs lack stability. Beliefs do not 'stick.' The cognizer is likely to change her mind again. This is remarkably close to the Stoic proposal.

[36]I am grateful for discussion of this idea—and the reasons for taking it seriously—to Isaac Levi. For a proposal that explores the idea that knowledge is true belief (albeit, in terms rather different from Socratic epistemology), cf. Isaac Levi, "Knowledge as True Belief," in Eric J. Olsson and Sebastian Enqvist (eds.), *Belief Revision Meets Philosophy of Science* (Dordrecht: Springer, 2011), 269–302.

other hand, this proposal fails, and knowledge is not well explained as true belief, then it seems that truth is not all we seek. And this suggests that, perhaps, *doxai* are not to be divided into 'good' (namely true) *doxai* and 'bad' (namely false) ones.

Consider more generally the question of how *doxa* relates to the truth. According to standard theories in contemporary epistemology, belief-formation aims at the truth. As others have noted, this claim could mean several things.[37] Taken descriptively, it might mean that for a cognizer to believe something is for her to hold it to be true. In this interpretation, the claim provides something like a definition of the attitude we today call belief, or alternatively, the attitude we call judgment. Judgment, here, is a term for a truth-claim, or for the acceptance of something (content, an impression, a proposition, a thought, etc., depending on the specifics of a given theory) as true.[38] The term describes a mental act without thereby evaluating it in any way or characterizing it further in ways that would lend themselves to normative concerns.

Arguably, it is an achievement of Plato's *Theaetetus* to first discuss these matters. Every truth-claim has the same structure: some content is accepted as true. This applies no matter whether the resulting attitude is a piece of knowledge, or whether it has the lesser status of ignorance or belief. Insofar as the *Theaetetus* takes seriously the option that *doxa* might simply be judgment, rather than a deficient kind of truth-claim, it discusses ideas that are close to today's notion of belief.[39] This idea from the *Theaetetus* is an ancestor of the framework of Stoic philosophy of mind, according to which every cognitive activity involves acceptance of (rejection of, or suspension of judgment with respect to) a given im-

---

[37]Cf. Pascal Engel, "Truth and the Aim of Belief," in D. Gillies (ed.), *Laws and Models in Science* (London: King's College, 2005), 77–79. Cf. Bernard Williams "Deciding to Believe," in *Problems of the Self: Philosophical Papers, 1956–72* (Cambridge: Cambridge University Press, 1974), 136–51.

[38]Notably, 'acceptance as true' is here meant to be full acceptance; that is, the partial acceptance involved in, say, assumptions, does not fall into the same class. For a different notion of acceptance as true, cf. Nishi Shah and David Velleman, "Doxastic Deliberation," *Philosophical Review* 114 (2005): 497–534. Shah and Velleman refer to believing that p, assuming that p, and imagining that p as accepting that p.

[39]Levett, Burnyeat, and McDowell translate *doxa* in the *Theaetetus* as 'judgment,' thus capturing this point. *The Theaetetus of Plato*, revision of M. J. Levett's translation by Myles F. Burnyeat (Indianapolis: Hackett, 1990); *Theaetetus* trans. John McDowell (Oxford: Clarendon Press, 1973).

pression. The normative question of how these acceptances fare, and whether they qualify as knowledge, is considered a separate question, one that is turned to after the basic structure of cognitive operations has been described.

In Plato, the notion of belief-as-truth-claim competes with the Socratic intuition that beliefs are a particular kind of truth-claim, namely deficient truth-claims. This competing conception immediately includes a normative perspective. Arguably, it is the nature of belief that, when we form a belief, we aim to accept as true what really is true.[40] A cognizer might fail and accept something as true that is not true. Moreover, and this is a point of particular relevance for Socratic epistemology, cognizers can fail to properly *aim* at the truth in forming beliefs.[41] They might 'jump to conclusions,' or in some other way accept something as true without having considered it carefully. The proposal is not that cognizers can 'decide to believe' or 'believe at will.'[42] In a suggestive formulation, one could say that, though cognizers cannot believe at will, they often believe as they please. Not adhering as closely as they should to norms of belief-formation, they may accept as true a nasty story about someone they do not like, or a positive one about their friend, without pausing to consider whether their interlocutor is just repeating gossip.[43] In cases like these, cognizers fail to aim at the truth because they do not make enough of an effort to distinguish between what seems true and what they would like to be true.

According to this proposal, beliefs aim to represent the world as it is, even if 'believers' fail to aim at the truth.[44] This distinction is important.

[40]Cf. for example David Velleman, "On the Aim of Belief," in Velleman, *The Possibility of Practical Reason* (Oxford: Oxford University Press, 2000), 244–81.

[41]For an explicitly normative formulation of this idea, cf. Christopher Peacocke, *The Realm of Reason* (Oxford: Oxford University Press, 2006), 15: "A mental relation to a content *p* is the judgement that *p* only if the thinker aims to make this the case: that he stands in that relation to *p* only if it is the case that *p*."

[42]For some recent discussions of this issue, cf. Jeff Kasser and Nishi Shah, "The Metaethics of Belief: An Expressivist Reading of 'The Will to Believe,'" *Social Epistemology* 20.1 (2006): 1–17; Nishi Shah, "How Truth Governs Belief," *Philosophical Review* 112.4 (2003): 447–82; Shah and Velleman, "Doxastic Deliberation."

[43]Philosophers interested in friendship have recently started to explore these epistemological questions. They proceed on the above observation: we are rather strongly inclined to believe positive stories about our friends. Cf. Sarah Stroud, "Epistemic Partiality in Friendship," *Ethics* 116 (2006): 498–524.

[44]Accordingly, this kind of perspective disputes an idea that Williams formulates at the beginning of his discussion, that a cognizer who realizes that her belief is false gives up on

In recent discussions, the idea that beliefs aim at the truth has been ridiculed, as if it implied that we think of beliefs as little archers, aiming to hit a target.[45] With a view to how strange an idea this seems to be, it has been suggested that the dictum must be about cognizers, not about beliefs: cognizers aim, or should aim, at the truth in forming beliefs. This move is too quick. One can think of beliefs as having their own kind of directionality without imagining them as mini-agents. Beliefs, then, are the kind of attitude that aims to represent the world as it is. A cognizer might fail in aiming for the truth, accepting, for example, a view that feels good to her, and yet by thus forming a belief have an attitude that aims at the truth. One might say that precisely this is the problem: cognizers who fail to aim at the truth still end up with truth-claims.

Some of the interlocutors who populate early Socratic dialogues exemplify how far things can come apart. They make unmitigated truth-claims, and they fall awfully short of adhering to norms of belief-formation. Somewhat polemically, one might say that their beliefs represent things as they would like them to be. First of all, their beliefs represent them, the speakers, as smart and authoritative. Second, their beliefs represent other matters in ways that fit this self-image. Third, their belief-formation avoids intellectual work: they prefer to accept something as true if this acceptance does not call for the revision of other beliefs. Fourth, they are inclined to accept as true what in one way or another feels good. Fifth, they tend not to be aware of the fact that they might not be acquainted with relevant concepts, thus buying into ideas that they hardly comprehend. Sixth, they display a propensity for belief-formation as opposed to abstention from belief-formation.

Consider an example, the priest Euthyphro, Socrates' interlocutor in the dialogue *Euthyphro*. Euthyphro is presented as someone who sees himself (and is seen by the city) as an expert in matters of piety and justice. As a consequence, he is brazenly confident in his own legal judgment, though it concerns a complicated case—a case that could either be intentional murder or mere negligence (2a–5d). The thought

---

her belief ("Deciding to Believe," 137); often cognizers divert their attention, or do something else that makes it possible for them not to give up on views that are—perhaps just momentarily—recognized as false.

[45]Cf. Ralph Wedgwood, "The Aim of Belief," *Philosophical Perspectives* 16 (2002): 267–97.

that he might misjudge the facts does not cross his mind; instead, he compares himself to Zeus (6a). When Socrates calls his views into question, and he no longer knows how to defend them, he leaves (15d–e). Clearly, he is not going to revise any of his judgments in the light of arguments. In the course of the conversation, Euthyphro accepts a number of premises without having given them due consideration. In particular, he accepts ideas that sound good to him, for example, ideas that vaguely fit his notion that the gods are amazing and incomprehensible (6b–c). In a famous passage, Socrates asks Euthyphro whether everything that is pious has the same *idea* (5d, 6d–e) and is pious through the same *eidos* (6d), using the Greek terms that eventually become central to Plato's thought about the Forms.[46] Euthyphro quickly says yes. A more careful interlocutor would have said that she neither knows how to understand the locution 'through' in Socrates' proposal, nor what *idea* and *eidos*, both words with wide-ranging nontechnical uses, precisely mean here. Euthyphro is unaware of such issues, and he prefers to take a stance.[47]

Euthyphro is exemplary in displaying tendencies of the mind that Socrates battles against. A willingness to gloss over what one does not comprehend; an inclination to accept as true what one is in no position to judge; inflated confidence in one's judgment, nourished by self-aggrandizing claims; and a preference for ideas that feel lovely ("The gods are amazing!") as opposed to less pleasurable, but more realistic ideas ("I have no idea what the gods are"). In sum, the Socratic proposal is that it is not a fact about human faculties that in forming beliefs cognizers aim at representing the world as it is. Instead, they often aim at feel-good beliefs and at seeing themselves in a positive light.[48]

---

[46]Given the difficulties of establishing a precise relative chronology, as well as the difficulties of saying anything specific about the development of Plato's thought about Forms, it is best to abstain from precise claims about the role of this passage.

[47]At some point, however, even Euthyphro realizes that he does not understands what Socrates says (cf. 10a4).

[48]In the language of contemporary discussions, the behavior of Socrates' interlocutors could be described as 'data' that are to be explained, data that are relevantly similar to the findings of some recent empirical research. For example, studies about 'moral dumbfounding' look at the ways in which people who find themselves unable to support their moral views in the face of critical argument nevertheless hold on to their views. Cf. Jonathan Haidt, Fredrik Bjorklund, and Scott Murphy, "Moral Dumbfounding: When Intuitions Find No Reason" (August 10, 2000), available online (as of March 10, 2012): http://faculty.virginia.edu/haidtlab/articles/manuscripts/haidt.bjorklund.working-paper.when%20intuition%20finds%20no%20reason.pub603.doc.

Aiming at the truth, accordingly, is a hard task. It is difficult to comply with the fundamental norm of belief-formation, namely, to aim to form beliefs that represent the world as it is. Depending on how this norm is interpreted, adhering to it might imply that one holds back from forming beliefs pretty much all the time. Alternatively, adherence to this norm might imply that one takes seriously criteria of truth—criteria that are taken to indicate that a given thought indeed represents things as they are. One way or another, it is clear that, as compared to widespread habits of belief-formation, the Socratic perspective is likely to call for less judgment, slowed-down judgment, and more cautious judgment.

Against this Socratic perspective, one could argue that it is often better to form a belief as opposed to not forming a belief. This kind of objection can be raised from several perspectives.[49] For example, one might think that, in many situations, one is better off holding a belief, even if the risk that it might be false cannot be ruled out.[50] Moreover, certain situations might call on agents to take a stand, so that abstaining out of cautiousness involves a moral failure. Relatedly, one might think there can be virtue in holding on to an intuition, even if one cannot find proof. Presumably, this tension is made vivid in Plato's *Phaedo*, where it seems that Socrates is unwilling to give up on his view that the soul is immortal, even though it remains unclear whether any of the arguments to that effect is conclusive.[51] Similar points are raised within the ancient Socratic tradition, in particular, against the Pyrrhonian skeptics, who are perceived as arguing for extreme epistemic norms, favoring the avoidance of deficient

[49]The pragmatist tradition engages with similar issues. Peirce argues that doubt, understood as a state in which one neither believes a given proposition nor its negation, is unpleasant; it motivates investigation; belief generates relief. In a sense, Socratic epistemology agrees, though these phenomena receive a different evaluation. Being comfortable with less than (full) belief might be an acquired taste, but one that one *should* acquire. Peirce's diagnosis hangs partly on a presumed relationship between belief and action; cf. Richard Holton, "Partial Belief, Partial Intention," *Mind* 117 (2008): 27–58; and Eric Schwitzgebel, "Acting Contrary to Our Professed Beliefs; or The Gulf between Occurrent Judgments and Dispositional Belief," *Pacific Philosophical Quarterly* 91 (2010): 531–53.

[50]For a position of this sort, cf. Ernest Sosa, "Value Matters in Epistemology," *Journal of Philosophy* 107.4 (2010): 167–90.

[51]Cf. Raphael Woolf, "Misology and Truth," in John J. Cleary and Gary M. Gurtler (eds.), *Proceedings of the Boston Area Colloquium in Ancient Philosophy* 23 (2007): 1–16.

judgment over any other epistemic aim. These objections fuel a famous antiskeptical argument, the so-called Apraxia Charge. The charge comes in a number of versions, including one according to which the skeptics cannot survive, one according to which they cannot act in any robust sense of 'action,' and one according to which they cannot adhere to any kind of ethical values.[52] As I hope to show throughout the book, the intuitions on the side of Socratic caution are strong. This does not mean that critics who point to the role of belief in action, or to the moral importance of taking a stance, refer to issues of little significance. On the contrary, much of the argument that Socratically inspired epistemologists must provide is that more or less distant relatives of belief—hypotheses, 'seemings,' assumptions, and the like—can fulfill the functions that are greatly relevant. Notably, the skeptics and Stoics do not speak loosely of belief, as if assumptions or suppositions were kinds of belief. It is important to them to draw a distinction between the attitude of belief on the one hand and attitudes that involve some distancing or open-mindedness on the other hand.[53]

The Pyrrhonian skeptics develop sophisticated methods of staying away from beliefs. In particular, they employ so-called modes of arguments when they investigate philosophical questions. Contemporary scholars have complained that someone who employs such modes, thereby regularly arriving at suspension of judgment, cannot seriously call herself an 'investigator' (*skeptikos*), as the skeptics do. The skeptics, they argue, aim at suspension of judgment, not at truth. This charge was not raised among the contemporary critics of the skeptics, who were otherwise vocal and imaginative critics of skeptical philosophy, able to detect many potential weaknesses. As I suspect, it was not raised because prominent interlocutors of the ancient skeptics shared with them Socratic premises about a life devoted to investigation. The value of truth has two sides: it is valuable to attain truths, and it is valuable to avoid the

---

[52]Cf. Vogt, "Scepticism and Action," in R. Bett (ed.), *The Cambridge Companion to Ancient Greek Scepticism* (Cambridge: Cambridge University Press, 2010), 165–80; Richard Bett, "Scepticism and Ethics," in Bett, *Cambridge Companion to Ancient Scepticism*, 181–94.

[53]This intuition is not wholly foreign to contemporary epistemology. For example, Bas C. van Fraasen argues that belief involves a certain degree of commitment (he invokes a passage in Augustine that employs Stoic vocabulary of assent, but that, via Augustine's preoccupations, leads toward voluntarist intuitions, and thus away from Socratic epistemology). "Belief and the Will," *Journal of Philosophy* 81 (1984): 235–56.

acceptance of falsehoods. The value of truth can thus be responded to in several ways, depending on how one construes the relationship between these two aims. If one shares the Socratic intuition that it is paramount to avoid the acceptance of falsehoods, and that it is preferable to make no truth-claims as opposed to false ones, then skeptical investigation might be the most convincing response.

1

What Is Ignorance? Plato on Presumed Knowledge, Wishful Thinking, and Not Understanding Your Own Thoughts

Socrates: Now, ignorance is a vice, and so is what we call stupidity [...] Are there not necessarily three ways in which it is possible not to know oneself? [...] (i) if someone thinks himself richer than in fact he is [...]; (ii) even more consider themselves taller and handsomer than in fact they are, and believe that they have other such physical advantages [...] (iii) but an overwhelming number are mistaken about the third kind, which belongs to the soul, namely virtue, and believe that they are superior in virtue, although they are not.
(Philebus 48c–e)

It is probably hard to find a human being who considers herself ignorant. It is perhaps even harder to find someone who denies that ignorance is a bad state. Beyond our almost instinctive assumptions when it comes to ignorance, however, it is not clear what precisely ignorance is, and what is bad about it. Once one begins to think about these questions, it becomes likely that there are different kinds of ignorance. Not all of them seem to be bad, or bad in the same sense. For example, one might be no worse off for not knowing how many blades of grass are in one's garden. Some instances of ignorance seem disadvantageous though they do not reflect badly on the cognizer, like not knowing that a disgruntled colleague placed a bomb in your spacious new corner office. The badness of other kinds of ignorance is best expressed by saying that ignorance is worse than knowledge: wherever we value knowledge—say, in mathematics—it makes sense to think of ignorance in this field as bad. Then there are instances of ignorance that seem to be not just worse than knowledge, but blameworthy.[1] Consider an agent who likes to think of herself as a kind person. Inspired by this view of herself, she tells someone to take a medication because she heard of a similar case where it helped, mistaking her recollection of the particular case for medical knowledge. This kind of ignorance interests Socrates, as presented in some Platonic dialogues.[2]

According to the texts I shall discuss—*Apology*, *Ion*, and *Philebus*— blameworthy ignorance involves self-aggrandizing modes of thought. It is not primarily to be located in deficient judgments that cognizers make about the matters they are ignorant about. Instead, certain background assumptions about ourselves—claims to the effect that one is richer, handsomer, wiser, or indeed, more genuinely kind, than one really is— throw us off track. They diminish our abilities to make careful judgments and mislead us into overly confident claims to knowledge and expertise. I shall refer to this kind of phenomenon as *transferred ignorance*: blameworthy ignorance involves a transition from an inflated self-image to an inflated view of one's ability to assess matters other than oneself. Even worse, when we, thus encouraged, put forward what we claim to know, we often formulate ideas that figure in our thoughts because we picked them up from others. While we indulge in our overly optimistic self-image, we forget that we do not even comprehend what we say.

After a brief sketch of different kinds of ignorance (section 1), I discuss ignorance in the best-known Platonic text on these matters, the *Apology* (section 2), as well as the *Ion*, a dialogue about a paradigmatically ignorant expert (section 3). Finally, I turn to the passage from the *Philebus* cited in the epigraph to this chapter, and the claim that thinking of oneself as richer, handsomer, more virtuous, and wiser than one really is can figure centrally in Socratically blameworthy ignorance (section 4).[3]

---

[1] By 'blameworthy' I do not mean 'morally blameworthy', but 'deserving of ethical criticism'.

[2] I am leaving aside 'ignorance is bliss' attitudes in their various—sometimes playful, sometimes more serious—manifestations. These matters would lead beyond the scope of this chapter.

[3] An inflated self-image is neither a necessary nor a sufficient condition for Socratically blameworthy ignorance. For example, another kind of Socratically blameworthy ignorance might involve one's underestimating the abilities of others, or the members of certain groups. Socrates' respectful attitude to craftsmen, whom others regard as too humble to be real interlocutors, as well as his attitude of taking the words of others at face value might be cited as evidence. For example, when Socrates is faced with the charges against him, he does not ascribe them to ill will on the part of Meletus, or to misconceptions on the part of the Athenians.

1. Kinds of Ignorance

Transferred ignorance has a surprising structure. It will help to differentiate it, for the time being somewhat schematically, from other kinds of ignorance.

Case 1: Ignorance as mental blank

The cognizer has never even heard of a given subject-matter and accordingly has no attitudes whatsoever with respect to the relevant range of content.[4]

Case 2: Ignorance as conscious ignorance

The cognizer is aware that there is a given subject-matter, and that it is concerned with such and such questions; but she holds no views about this subject matter.[5]

Case 3: Ignorance as mere belief

The cognizer has some views relevant to a given subject-matter, but these views fall short of being knowledge. They may be either false, or deficient insofar as they are not firmly rooted in her mind (she would not know how to explain them, how they hang together, etc.). The cognizer is aware that her attitudes are 'mere beliefs.'

Case 4: Ignorance as presumed knowledge

The cognizer has some views relevant to a given subject-matter, but these views fall short of being knowledge. However, she fully endorses these views and puts them forward as knowledge claims.

He thinks that, if others arrive at these views, they must take themselves to have reasons (cf. *Apology* and *Euthyphro* 2b–3a). Utterances of this kind are sometimes taken to express Socrates' irony. Though this may well be accurate, it does not mean that they cannot be, in another sense, sincere. Cf. Jonathan Lear, *A Case for Irony* (Cambridge: Harvard University Press, 2011).

[4]This kind of ignorance might be included in *Republic* V (476c–479d), where Socrates says that ignorance is about 'what is not'; the idea that ignorance is a kind of 'darkness' (478b) could, at the extreme end of complete darkness, capture such cases.

[5]For the Plato of the middle dialogues, this kind of ignorance can be ethically relevant. For example, Plato thinks that extended study of mathematics is necessary to shape our psychologies. Cf. Myles Burnyeat, "Why Mathematics Is Good for the Soul," in Timothy Smiley (ed.), *Mathematics and Necessity: Essays in the History of Philosophy* (Oxford: Oxford University Press, published for the British Academy, 2000), 1–81. Cf. also Raphael Woolf, "Truth as a Value in Plato's *Republic*," *Phronesis* 54 (2009): 9–39. Woolf argues that, in the *Republic*, only philosophical truth is considered valuable in itself.

Cases 1 to 4 have in common that ignorance is thought of as relating to a relatively well-defined range of subject matter.[6] For example, I might know nothing about astronomy in either of these four ways. Case 4 is often thought of as the central case of Socratically blameworthy ignorance: someone takes herself to have knowledge, though she is in no position to make knowledge claims. This kind of attitude is standardly diagnosed in Socrates' interlocutors in the *Apology*. While Socrates knows that he does not know the answers to certain questions, his interlocutors take themselves to know about these things. However, they do not have this knowledge; their ignorance is blameworthy—while Socrates' is not—because they presume to have knowledge that in fact they do not have. And yet this diagnosis is incomplete. The problem is not fully described when we say that blameworthy ignorance is presumed knowledge. Case 4 envisages presumed knowledge about a certain content, without any reference to the image that the cognizer has of herself. As it stands, Case 4 could be comparatively harmless, occurring, say, when I assert that a given shirt is in a given closet, thus implying that I know where it is, when ideally I should say that, as far as I recall the shirt is in that closet. The ignorance of some of Socrates' interlocutors has a further dimension.[7]

Case 5: Transferred ignorance

The cognizer holds an inflated view of herself and feels empowered by this view to make overly confident knowledge-claims.

---

[6]Further complexities would arise if the relationship between ignorance and falsehood was studied. For example, one might ask whether the "noble lies" of the *Republic* make those who are lied to ignorant or not; if yes, this would be a kind of ignorance that Plato judges to be beneficial. However, this question leads beyond my current purposes. Cf. Woolf, "Truth as a Value," on noble lies and the value of truth.

[7]Raphael Woolf discusses the ignorance of Socrates' interlocutors in terms of first-person authority and access to one's own mental states ("Socratic Authority," *Archiv für Geschichte der Philosophie* 90 [2008]: 1–38). He observes that Plato's view seems to be diametrically opposed to the Cartesian idea that access to one's own mind is direct, while access to the mental states of others is problematic. "First-person authority […] is depicted in the dialogues as very rare. Only Socrates, as we have seen, has the authority to make epistemic self-ascriptions that are immune from challenge" (20). In taking my cue from the *Philebus* quote, I aim to suggest that the gulf between Plato's concerns and modern preoccupations is even larger. Though ignorance can involve not understanding one's own thoughts, Plato also points to the role of an inflated self-image.

Transferred ignorance is a pervasive phenomenon: self-aggrandizing claims negatively affect our ability to judge *all* other matters. An ignorant person can fare relatively well if she has a realistic conception of her competence, and consults others who know better.[8] Similarly, the deficient beliefs of the learner are—though worse than knowledge—ultimately not worrisome. Many of Socrates' interlocutors in the middle dialogues (beginning already with the *Meno*) are on a positive trajectory. As students, they are making progress. Though they do not possess knowledge, and are thus strictly speaking ignorant, they are not the target of the Socratic idea that ignorance is a vice. For example, the eagerness of someone like Meno makes him a promising student.[9] Arguably, a certain kind of optimism about one's ability to learn might even fuel one's thought processes, enabling a student to formulate ideas and grasp connections.[10] The ideal here is thus not that one takes a self-deprecating or pessimistic view about one's intellectual abilities. Instead, the ideal is that one become aware of the difficulty and importance of getting things right, rather than conclude that, because one has a certain social position or a particular competence in a well-circumscribed field, one has knowledge in other areas. This is the

---

[8]In the *Theaetetus*, Plato describes such ignorance as lack of learning (*amathia*) (170a–b; cf. 170c8). Plato envisages people who encounter a medical emergency, a storm at sea, or a drastic situation during a military campaign (170a). The cognizer is aware that, in these matters, things can go terribly badly for her because she lacks insight. She thus turns to someone else for advice and teaching.

[9]The call for less self-flattery should not be mistaken as the injunction to be pessimistic. The influential (though controversial) findings of Shelley E. Taylor and Jonathan D. Brown, according to which people with realistic views of themselves tend to be depressed, do not raise immediate problems for the matters I discuss in this chapter. Taylor and Brown, "Illusion and Well-Being: A Social-Psychological Perspective on Mental Health," *Psychological Bulletin* 103 (1988): 193–210.

[10]What then about people who underestimate themselves? This question is too large to address here; I shall limit myself to three brief points. First, Socrates' attitude implies that a model teacher treats *all* students as capable, and aims to instill that kind of self-image in them. Second, the Plato of the *Republic* recognizes no traditional assumptions about the distribution of intellectual talents; the so-called "second wave" argues against a society that does not trust women with the same kinds of intellectual tasks that men are thought capable of. Third, *Republic* VIII–IX could arguably account for the destructive forces of certain self-deprecating views, say, thinking of oneself as less good-looking than one really is and adopting destructive pleasure and pain attitudes (say, taking pleasure in the pain of highly controlled eating habits), attitudes that may cloud one's judgments on a number of things. Cf. Vogt, "Plato on Madness and the Good Life," in W. Harris (ed.), *Mental Illness in Antiquity* (forthcoming).

attitude of another type of Socratic interlocutor—of priests, politicians, poets, and so on. These people see themselves as experts, and they have a social standing that lends some credibility to these claims.[11] Some of them are shockingly conceited and turn out to be ignorant in a blameworthy way.

2. Two Puzzles of the Apology

The best-known Platonic text on ignorance is the *Apology*. Note first that, in the *Apology*, Plato proceeds on the assumption that every cognitive attitude toward a given content that falls short of knowledge counts as ignorance. Plato employs a binary distinction: either one has knowledge, or one is ignorant. Attitudes that he later discusses in terms of belief—say, getting the answer right without being able to defend it, or without being able to reliably arrive at the correct answer—hence simply count as ignorance. While Plato uses cognates of *doxa*, such as the verb 'it seems (*dokei*) to me,' he does not use the noun *doxa*, belief. He does not operate with the threefold distinction between ignorance, belief, and knowledge that is developed in the *Meno* and later dialogues; nor does he operate with the threefold distinction between ignorance, true belief, and knowledge that is discussed in the *Symposium*.[12] Ignorance is taken quite literally: as long as one does not know something, one is ignorant of it. The most general thing to say about ignorance in the *Apology*, then, is that any truth-claim that fails to qualify as knowledge is a piece of ignorance.[13]

[11]Compare this to recent studies of the so-called Downing effect: people with a below average IQ tend to overestimate their IQ, and people with an above average IQ tend to underestimate their IQ (cf. J. E. Davidson and C. L. Downing, "Contemporary Models of Intelligence," in R. J. Sternberg (ed.), *Handbook of Intelligence* (New York: Cambridge University Press, 2000), 34–49. It is conceivable that Plato would argue that people of high standing often have lesser abilities than ordinary craftsmen, simply because there is nothing of real value that they are competent in, whereas, say, making shoes is a valuable activity.

[12]Cf. *Symposium* 202a on the idea that true belief is genuinely *in between* knowledge and ignorance.

[13]Accordingly, an interpretation of the *Apology* should not invoke a notion of true belief that implies that true belief, while still falling short of knowledge, is better than and different from ignorance. Terence Irwin's proposal, in *Plato's Moral Theory* (Oxford: Clarendon Press, 1977), that Socrates disavows knowledge, but not true belief, does not sit easily with the earliest Platonic presentations of Socrates. Similarly, Gail Fine ("Does Socrates Claim to Know That He Knows Nothing?" *Oxford Studies in Ancient Philosophy* 35 [2008]: 49–88) assumes that we can stipulate a distinct category of true belief in interpreting the *Apology*.

Scholars have studied the *Apology* with a view to the ignorance of Socrates' interlocutors, as well as with a view to Socrates' own proclaimed ignorance. Both kinds of ignorance, I want to suggest, are relevant to understanding what is bad about transferred ignorance. Socrates' interlocutors are ignorant in that they take themselves to have knowledge that they do not have, and as I argue, they feel entitled or encouraged to do so by their specific skills or social standing. Socrates' ignorance is an accomplishment because it involves precisely the opposite: he does not think of himself as a better cognizer than in fact he is. Both kinds of ignorance are furthermore characterized by how a cognizer relates to a specific domain: the domain of 'fine and important questions.' When Socrates describes himself as not having knowledge, he refers to these matters; the transferred ignorance of his interlocutors is particularly blameworthy because they pronounce views on questions of major relevance.

The *Apology*—literally, "defense speech"—is about Socrates' trial. In response to the charges brought against him, Socrates admits to a certain kind of human wisdom (*anthrōpinē sophia*, 20d6–7). Human wisdom, it will turn out, is a kind of wisdom; but it is not wisdom of the best kind. Socrates proceeds to explain his wisdom through an interpretation of the Delphic oracle, according to which no one is wiser than Socrates. Arguably, it could be true that no one is wiser than Socrates if everyone, including Socrates, were equally ignorant. But Socrates takes the oracle to be making a comparative assessment according to which he is in a better position than others. This better position is described as human wisdom.

Oracles are pronouncements that are typically obscure to those who receive them; they are taken to be true; they may well seem to contradict other things one takes oneself to know; they need to be interpreted by experts trained or gifted for this task; often, their meaning only becomes clear when events unfold. To receive an oracle, then, is to be sent on a puzzle-solving expedition. It is assumed that, no matter how unlikely or incomprehensible, the oracle reveals something true. This is how Socrates engages with the Delphic oracle (20c–24b). He takes it to be true, and asks how its truth can be compatible with another truth, namely that he is not wise.[14]

---

[14]More could be said about the status of the oracle: it is true, but it is not presented as anyone's knowledge. It is conceivable that Plato ultimately regards oracles as *so* obscure that the interpretive task is not genuinely to figure out how they can be true, but to reformulate them so that something true is being said.

Oracle Puzzle[15]

(1) I (i.e., Socrates) am not wise.

(2) The Delphic oracle (according to which no one is wiser than Socrates) does not lie.

Trying to solve the riddle, Socrates interrogates politicians, poets, and craftsmen. In a first round of conversations, Socrates talks with politicians (21c–22a). On the whole, they are a disappointment. They take themselves to be wise (*sophos*), though they are not. However, there is some variation. The most famous politicians are worst; those with less prestige seem to Socrates to be somewhat more sensible (*pros to phronimōs eichein*; 22a6). The implication of this gradation becomes clear as the text proceeds: with less social standing, these minor figures are less tempted to overestimate their own faculties. Next, Socrates talks to poets (22a–22c). Socrates interrogates them about the meaning of their verses. It strikes him as rather shocking that, of everyone present at these conversations, the poets are least able to say anything about the meaning of their creations. The poets compose their verses by nature and by inspiration, not by any kind of understanding. They are like prophets in that they say many fine things, but "know none of the things they say" (22c3). Finally, Socrates talks to craftsmen (22c–e). The craftsmen differ from Socrates in actually being experts on something. Their mistake, Socrates says, is somewhat like the mistake of the poets (22d). They infer from the fact that they know something in an expert way that they are also wise about fine things. Their folly, Socrates says, hides their wisdom (22d8–e1). This is an important feature of transferred ignorance: with respect to her state of mind as a whole, a person can fare badly even though she has her field of expertise. The faulty inference from a limited competence to larger-scale

---

[15]According to Woolf ("Socratic Authority," 3–5), Socrates "faces down the oracle": Socrates says he will put the oracle to the test (21c1–2). But as Woolf admits, Socrates also says that the oracle should remain unrefuted (22a7–8). In my view, Socrates responds in traditional fashion: oracles *are* oracular. They can appear incomprehensible to the point of not making sense to those who receive them; but one shall have to decipher them (even if this involves drastic reinterpretation) under the assumption that they are true. For earlier discussions of this matter, cf. Alexander Nehamas, "Socratic Intellectualism," in John J. Cleary (ed.), *Proceedings of the Greater Boston Area Ancient Philosophy Colloquium*, vol. 2 (Washington, D.C.: University Press of America, 1986), 275–316; and Thomas Brickhouse and Nicholas Smith, *Socrates on Trial* (Oxford: Oxford University Press, 1990), 96.

insights throws a shadow. It pushes the particular bit of expertise a person has, though it is in itself valuable, into the periphery of what matters.

As it turns out, Socrates is wiser than all these people insofar as he does not take himself to know what he does not know. Consider more specifically the subject matter at issue. Neither Socrates nor the politicians know anything fine and valuable (*kalon k'agathon*) (21d4).[16] Each of the craftsmen thinks that, because he performs well in his craft, he is also most wise in the greatest things (*megista*) (22d7).[17] Transferred ignorance, then, involves a move from one's own competence (or social status) toward knowledge claims in a specific, elevated domain.

The Greek words Socrates uses to characterize this domain indicate value and significance.[18] What are these things? First, Socrates' discussion of care of the soul toward the end of the *Apology* makes clear that questions of 'life and death' are important questions. Second, questions about divinity seem to count as important. We can take this to be implied by Socrates' respect for the god who tells him to engage in philosophy; it is reflected in Socrates' attitude to the Delphic oracle, and his interest in the limitations of mortal life. Third, questions about the nature of the universe—in particular since such views involve religious and theological

---

[16]Gareth Matthew translates "fine and good" in "Socratic Ignorance," in Benson, *A Companion to Plato*, 103–18. Cf. Richard Bett on the range of relevant questions ("Socratic Ignorance," in Morrison, *Cambridge Companion to Socrates*, 215–36, esp. 219–26). Bett argues, in my view convincingly, against Thomas Brickhouse and Nicholas Smith, who address the issue via a distinction between expert and ordinary knowledge, *The Philosophy of Socrates* (Boulder, Colo.: Westview Press, 2000), 108–9.

[17]Gail Fine translates what Socrates says in 21b4–5 as "I am aware of being wise in nothing, great or small" ("Does Socrates Claim to Know," 56). However, once we see that a notion of 'great questions / important issues' matters to the discussion of Socrates' wisdom in the *Apology*, we might be inclined to go with a different translation: "I am aware of being neither greatly nor a little wise." This corresponds to Friedrich Schleiermacher's translation, here as elsewhere astonishingly philosophically acute.

[18]Eric Schwitzgebel, "Self-Ignorance," in JeeLoo Liu and John Perry (eds.), *Consciousness and the Self: New Essays* (Cambridge: Cambridge University Press, 2011), 184–97, 191, though not an ancient scholar and not writing on the *Apology*, is particularly explicit and poignant on this issue. As he puts it, "The oracle was presumably not concerned about whether people knew their attitudes about the April weather. To the extent that the injunction to know oneself pertains to self-knowledge of attitudes, it must be attitudes like your central values, and your general background assumptions about the world and about other people."

matters—count as important.[19] These questions bear directly or indirectly on how one should live. Accordingly, they are plausibly seen as questions that Socrates takes very seriously. When Socrates says that neither he nor his interlocutors know anything fine (valuable, great), I take it he refers to this domain.

Socrates' preoccupation with 'human' matters has sometimes been interpreted as if Socrates were a moral philosopher. Vlastos, for example, thinks that Socrates' human wisdom consists in having moral knowledge. Vlastos collects a number of passages from various dialogues in which Socrates says he knows something of this nature.[20] For example, in the *Republic* Socrates says that everyone who followed the argument up to a given point now knows that injustice is ignorance (351a5–6).[21] However, such examples show that ethics (as I would prefer to say) is not neatly separate from other fields in philosophy. If injustice is ignorance, questions of value immediately relate to epistemology.

More generally speaking, a Socratic ethics would have to be the study of how to lead a good life. For comprehensive answers to the relevant questions, many of the 'fine and great' issues would need to be known.

---

[19]It is a central charge against Socrates that he violates traditional religion, and Socrates is likely to be guilty as charged (cf. Burnyeat, 1997). Discussions among Socrates scholars, originating in responses to Vlastos's Socrates, both in *Socrates, Ironist and Moral Philosopher* (Ithaca: Cornell University Press, 1991) and his earlier *Platonic Studies* (Princeton, N.J.: Princeton University Press, 1973), often move too quickly to a distinction between ethical knowledge as gained through elenchus and other kinds of knowledge. The widespread view that Socrates is only interested in ethics sometimes goes along with pointing to his interlocutors: ordinary people, it is assumed, are unlikely to have views in physics. However, ordinary people can certainly have views about the nature of the universe: how everything does or does not depend on fate, how there is or is not 'reason' behind it all, and so on. Related issues seem to be relevant to the charges against Socrates: if he is some kind of sophist, if indeed he studied what earlier natural philosophers said, if he violates traditional religion, then it must appear that he does not see the universe as, from the point of view of his accusers, he should.

[20]Many scholars follow Vlastos, arguing for similar views. Cf. Annas, who thinks that "Socrates has firm and passionately held beliefs of a moral kind" ("Plato the Skeptic," 313).

[21]A number of claims are associated with so-called Socratic intellectualism (such as "Virtue is knowledge," "No one does wrong voluntarily," etc.) and considered candidates for what Socrates knows (e.g., Nozick, "Socratic Puzzles"). For recent discussion, cf. Thomas C. Brickhouse and Nicholas D. Smith, *Socratic Moral Psychology* (Cambridge: Cambridge University Press, 2010); Rachel Barney, "Plato on the Desire for the Good," in Sergio Tenenbaum (ed.), *Desire, Good, and Practical Reason* (Oxford: Oxford University Press, 2010), 34–64.

For example, what I referred to as questions of life and death matter immediately to how one lives. Similarly, how one views the workings of the universe might make a difference. Relatedly, insight into divine matters would be likely to have repercussions for one's way of life.[22] For Socrates to claim knowledge on questions of value he would have to take himself to have knowledge on these matters—which he says he has not. Accordingly, I suggest that we do not interpret Socrates' turn to human matters as a turn to 'morality.'

Socrates' concern with a good human life involves a broad set of questions. Moreover, it involves a view about how we ought to conceive of ourselves as investigators. Socrates picks up on the long-standing idea that our situation as cognizers is distinctively the situation of human beings. The Delphic oracle, Socrates says, means the following: among human beings, he is wisest who understands that in truth he is not worth anything with respect to wisdom (23a). Our ambitions in understanding the world, and knowing what a good life is, must be framed by an awareness of human limitations. The distinctively Socratic flavor here—as opposed to, say, the versions of this idea found in the Western monotheistic traditions—is that it is good to devote serious study to our life as it is lived inside of its own parameters. It would be misguided to want to leave behind this perspective in finding out how things are. To put this even more forcefully: we *ought* to be interested in how things are for us. Contrary to later (and earlier) traditions, characterized by the attempt to reconstruct how the world 'really' is—or what lies behind the surface of appearances-for-us, or why God created us with cognitive faculties with such and such limitations—Socrates embraces the Delphic inscription "Know thyself."[23]

It is a widespread assumption among scholars of ancient philosophy that Socrates' question-and-answer method in the early dialogues reflects a side of the Delphic "Know thyself" maxim. In finding out whether one can defend a thesis, one learns something about one's

---

[22]Socrates neither seems to claim that knowledge about divine matters is relevant to knowledge about how to live, nor seems to deny that it is. Instead, it is considered conceivable that this kind of knowledge would matter.

[23]Prior to its philosophical interpretations, this inscription warns religious visitors to the Delphic sites not to forget that they are merely mortals. Entering the sacred space, they are reminded of their human status; to be forgetful of this status—so-called hubris—is considered 'sin.'

state of mind; this kind of process is thought to be a progress toward self-knowledge. The Socratic appropriation of the maxim thus seems to inform Socrates' method of philosophical conversation.[24] This point is well taken, though one-sided. Socrates' version of the Delphic idea involves more than this. The *Apology* is rife with references to religion: Socrates is accused of violating traditional religion, and he engages with the Delphic oracle. Similarly, it contains an astonishing density of philosophically intriguing references to tragedy. A protagonist receives a pronouncement of an oracle that is incomprehensible to him. As he proceeds to decipher it, there is reflection on the standing of mortals.[25]

"Know thyself" also means: "Mortals you are, think mortal thoughts." Qua human thinker, one should and in some sense must concern oneself with matters as they figure in human life, and from a human perspective. Socrates stands for a philosophical version of a pronouncement from Euripides' *Bacchae* (395–97): "Wisdom (*sophia*) is not wisdom (*sophia*). And

---

[24]I shall not engage here with the wide-ranging literature on Socratic elenchus. In brief, I take it that Socrates' method is generally well described as a "question and answer" method, a term that is deliberately vague and wider than "elenchus." Moreover, Socrates is quite able to jump into different modes of conversation; witness for example the interpretation of poetry in the *Protagoras*. Accordingly, I avoid focus on the elenchus as if it were the paradigmatic Socratic mode of conversation. For a recent discussion of Vlastos's view, cf. James Doyle, "The Socratic Elenchus: No Problem," in Jonathan Lear and Alex Oliver (eds.), *The Force of Argument: Essays in Honour of Timothy Smiley* (New York: Routledge, 2010), 68–81. For the view that the Socratic dialogues display a common Socratic method, cf. Benson, "Socratic Method." Vlastos's Socrates, though often attacked, is still very much alive. In spite of problems with his views (see below), I think it is well deserved that Vlastos's reconstruction continues to figure in our discussions.

[25]I do not mean to suggest that he follows traditional religion. On the contrary, I agree with Myles Burnyeat's well-known point that Socrates is guilty as charged: Socrates violates traditional piety by not 'believing' in the gods of the city ("The Impiety of Socrates," *Ancient Philosophy* 17 [1997]: 1–12). On Socrates' attitude to religion, cf. Paul Woodruff, ed. with Nicholas D. Smith, *Reason and Religion in Socratic Philosophy* (Oxford: Oxford University Press, 2000). See also A. A. Long, "How Does Socrates' Divine Sign Communicate with Him?" in S. Ahbel-Rappe and R. Kamtekar (eds.), *Blackwell Companion to Socrates* (Oxford: Oxford University Press, 2006), 63–74; and Paul Woodruff, "The Skeptical Side of Plato's Method," *Revue Internationale de Philosophie* 156–57 (1986): 22–37. Mark McPherran and James Doyle explore the point that Socrates sees his way of life as a matter of piety: the god commanded him to philosophize, and he observes this command. McPherran, "Socrates and the Duty to Philosophize," *Southern Journal of Philosophy* 24 (1986): 283–309; Doyle, "Socratic Methods," forthcoming from *Oxford Studies in Ancient Philosophy*.

not to think mortal thoughts (*to te mē thnēta phronein*) is to see few days."[26] For a human cognizer to try to think other than human thoughts is not to be ambitious. It is like attempting a 'view from nowhere,' or alternatively a view from a divine perspective, as if that were a superior view for a human cognizer.[27] However, though it might in principle be a superior perspective, it is not one for us to strive for.[28] Consider an example from the end of the *Apology*. Fear of death, Socrates says, is a matter of misrepresenting one's own epistemic standing: in fearing death, one deems oneself wise (29a). One assumes that one knows what death is, which in fact we do not know.[29] To try to formulate a view about this is not an admirably ambitious intellectual project. Instead, it is a sure route to confusion. The most basic way in which one should not overestimate oneself, it turns out, consists in understanding one's status as *human* cognizer, as opposed to a cognizer of a better sort, who would be able to know things that, from our point of view, are inaccessible. Socrates' human wisdom also involves conscious ignorance, the ignorance of being able to identify, at least in outline, what it is that one does not know. These are significant accomplishments, which merit being seen as a kind of wisdom.

The distinction between human wisdom and genuine wisdom supplies a solution for the Oracle Puzzle.[30] Socrates is not wise in the sense of

[26]I owe this reference to Gregory Vlastos, "Socrates' Disavowal of Knowledge," *Philosophical Quarterly* 35 (1985): 1–31, 28.

[27]Though many of the framing premises are different, this point is similar to one that Thomas Nagel makes in *The View from Nowhere* (New York: Oxford University Press, 1986). As Nagel argues, if one were to try to fully occupy what he calls an 'objective' perspective, one would leave out something real, namely the subjective perspectives of cognizers. Socrates could agree that stepping back from one's particular perspective is not impossible. We can and do ask how things 'really' are. But in doing so, we are in danger of forgetting that our perspective is partially constitutive of how the world really is for us.

[28]Book X of the *Nicomachean Ethics* offers indirect evidence that this position figured importantly in the discussions in and around the Academy. Aristotle says that the advice "Mortals you are, think mortal thoughts" is misguided. On Aristotle's view, we should aim as high as we possibly can (1177b31–34). I follow Vlastos ("Socrates' Disavowal of Knowledge") in seeing this connection.

[29]Arguably, one might fear death because one does not know what it is; however, this option is not discussed. Socrates seems to assume that to fear death is to consider death a bad thing.

[30]M. Stokes argues that Socrates' wisdom is in between human and divine wisdom. Michael C. Stokes, in Plato, *Apology: With an Introduction, Translation and Commentary* (Warminster: Aris & Phillips, 1997). However, I see no reason to dismiss Socrates' own usage of the term human wisdom, as applied to himself. Surely, if other human beings were to strive for wisdom, they could take Socrates as a model of what is humanly achievable.

genuine wisdom; he is wiser than everybody else insofar as he has human wisdom. As I see it, the Oracle Puzzle is at the heart of the *Apology*. The notion of human wisdom references a set of questions where transferred ignorance is particularly poignant and worrisome. Socrates' awareness of his lack of knowledge in this domain is valuable—and makes him wise in the sense of human wisdom—because we are concerned with things of significance for human life.

Interpreters of the *Apology* tend to focus on a different puzzle, a puzzle I shall call the Knowledge Puzzle.

Knowledge Puzzle:

(3) I am aware of knowing nothing.[31]

(4) The things I do not know are the fine/great things.

(5) I know that p (for example, that it is shameful to do wrong, 29b).[32]

---

[31]When Socrates talks about his conversations with the craftsmen, he says "*emautō gar sunēdē ouden epistamenō*"—I was aware of knowing nothing (22d). This sentence has sometimes been rendered as "I know nothing." For example, Harold Tarrant says that Socrates' most famous claim is that "he knows that he knows nothing" ("Socratic Method and Socratic Truth," in Ahbel-Rappe and Kamtekar, *Blackwell Companion to Socrates*, 254–72, 263). This trend is in part inherited from the tradition that otherwise I hold in high esteem: the Hellenistic philosophers seem to have focused on the relevant passage, with Arcesilaus going as far as to misdescribe Socrates. Arcesilaus claims that Socrates said he knew nothing, and objects that this is negative dogmatism (cf. Cicero, *On Academic Scepticism* 1.45 and 2.74).

[32]Vlastos solves this puzzle (or rather, his version of it) by a mix of two moves. The first half of his argument is contextualist: when Socrates disavows knowledge and yet occasionally says he knows such and such, different contexts supply different standards for knowledge. It is perfectly consistent to disavow knowledge of an ambitious kind, which Vlastos associates with certainty and calls knowledgeC, and at the same time take oneself to have knowledge of a less ambitious kind. This latter knowledge results, *pace* Vlastos, from elenctic argument; Vlastos calls it knowledgeE. The second half of Vlastos's account is that he takes the elenchus to be concerned with moral questions. The kinds of things that Socrates knowsE are moral things (Vlastos, "Socrates' Disavowal of Knowledge"). Vlastos's reconstruction of Socrates has been subjected to multiple criticisms, many of them plausible. In particular, it seems misguided to me to assume that Socrates' method is throughout elenctic. On the contrary, Socrates seems to be a master at jumping from one mode of philosophical conversation to the next. Similarly, I would not describe any of Socrates' questions as concerned with 'morality,' arguably a modern concept; 'ethical questions' is a wider category. It also strikes me as an anachronism to say that the ambitious notion of knowledge that Plato and other ancient philosophers envisage focuses on *certainty*; this is a Cartesian,

The most obvious way to resolve the puzzle—or indeed, to argue that there is no puzzle—lies in a disambiguation of the words for 'knowledge'.[33] The quote from Euripides makes for a good warning.[34] It is very well possible to use a term in different senses. For example, one can say that '*sophia* is not *sophia*,' without falling into the traps of contradiction and self-contradiction.[35] People say this kind of thing all the time. Suppose your friend knows that you love to eat cake, and asks you why you chose not to order cake in a cafe where the two of you get together. You may well say in response, "Well, their cake isn't really cake," and imply that, according to your connoisseur standards, the cake on offer just is not the kind of cake you mean when you say that you love cake.

In saying that he is not 'a knower' (*epistamenos*) about anything, Socrates seems to employ a notion of *epistēmē* that is pervasive in early Socratic dialogues: knowledge as expertise. It is a commonplace that, in early Platonic texts, *epistēmē* and *technē*—and to some extent *sophia*, wisdom—are used interchangeably, or almost so. To be a knower in this sense is to be an expert on a given subject-matter, or, in other words, to be 'wise in X'.[36] The ambitious notion of knowledge that Socrates invokes

---

not an ancient, idea. Several other, unpromising routes have been explored. Surely, it is not enough to point to Socrates' famous 'irony'; the question of whether one claims to have knowledge is a serious one for Socrates. Interpretations that do not even recognize a problem, and rephrase Socrates' disavowal of knowledge simply as a disavowal of fully worked-out doctrines, seem peculiarly blind. Cf. Gregory Vlastos's remarks on Eduard Zeller, *Sokrates und die Sokratiker*, in "Socrates' Disavowal of Knowledge," 6 n. 13.

[33]Here I agree with Vlastos ("Socrates' Disavowal of Knowledge"), though I disagree on the details of how this should be done.

[34]Indeed, it is even quite possible that Socrates has Euripides in mind, and Euripides Socrates, when they say such things. It is relatively well attested that Socrates and Euripides were intellectual friends for a substantial period. Cf. Christian Wildberg, "Socrates and Euripides," in Ahbel-Rappe and Kamtekar, *Blackwell Companion to Socrates*, 21–35.

[35]In particular, this is easily comprehensible because of the mixed reputation of the Sophists (literally "wise men"): their wisdom is not considered real wisdom, and yet they are referred to as wise men. Cf. a related passage from the *Ion* (532d): Ion says to Socrates, "I love to hear you wise men talk." Socrates responds: "I wish that were true, Ion. But wise? Surely you are the wise men, you rhapsodes and actors, you and the poets whose work you sing."

[36]In her discussion of what we should take Socrates to be talking about when (and if) he says that he knows he knows nothing, Fine does not consider this option, though versions of it have already been defended by C. D. C. Reeve, *Socrates in the Apology: An Essay on Plato's Apology of Socrates* (Indianapolis: Hackett, 1989) and P. Woodruff, "Plato's Earlier Epistemology," in S. Everson (ed.), *Greek Epistemology* (Cambridge: Cambridge University

in (3) seems to be precisely this notion: Socrates is not an expert in anything. In making this claim, Socrates is entirely consistent with things he
said earlier in the dialogue (cf. 19e–20c). This is how he compares to all
his interlocutors, who take themselves to have either some kind of gener-
alized expertise or a specific skill.

This lack of expertise is compatible with having human wisdom, as
described above; thus (3) is compatible with (4). Further, it is compatible
with knowing all kinds of things outside of the domain of fine and important matters; (3), (4), and (5) are compatible.[37] For example, Socrates says
he knows that people hate him because he is such an unpleasant interlocutor (24a).[38] Notably, Socrates also ascribes knowledge of mundane
facts to the audience of his defense speech. For example, they know as well
as he knows that what he says is true, namely that he is rather unpopular
(28a). Other pieces of Socrates' knowledge are weightier, for example,
that one should not disobey the gods. But Socrates takes himself to know
this without, at the same time, having any kind of expertise on divine
matters. Instead, it appears that this is a commitment one might have,
whatever might turn out to be true about the gods and their commands.
Similarly, Socrates makes some almost conceptual claims; for example, he
says he knows it is bad and shameful to do wrong (*adikein*) (29b). It is

---

Press, 1990), 60–84. Reprinted in Hugh Benson (ed.), *Essays on Socrates* (Oxford: Oxford
University Press, 1992). Fine does not seem to recognize an early, Socratic phase in Plato's
epistemology, a phase that is not yet concerned with a threefold distinction between ignorance, belief, and knowledge. Fine draws on the *Meno*, and proposes that according to a
minimal and uncontroversial conception, knowledge is "a truth-entailing cognitive condition that is appropriately cognitively superior to mere true belief" ("Does Socrates Claim to
Know," 55). As I see it, this is neither uncontroversial nor plausible as the relevant notion of
knowledge for our purposes. In the *Apology*, Plato does not recognize a category of belief as
distinct from knowledge and ignorance. Whatever we say about the relevant conception of
knowledge, it should not be phrased in terms of how this attitude is superior to true belief.

[37]Moreover, Socrates insists several times that what he says is true, in terms that go
beyond the idea that he is truthful or honest: Socrates says that he is speaking the truth (cf.
17c, 22a, 22b, 24a, 28e; cf. *Ion* 532d). It is one thing to claim that one says what is the case,
which is how I would paraphrase Socrates' truth-speaking, and quite another thing to say
that one is putting forward knowledge qua expertise about something.

[38]This is one of many examples that show the limitation of Vlastos's proposal, namely
that Socrates' knowledge is moral knowledge gained via elenchus. Surely, Socrates did not
learn that others hate him via elenctic argument, though he may have registered in the
course of elenctic conversations that people see him, as he puts it, as a "pestilential fellow"
(23d).

possible to know this, as it were, by understanding the words—but this does not tell one what kinds of things are bad and shameful.[39] That is, one can know this without knowledge of fine and valuable things. In order to have the kind of knowledge relevant to leading a good life, one would need to know what is bad and shameful, not just that the bad and shameful is not to be done. The Knowledge Puzzle, I take it, can be resolved: Socrates knows a number of things without being an expert in anything, and at the same time he has human wisdom.

Part of the upshot of my reading, which focuses on the notion of human wisdom and the domain of important matters it delineates, is that transferred ignorance is ultimately a problem for those of us who are scholars, lawyers, politicians, and so on. Among Socrates' interlocutors, the craftsmen fare comparatively best. The chef who explains the world to you might be forgiven: at least he can make excellent soup. He should talk less confidently about the afterlife, the gods, and the universe. And yet he is a good chef. Socrates' preference for craftsmen seems well taken. A philosopher who got all excited about the ignorance of ordinary people would not just seem to be a rather unpleasant person. She would overlook something relevant: ordinary skills are valuable. The study of blameworthy ignorance plausibly turns to our own camp, that of people who deal, in one way or another, with words and with a wide range of questions. It is hard to deny that people with these occupations have some kind of ability; but what is it? This question belongs to the core repertoire of Socratic worries. The Sophists, for example, literally 'wise men,' claim to make those they educate better people. Parents hire them for their sons, as they hire someone to take care of the horses, with the expectation that there is some specific ability that people offer. Those who take care of the horses have a well-defined expertise. In the case of those who concern themselves with human beings and a good human life, however, it is unclear whether any such expertise can be detected (e.g., *Apology* 20a–b).

The poets and politicians Socrates talks to are in the same position that philosophers find themselves in. Their field is 'everything and nothing': they talk about all things relevant to human life. That is, their endeavor

---

[39]This kind of issue is discussed in the *Euthyphro* 8c-d. Everyone agrees, Socrates says there, that the wrongdoer should be punished. But we all disagree about which actions are wrong, who did what, and how to categorize particular actions. Thus, to 'know' something like 'wrongdoing is bad' is to know almost as little as if one just knew the meanings of the words: the bad things are those that are not to be done. But which things are bad?

might not even lend itself properly to expertise; there is no well-defined specialization. Their typical mistakes, thus, are more complicated than the faulty claims to knowledge made by craftsmen. Poets, Sophists, and politicians are in a peculiar situation. The fact that somehow everything is relevant to what they do, and that they are good at some of the skills relating to language and argument, can mislead them into thinking that they are knowledgeable about everything. This is the topic of the *Ion*, a dialogue that is badly neglected by philosophers, though it is close to home. Its protagonist, Ion, is rather like many who populate colleges and universities.

3. Not Understanding Your Own Thoughts

Ion is a master in reciting and interpreting Homeric poetry. The dialogue, named after its protagonist, tends to be studied by literary theorists: its ostensible topic is divine inspiration as it figures in artistic creativity and performance. Outside of literary criticism and aesthetics, the *Ion* is rarely referred to.[40] However, its central topic is whether Ion is an expert, and what it would mean for him to be an expert. According to long-standing scholarly assumptions, Plato's earliest (and presumably most Socratic) epistemology is conceived in terms of expertise (*technē*) rather than knowledge. That is, insofar as Plato uses words for 'knowing' in an elevated sense, he does not refer to instances of knowing that p; instead, he refers to the idea that someone masters a given field.[41] This view, almost a platitude in Plato scholarship, is not often applied to the *Apology*. But it has been explored with respect to other texts. What, then, is knowledge qua *technē*?[42]

[40]A notable exception is Nickolas Pappas, "Plato's 'Ion': The Problem of the Author," *Philosophy* 64 (1989): 381–89. Pappas discusses both the Romantic appropriation of some of the dialogue's ideas via Shelley, and the philosophical problems regarding Ion's ignorance. On the question of whether Plato is indeed a forefather of Romantic aesthetics, cf. Suzanne Stern-Gillet, "On (Mis)interpreting Plato's 'Ion,' " *Phronesis* 49 (2004): 169–201.

[41]I shall not pursue here the long-standing question of whether *technē* has a practical aspect of knowing how to do X, and how such a practical side might relate to the relevant body of knowledge.

[42]Plato mentions a broad range of expertises (*technai*) in the *Ion*—ranging from arithmetic to chariot driving, to poetry, flute-playing, medicine, and divination—without categorizing them as falling into distinct groups. In a general discussion of early Socratic dialogues, Paul Woodruff proposes a distinction between subordinate *technai* and important ones. I won't employ this distinction. Contrary to Woodruff, I would hesitate to refer to crafts as 'subordinate'; Socrates has much appreciation for them. I would similarly hesitate

The *Ion* begins with the idea that, for Ion to be an expert on Homer, he must not only be able to recite Homeric verses, but also understand their meaning (530c). Socrates takes this to imply that Ion has to expertly understand the subject matter that is the topic of a given verse (531b). Since several poets talk about the same sets of topics, a Homeric rhapsode runs into a problem. How can Ion claim to be an expert on Homer and not on Hesiod, if there are things that both of them talk about? For example, if Homer talks about soothsaying, then Ion must, qua expert on Homer, be an expert on soothsaying; but Hesiod too talks about soothsaying, and insofar as Ion is not an expert on Hesiod, he is not an expert on soothsaying. Further, how could he formulate a judgment on how good a speaker Homer is on a given issue if he does not study what others have to say on the same topic (531e–532b)? For something to be an expertise, it must be separate from other *technai*: what one knows by one expertise one does not know by another; one expertise is about one kind of thing, the other about another thing (537d–538a). Accordingly, it appears that every passage in Homer can be better judged with respect to whether it is well said by the respective specialist—the seer, fisherman, charioteer, and so on, as opposed to Ion. No subject matter is left for Ion to be an expert about (538b–540a). Ion's specialty—reciting and interpreting Homer—apparently does not meet the criteria for expertise (532c, 535d).[43]

According to Socrates, Ion is instead divinely inspired. The chain of inspiration begins with the way in which muses put verse into the poets' minds, then moves on to interpreters like Ion, and finally to the audience (533d–535e). Ion himself is not possessed by a god; he is possessed by

---

to see rhetoric, poetry, and politics as straightforwardly 'important' (as they are de facto practiced, these arts may not merit this epithet). Finally, it seems that a number of *technai* such as medicine or architecture do not fit neatly into Woodruff's categories. Moreover, there is no classification of kinds of expertise in the *Ion*. Cf. "Plato's Earlier Epistemology." See also Woodruff's "Expert Knowledge in the Apology and the Laches: What a General Needs to Know," *Proceedings of the Boston Area Colloquium in Ancient Philosophy* 3 (1987): 79–115. Though I'm sympathetic to many of Woodruff's cautionary notes regarding the interpretations and appropriation of Socrates, I do not share his assumption that expertise in the *Apology* is about knowledge of definitions.

[43] In other dialogues, Plato associates expertise with teachability. Something is an expertise if it can be taught and studied. This idea does not figure in the *Ion*, perhaps because it would make all too obvious that Ion, a singer who presumably is divinely inspired, is not an expert. Whatever comes to a person from mysterious external forces is certainly not the kind of thing one could learn by taking a class.

Homer—that's why his 'soul dances' when people talk about Homer, and
falls asleep when they talk about other poetry (532b–c; 536b–d). In doing
what he does, he is out of his mind (535d). Ion does not like this description. As he sees it, he is not mad when he talks about Homer (536d). And
yet at the end of the dialogue he accepts the reformulation of this proposal, namely that he is divine (542b). This attitude is a symptom of Ion's
state of mind: as long as his condition can be described in nice terms, he
does not really care whether he has knowledge.

How should we assess this exchange? Socrates got Ion to agree that,
in being an expert on Homer he is also an expert on everything Homer
says. Quite likely, Ion should have hesitated, and insisted on a more
complicated picture. Qua interpreter of Homeric poetry, Ion engages
with practically every aspect of human life. Homer talks about military
strategy, love, friendship, medicine, athletic games, shipbuilding, and so
on. Ion takes himself to be immediately concerned with all these matters. The dialogue shows that this is absurd: one does not become a general by studying the *Iliad*.[44] And yet Socrates is right to say that mere
recital or analysis of the formal aspects of poetry is not enough. The best
contributions to literary criticism seem to contain much thought about
the ideas that figure in a given work.[45] Perhaps Ion should have said that,
by studying the *Iliad* and the *Odyssey*, one engages with certain dimen-
sions of warfare—not military strategy, but, say, the trauma of fighting
far from home, or the ways in which petty disputes serve as pretexts for

[44]Ion's mistake should not be misunderstood as the crazy aberration of an unusual
person. Allegedly, many a German Latin teacher in the 1920s seems to have felt like a general while translating Caesar. With maps of the battles on the wall, *De bello Gallico* came
alive; everyone seems to have had views about where to dig trenches and where to attack.

[45]Pappas (1989) argues that by studying Homer one does not become an expert on X,
but on X-in-Homer. That seems too little: surely, literary critics have been able to make
contributions on central questions of human life via engagement with literature. Accordingly, I think that Pappas's further proposal, that Ion's mistake lies in seeing the
world through Homer's eyes and thus, by aiming to occupy this individual perspective,
rejecting the aim to learn something about the world, is not convincing. If one can learn
something about the world by thinking one's way through Parmenides, then why not
similarly by thinking one's way through Homer? Plato seems to do both. T. F. Morris,
"Plato's *Ion* and What Poetry Is About," *Ancient Philosophy* 13 (1993): 265–72, considers
it naive to assume that poetry is, say, about war; he thinks this would mean that Homer
merely talks about "events" (271). Though there is obviously much to be said about
poetry, I propose to hold on to the idea that Homer talks, in some relevant sense, about
war, friendship, and so on.

long-planned usurpations. Quite plausibly, a literary scholar could write about such issues in illuminating ways.[46]

These are arguments that, surprisingly, scholars do not engage with. And yet they concern a serious point. Literary criticism of a certain kind engages with central issues in human life, via works of art that engage with these issues. This kind of literary criticism is obviously highly demanding. An expert in it must, for example, specialize in Homer, and also think widely about such diverse issues as the trauma of war, the difficulties of returning home after war, friendship, death, and so on. If Ion were to master this art, he would surely achieve something significant.

Ion, however, makes a mistake. As reciter of Homer, he sees himself as a mouthpiece of Homer. When he sings about Agamemnon and Nestor consulting about the next move in the war, he takes himself to be a general. As rhapsode, Ion memorized many sentences. He keeps repeating them in his mind, and speaking them out loud. Someone else is the author of these sentences; by now, they have become Ion's repertoire. What happened, then, was that he forgot that these thoughts—and that is, not the artistic side of the verses, but content like "attack at dawn"—are not his own thoughts. Rather than see himself as having memorized someone else's thoughts and engaging with them qua work of art, he takes these thoughts to be his own.[47]

His mistake is a particularly poignant version of a phenomenon that figures in a number of Plato's dialogues. In response to a question, someone makes a proposal that is, in some sense, not his own. For example, Meno is presented as having picked up ideas from a teacher; Glaucon and Adeimantus say they have heard certain arguments and proposals,

[46]A contemporary example of this kind of contribution might be (though Sherman is a philosopher) Nancy Sherman, *Stoic Warriors: The Ancient Philosophy behind Military Minds* (Oxford: Oxford University Press, 2005). Certainly, Sherman is not an expert military strategist. And yet she has interesting things to say about war.

[47]One could also make the opposite mistake. Perhaps Plato at some point ascribes thoughts to Socrates that in fact are his thoughts; or more generally, a student could ascribe thoughts to a teacher that in fact are her thoughts (I am grateful to Avery Archer for drawing my attention to this phenomenon). A similar case might occur in the interpretation of poetry: perhaps the Socrates of the *Protagoras* ascribes thoughts to Simonides that are his/Plato's thoughts. Arguably, this kind of mistake is less worrisome from a Socratic-Platonic perspective: in spite of the false ascription, one would be genuinely thinking the thought one thinks, and thus arguably have a better chance at understanding it; historical accuracy in the ascription of thoughts to others appears to be less of a concern for Plato than it might be for us.

and that they want to explore them. These examples show that being acquainted with the ideas of others can take different forms: one can take oneself to have adopted a certain thought as one's own thought, or one can be aware that a certain thought is not one's own. Ion is at the far end of a spectrum. He takes himself to, as it were, 'own' Homeric verses as his own thoughts.

When Ion ends up saying that, yes, he is an excellent general and Athens should hire him for their next war, Socrates switches gears (541b–d). Rather than be his painstaking self, he becomes charming, calling Ion divine, a sure sign that he has given up on him (542b). It shall not be possible to explain to Ion how far off he is. Ion turns out to be ignorant in a Socratically blameworthy way. Not understanding the status of his own thoughts, he arrives at self-aggrandizing knowledge claims, claims that are so ridiculous that they do not even merit refutation. Instead, we can laugh and say, "You must be divine." Compare this to a sentence said by Socrates in the *Apology*. When Socrates begins his story about the Delphic oracle, talking about his human wisdom, the audience grumbles. In response, Socrates says, "do not interrupt me with noise, even if I seem to you to be boasting; for the word (*logos*) which I speak (*legō*) is not mine"—as it turns out, it is the word of Pythia, the Delphic priestess, pronouncer of the oracle (20e). Part of Socrates' strength is that he can distinguish between his own thoughts and those of others, though these other thoughts may figure in his mind. He is aware that, though he is by now familiar with the oracle, he could not have been the author of this kind of thought himself. He can repeat it and ex-plore it; but he is looking at it, as it were, from the outside.

This interpretation of the *Ion* helps make sense of another under-discussed feature of the text. Scholars who read the *Ion* in the context of studying Plato's views on poetry have little to say about the reasons why Plato would choose to discuss a rhapsode. Why study the specifics of being an expert reciter? Arguably, Ion's skill is a particularly interest-ing one. A rhapsode is the archetypal mouthpiece for other people's thoughts. Ion thus exemplifies a phenomenon that is rather widespread: we find ourselves with thoughts that someone else—who knows who—understands, thoughts that traveled from person to person. We say things that we picked up somewhere. This is how many of Socrates' in-terlocutors arrive at their replies to his questions (and arguably, how people quite generally communicate about issues of some complexity); they say, sometimes openly, sometimes implicitly, things along the lines of "I guess I heard someone say that p."

Such replies highlight a difficulty that is relevant to the topic of blame-worthy ignorance. We often do not know how we came to have a certain idea among the repertoire of things we can think of; it is hard to keep apart the thoughts of others that we picked up, and our own thoughts. We say things that we do not actually understand, and that we would be in no position to formulate by ourselves. This phenomenon provides a pattern for many Socratic conversations, or parts thereof. Socrates' interlocutors make a proposal, and when Socrates pushes them to explain what they are proposing, they realize that they did not know in the first place what they were saying. That is, the problem that is exposed in many replies is not that they can be refuted, or that they are false, or inconsistent with other views the speaker holds, as it has often been argued. The fact that Socrates' inter-locutors cannot defend their views often reflects an even more basic prob-lem: they said something that sounded good to them, or that they have gotten used to thinking because they hear it all the time; but they actually do not understand what they are saying. The kinds of things cognizers are encouraged to put forward as knowledge by indulging in self-flattery—in Ion's case "I am divine!"—may not even be the speaker's thoughts.

4. Wishful Thinking

Return now to the *Philebus*, or rather, a short section from it, cited at the outset of this chapter. The *Philebus* is considered one of Plato's latest dia-logues. It is a markedly Socratic text, both in terms of Socrates' persona and in terms of the content of the conversation.[48] Plato seems to recon-sider some questions that are central to his middle dialogues—questions in ethics and metaphysics, and in the psychology of pleasure—in ways that are plausibly associated with the Socrates figure of early dialogues.[49]

[48]For general discussion of these matters, cf. Dorothea Frede's introduction and commen-tary in *Philebos*, vol. 3.2 of *Platon Werke* (Göttingen: Vandenhoeck und Ruprecht, 1997).

[49]For example, one might think that Plato's extended argument in the *Philebus*, accord-ing to which the good is the good life, is deeply Socratic: the good is not discussed as a Form, but as something situated in our lives. That is, the argument that the good is the good life is not only a detailed discussion of an idea that Aristotle, in the *Nicomachean Ethics*, presents as if it was obvious; it is at the same time a reconsideration of the Socratic intuition that we should try to say something about things as they are within our lives. For a discus-sion of the central argument to this effect, cf. my "Why Pleasure Gains Fifth Rank: Against the Anti-Hedonist Interpretation of the *Philebus*," in John Dillon and Luc Brisson (eds.), *Plato's Philebus* (St. Augustin: Akademia Verlag, 2010), 250–55.

The passage I cited marks a moment of hand-waving toward Socratic insignia, such as the Delphic oracle, ignorance as vice, self-knowledge, and so on. Plato apparently signals that he shall refer to ideas his readers are already familiar with, and should associate with an early Socrates.

The passage begins with a statement of the Socratic idea that ignorance and stupidity are vices.[50] Note that 'vice,' here, is a conventional but imperfect translation. Socrates talks about a bad state or about 'a bad [thing]' (*kakon*). This formulation corresponds to the way in which Greek ethicists talk about 'goods' (*agatha*) and 'a good' (*agathon*). Accordingly, the claim that ignorance is a *kakon* could simply mean that it is a bad thing. The conventional rendering of the text, where Socrates says that ignorance is a vice, is nevertheless legitimate: the thought is immediately rephrased in terms of *ponēria*, that is, badness in the sense in which one might say that someone's badness is shameful. And yet the relevant idea is different from 'vice' in a moral sense. A *kakon*, understood as a *ponēria*, is a bad state for the person to be in. To be in this state is bad for her, and quite generally speaking, a bad thing.

> Socrates: Now, ignorance (*agnoia*) is a vice (*kakon*), and so is what we call stupidity [...].
>
> What conclusions do you draw from this about the nature of the ridiculous? (48c)

The occasion for this remark is provided by a discussion of comedy.[51] Plato is interested in the nature of those protagonists who are laughed at by the audience. They are ridiculous.[52] The ridiculous is the kind of badness (*ponēria*) that would result from adhering to the opposite

[50]Another relevant passage is *Euthyphro* 2a–3d. Socrates talks about the charges that Meletus brings against him, including the charge that he corrupts the youth. This charge implies, *pace* Socrates, that Socrates is ignorant—for otherwise he would not do anything bad. Notably, since Socrates rejects the charge that he corrupts the youth, he also rejects the charge of being ignorant in the relevant sense (vice, badness, wrongdoing).

[51]Again, this is a case where scholars divide up into their respective fields, and interesting questions get lost: this bit of text is almost exclusively studied by literary theorists working on the history of comedy; it is not read as relevant to Plato's epistemology.

[52]Interpreters sometimes think that Plato discusses the nature of the ridiculous as if he was concerned with 'what is ridiculous' in a general way; however, he is concerned with the nature of ridiculous people, and with the idea that they display the vice of ignorance in a specific fashion.

recommendation of the Delphic "Know thyself," namely "Do not know yourself at all" (48c–d). The resulting condition is now subdivided.

Are there not necessarily three ways in which it is possible not to know oneself? [...] (i) if someone thinks himself richer than in fact he is [...]; (ii) even more consider themselves taller and handsomer than in fact they are, and believe that they have other such physical advantages [...] (iii) but an overwhelming number are mistaken about the third kind, which belongs to the soul, namely virtue, and believe that they are superior in virtue, although they are not. [...] And again, among the virtues, is it not especially to wisdom that the largest number of people lay claim, puffing themselves up with quarrels and pretensions to would-be knowledge? (*Philebus* 48d–49a)

Socrates proposes that there is a kind of ignorance, and thus a kind of badness, that is typically tied to thinking of oneself as better than in fact one is. Notably, lack of self-knowledge is here not introduced as, say, a matter of access to one's mental states. It includes such matters as thinking oneself *richer* than one is. Falling prey to one's wishful thinking, seeing oneself as taller, richer, more beautiful, and so on, than one is count as ways to lack self-knowledge.[53] Thinking that one is smarter and more virtuous than one is has the same structure. Though now one is concerned with one's soul rather than one's physical or material advantages, one is basically doing the same thing: one indulges in an inflated self-image. I put the quote from the *Philebus* at the very beginning of this chapter because, as I see it, it involves a significant leveling-down of what philosophers tend to expect when they discuss a lack of self-knowledge. Plato is concerned with wishful thinking about one's own positive traits, and with how such self-flattery leads to inflated knowledge-claims.[54]

The text continues with an important qualification. Such conditions, Socrates says, play out differently, depending on whether the person is strong and powerful, or whether she is weak (49b). Ridiculous people are

[53]Plato's well-known example for a false pleasure recalls the cartoons of Dagobert Duck in his gold chamber. Plato envisages a person who is greatly pleased by the thought of herself sitting on top of a pile of gold. Cf. D. Frede, "Rumpelstiltskin's Pleasures, True and False Pleasures in Plato's Philebus," *Phronesis* 30 (1985): 151–80.

[54]This doesn't mean, of course, that he is exclusively concerned with this point. As discussed in the case of Ion, he is also interested in mistakes cognizers make with respect to whether they understand their own thoughts; and whether the things they say are indeed, in a full sense, *their* thoughts.

weak: they are the ones who are not in a position to revenge themselves when they are laughed at. Strong people with the relevant ignorance, however, take revenge and become dangerous and hateful when they are laughed at for their stupidity. "[I]gnorance on the side of the strong and powerful is odious and ugly"; it is harmful (*blaberon*) not only for the person herself, but also for those next to her (49c).

This proposal is, I think, the upshot of much that is discussed in the *Apology* and *Ion*, and in other early dialogues such as the *Euthyphro*, where Socrates talks with a singularly conceited priest. Plato makes explicit what is most remarkable about the Socratic proposal. Blameworthy ignorance involves self-aggrandizing thoughts; it is harmless in people of modest standing, and dangerous in those with power. Claims to the effect that we are better than we really are, Plato proposes, have a pervasive influence on how we fare in our other thoughts. This proposal is tied to an analysis of our reactions. Where the ignorant person is a 'nobody,' we laugh about her stupidity. However, where the ignorant person is in power, things are more complicated. Such people are also pathetic. But if one were to laugh about them, they would lash out. This discussion adds to the *Apology*'s distinction between craftsmen on the one hand, and politicians and poets on the other hand. Ordinary people who think too highly of their wisdom deserve less blame than intellectuals in the same predicament; moreover, they only harm themselves through their condition, not doing harm to others. Socratically blameworthy ignorance is at its worst when displayed by persons in power— arguably, not just politicians and priests, but also scholars.

It is hard to say what someone is good at who is a good interpreter of poetry, or a good speaker in political assembly. Surely, such people must in some sense be good thinkers; and surely, they must take an interest in a wide range of questions. But if you are a good thinker, and if many questions figure in your thoughts, how are you to still draw the line, and recognize what knowledge claims you are entitled to? Plato's criticism of blameworthy ignorance is not an arrogant dismissal of the things ordinary people say. It is best read as addressing philosophers and others in similar walks of life. It points to a deep difficulty in how to do philosophy, or poetry, or politics, and so on. As will become clear throughout the book, I think that this line of thought leads toward the investigative techniques and epistemic norms of ancient skepticism—a kind of philosophy that emphasizes the struggle against one's own ignorance, as opposed to the attempt to formulate and defend one's own theory.

Bryant & Stratton
2College Library
Virginia Beach College

Belief and Investigation in the *Republic*

From the point of view of contemporary ethics, and from the point of view of ordinary talk about our ethical lives, it seems obvious that we have beliefs about the good—beliefs about what kinds of things are good, what makes good things good, and so on. Starting from such beliefs, we might try to formulate a theoretical account of these matters. It would seem that an ethical theory according to which one cannot conduct this type of investigation must be misguided.[1] Surprisingly, Plato scholars have been content with an interpretation of the *Republic* according to which Plato cannot allow for beliefs about the good—even though, arguably, quite a few beliefs about the good are discussed. Indeed, it might seem that one cannot even begin to think about the good if one is not going to ask oneself and each other what one believes about it. What, then, is the role of beliefs in investigation?

The *Republic*'s conception of belief makes room for what I see as three distinctively different ways of believing. Plato ascribes features to beliefs—such as, that belief is with or without knowledge, that belief is ugly and blind, and so on—that allow us to draw a distinction between beliefs about the objects of belief, beliefs *without* knowledge about intelligible objects, and beliefs *with* knowledge about intelligible objects.[2] Plato's

[1]Note that such beliefs can be of quite different kinds. Theorists will differ on whether ethics should begin from 'intuitions.' Even if it does not, it will begin from some considerations, and as long as these are subject to revision, they will count, in Plato's framework, as beliefs.

[2]One might object that, rather than introduce a distinction between three modes of believing, we should keep apart a strict and a loose sense of belief. In the strict sense, belief is belief about believables. This proposal seems right to me insofar as beliefs about believables are, as I see it, the 'core' case of belief: here belief is applied in the manner that most

51

conception of belief explains that the proper objects of belief are not knowable. The proper object of belief is the 'believable' (*doxaston*), or that which is and is not. To have beliefs about such matters is not second best. In relation to such matters, belief is entirely adequate. The fact that there are beliefs about intelligible objects helps Plato account for investigation. Investigation begins from beliefs about matters that we ultimately want to know about. Our initial beliefs can be examined, dismissed, and reformulated.[3] Some myths and stories are beliefs.

But in important respects, they are not about believables. For example, a story about a hero may involve many believables. In these respects, and thus in a quite literal sense, it may be true or false. But the story may also contain truths about courage, or friendship, and so on. Insofar as it does, it still has the status of belief (note that these matters are likely to be expressed in images), but it is not about believables. The story can lead those who listen to it toward the truth, and it can thus have an element of understanding to it. In this sense, it is a belief with knowledge, or at least, it is not without knowledge.

Consider the passage that leads up to the similes of the Sun, the Line, and the Cave.[4] As Socrates reports, Adeimantus has often heard

---

immediately reflects the nature of belief. But I do not think that beliefs about intelligible matters are beliefs in a nonstrict, and thereby ordinary sense. Beliefs about intelligible matters are as much the subject matter of epistemological theorizing as beliefs about believables. As will become clear from my argument, beliefs about intelligible matters are beliefs in a lesser sense insofar as, in these beliefs, the faculty of belief is not employed in the manner that most fully represents its nature.

[3]Cephalus's, Polemarchus's, and Thrasymachus's beliefs about justice, as well as Socrates', Glaucon's, and Adeimantus' reactions to them, figure prominently in the *Republic* as a whole. Similarly, the saying of the poet Simonides, that justice is to give everyone his due (*Rp.* I, 331e), is an important starting point of the discussions in the *Republic*. Again, this is not presented as a piece of knowledge. It is someone's view, and one that is worth engaging with.

[4]According to Charles H. Kahn, the passage is a "dramatical aside," "without consequences for the doctrinal account of *doxa*." As Kahn goes on to say, "In every careful statement of the basic dichotomy, *doxa* and sense perception belong together as taking *to gignomenon* as their object (e.g. *Tim.* 28A 2), whereas the reality of the Forms is *adoxaston* (*Phaedo* 84A 8)." "The Presentation of the Forms," in *Plato and the Socratic Dialogue: The Philosophical Use of a Literary Form* (Cambridge: Cambridge University Press, 1996), 329–70, esp. 361. Cf. J. Annas, *An Introduction to Plato's Republic* (Oxford: Clarendon Press, 1981), 194.

people discuss the question of what the good is. To most people, pleasure seems to be the good, and to some, wisdom (VI, 505b).[5] It takes just a brief remark by Socrates to remind us of well-known problems with these views.[6] Adeimantus wants Socrates to say what *he* thinks about the good. Socrates declines; he does not know what the good is. Adeimantus, however, insists. Why should one not say what one believes, stating it as something that one believes, without implying that one knows it (506c)? Socrates replies by asking Adeimantus whether he has not realized that beliefs without knowledge (*aneu epistēmēs doxai*) are ugly (*aischrai*), and that even the best of them are blind (*typhlon*) (506c).[7] Then, however, he relates the similes of Sun, Line, and Cave, and refers to them as 'what seems to him.' Clearly, this indicates that the similes in some way capture Socrates' beliefs about the good.

The traditional interpretation of the *Republic* cannot explain this passage. But neither can an interpretation that has been put forward in order to resolve the obvious problems of the traditional interpretation, an interpretation that I shall call countertraditional.[8]

[5]For discussion of the two theses 'pleasure is the good' and 'wisdom is the good' in other dialogues, cf. *Euth.* 281d–282e, 288d–289d (wisdom), *Gorgias* 494c–505a (pleasure), and the *Philebus*.

[6]Pleasure cannot be the good because there are also bad pleasures. When we ask the proponents of 'wisdom is the good' what it is that one is to be wise about, their answer is 'the good.' Thus while they presumably tell us what the good is, they at the same time assume that we already know it (VI, 505b–d).

[7]He also adds a third predicate to 'ugly' and 'blind': *skolia*, 'crooked'; and he contrasts these three predicates with 'clear' (*phana*) and 'beautiful' (*kala*) (506c–d). Throughout this book, I am translating *doxa* as 'belief'. For a detailed discussion of traditional translations of *doxa* in Plato (opinion, belief, judgment), cf. Jürgen Sprute, "Der Begriff der DOXA in der platonischen Philosophie," in *Hypomnemata: Untersuchungen zur Antike und ihrem Nachleben*, vol. 2 (Göttingen: Vandenhoeck & Ruprecht, 1962).

[8]The Two Worlds Doctrine is often presented in terms of a distinction between *being* and *becoming*; scholars tend to draw, next to the *Republic*, on the *Phaedo, Symposium*, and *Timaeus*. There is no consensus on whether the *Meno* and the *Theaetetus* should be interpreted as departures from the Two Worlds Doctrine, or merely as exploring knowledge from different perspectives. The idea that knowledge is true belief tied down by an account (*Meno* 98a), or true belief with an account (see the third part of the *Theaetetus*), may seem to not fit in with the idea that knowledge and belief each have their own objects, or it may only seem to fit in if we suppose that, once we are able to justify them or to provide an account, true beliefs *turn into* knowledge.

Traditional interpretation (T)[9]

(T1) There is no knowledge about the objects of belief (perceptible things), and no belief about the objects of knowledge ('what is'). Each cognitive power is *exclusively* related to its objects.

(T2) 'What is' refers to the Forms.

Countertraditional interpretation (C)[10]

(C1) We can have knowledge about perceptible things, and beliefs about 'what is.' Knowledge and belief engage with propositions—true propositions in the case of knowledge, true and false in the case of belief—not with this or that kind of object.

(C2) 'What is' does not refer to the Forms, but rather to what is true.

Neither of these interpretations can explain the conversation between Socrates and Adeimantus. T cannot accommodate the fact that people (including Socrates) have beliefs about the good. C cannot explain why there is anything wrong with beliefs without knowledge, other than that they may be false. Why should beliefs without knowledge, even if they are true, be ugly and blind? Both T and C rely on the idea that knowledge and belief relate to their objects in such a way that they cannot be *deficiently applied to other things*. This is not how Plato characterizes the relationship between cognitive powers and their objects. Rather, knowledge is directed toward and fitted for what is, and belief is directed toward and fitted for what is and is not. The claim that belief and knowledge have different objects does not imply that one *cannot* have beliefs

---

[9]Francis M. Cornford may be considered a proponent of this position, in *Plato's Theory of Knowledge* (London: K. Paul, Trench, Trubner, 1933). However, I am not engaging with any one interpretation specifically. Rather, I take it that these assumptions figure in many discussions of Plato's middle dialogues.

[10]Gail Fine offers the most elaborate account of this kind. Fine has presented her views in several publications—first in "Knowledge and Belief in Republiv V," *Archiv für Geschichte der Philosophie* 1978, 121–39; then in "Knowledge and Belief in Republic V–VII," in S. Everson (ed.), *Epistemology*, Companions to Ancient Thought 1 (Cambridge: Cambridge University Press, 1990), 85–115; reprinted in Fine (ed.), *Plato*, vol. 1, *Metaphysics and Epistemology* (Oxford: Oxford University Press, 1999), 215–46 and in Fine, *Plato on Knowledge and Forms: Selected Essays* (Oxford: Oxford University Press, 2003), 85–116. For an earlier, influential rejection of T cf. J. C. Gosling, "*Doxa* and *dunamis* in Plato's Republic," *Phronesis* 13 (1968): 119–30.

about the objects of understanding. It implies that belief about intelligible matters is inherently deficient—deficient because it is generated through a kind of cognitive activity that is naturally adapted to a different task.

I begin with a close look at C (section 1). C has a great advantage over T: it can explain philosophical investigation. But philosophical investigation can be explained in an even better way—and can be understood in a more nuanced fashion—if we resist C, and revise T. This revision relies in part on a retranslation of some key expressions in *Republic* V (section 2). Beliefs about intelligible objects play an important role in philosophical investigation (section 3).

1. The Countertraditional Interpretation

T and C refer to a number of passages in the *Republic*. Most importantly, they aim to interpret an argument at the end of Book V (476e–478e). Both the lover of sights and sounds and the philosopher *'love to see'* (V, 475d–476e). But they look at different things. The lover of sights and sounds loves to see the many beautiful colors and shapes of perceptible things. He sees these things as beautiful, and does not concern himself with the question of whether this is all there is to beauty. In contrast with him, the philosopher loves all knowledge, and seeks the Beautiful itself. Philosophers and lovers of sights and sounds differ with respect to where they turn their souls. This idea is part of a larger discussion in the *Republic*. Education in the best city is a *turning around of the soul (psychēs periagōgē)*, out of a nightlike day into a 'true day of being' (VII, 521c5–8).[11] From the very beginning, it aims to turn the soul toward the Forms, and to inspire love for them.[12] The lover of sights and sounds has his soul turned the other way, toward the many beautiful sights and sounds. For this reason, Socrates says that he can only have beliefs (476d).

This inference needs an explanation, and Socrates proceeds to clarify it (476e–478e). Knowledge engages with what is (*to on*); ignorance with

---

[11] On the importance of 'turning around' cf. Burnyeat, "Why Mathematics Is Good," esp. 42–45.

[12] Musical education, Socrates says, should end in love of the Beautiful (403c6–7). The kinds of games children are to play are conducive to producing a correct order in their soul, an order that mirrors the order of the law (IV, 424e–425a).

what is not (*to mē on*). Belief (*doxa*) is a different power (*dunamis*) than knowledge (*epistēmē*).[13] Just as the powers of sight and hearing are directed at different objects, belief is directed at something other than knowledge. Accordingly, belief cannot be directed at what is. But belief is directed at something, not at nothing. The objects of *doxa* must be in the middle between what is and what is not: belief is 'darker' than knowledge, but 'brighter' than ignorance. Knowledge knows 'knowables,' belief believes 'believables,' and the latter are explained as 'what participates in being and not-being,' or 'what is and is not.'[14] The lover of sights and sounds is confined to beliefs because he spends his life with 'what is and is not'; among the many beautiful things, there is not one that would not, at the same time, be ugly (479a–b). He does not even acknowledge that there are things other than the many beautiful things, for example, the Beautiful.

It is a core intuition of T that the Beautiful is an example of 'what is,' while things that are beautiful and ugly are examples of 'what is and is not.'[15] I want to hold on to part of this assumption: that 'what is' refers to the Forms (T2).[16] My argument for this claim is indirect. Even the proponents of C admit that the philosopher ultimately aims to know Forms,

---

[13]Other words for knowledge that Plato uses in this passage are *gnōmē* and *gnōsis*.

[14]478e1–2 and 478d5–6. In addition to Book V, interpretations of Plato's epistemology in the *Republic* draw on the similes and X, 601b–602b. In *Republic* X, Socrates explains how only the user of something, e.g., a flute, knows what a useful and a bad flute is. The maker of the flute needs to trust him; he has only correct belief (*pistis orthē*). I cannot engage with the complex questions pertaining to this passage. But it seems important to note that it does *not* suggest that users and makers have knowledge versus mere belief of perceptible particulars, like 'this flute.' Rather, the user of flutes knows what it is for a flute to be a good flute; this is knowledge of a theoretical matter. The beliefs of the maker engage deficiently with this theoretical matter.

[15]J. C. B. Gosling argues that the idea that beautiful particulars are also ugly does not make sense ("*Republic* V: *to polla kalla* Etc.," *Phronesis* 5 [1960]: 116–28). If we accept this assessment (which I do not share, but do not have the room to discuss), it may seem less plausible that 'what is' refers to the Forms.

[16]Much of the research on *Republic* V, 476e–478e employs a distinction between a predicative, an existential, and a veridical use of 'is' (*esti*); however, this distinction has also been subjected to much criticism. For the distinction between different uses of '*esti*' cf. C. Kahn, "The Greek Verb 'Be' and the Concept of Being," *Foundations of Language* 2 (1966): 245–65, as well as "Some Philosophical Uses of 'to be' in Plato," *Phronesis* 26 (1981): 105–35. While my argument engages with the veridical reading, it steers clear of many intricate issues pertaining to the existential and the predicative reading, both of which may seem to be closer to T than the veridical reading.

and that, in many passages in the *Republic*, Plato says that the Forms *are* (or that he refers to them as '*ta onta*', the things that are). I see no reason to suppose that Socrates, at *Republic* V, 476e–478e, does *not* use 'what is' as a label for what, at other passages in the dialogue, is referred to as Forms (T2).

According to C, T2 is precisely where the traditional interpretation goes wrong. Once we take 'what is' to refer to the Forms, so goes the suggestion, we fall into the trap of not being able to account for philosophical investigation. If 'what is' and 'what is and is not' refer to different kinds of objects, belief and knowledge do not *share* any objects. Apparently, we cannot progress from belief to knowledge. Gail Fine proposes a reading that aims to remedy this, and thus to account for philosophical investigation: in core sections of *Republic* V, 476e–478e, 'is' should be understood in a *veridical* sense.[17] According to this suggestion, what we know is true, while what we believe can be true *or* false. The objects of knowledge are true propositions, and thus are the objects of true belief. In this way, there are not two separate ontological realms, each with its own kind of object. Investigation engages, at every point, with propositions.[18] This interpretation has the great advantage of appealing to a core intuition about knowledge: that what we know is true. But what, in *Republic* V, 476e–478e, indicates that '*esti*' should be read in the veridical sense? Certainly (and this is not disputed by Fine), the rest of the middle books make it clear that philosophers aim at knowledge of the Forms, and that the Forms 'are' in the highest sense. It might seem overwhelmingly more plausible to assume that this is also at issue in *Republic* V, 476e–478e.[19]

---

[17]It is relatively uncontroversial that the Greek *esti* can mean something like 'is true.' Fine gives a very helpful summary of her views in the introduction to *Plato on Knowledge and Forms*, 1–43.

[18]For this reason, Fine calls her interpretation a contents analysis, rather than an objects analysis of Plato's epistemology (*Plato*, 221).

[19]I do not discuss the individual lines of the passage with respect to whether the veridical reading makes sense. That this reading is at several places problematic has been argued by F. G. Gonzalez, "Propositions or Objects? A Critique of Gail Fine on Knowledge and Belief in *Republic* V," *Phronesis* 41 (1996): 245–75. Some similar points are made by Job Van Eck in "Fine's Plato," *Oxford Studies in Ancient Philosophy* 28 (2005): 303–26. I engage with a premise of Fine's argument that is more widely accepted than the veridical reading: That in *Republic* V, 476e–468e, Socrates talks with the lover of sights and sounds. For a discussion of Fine's interpretation that disagrees with the veridical reading, but agrees with the view that Socrates is, at this point, in an important sense *not* talking with Glaucon, see M. Stokes, "Plato and the Sightlovers of the *Republic*," *Apeiron* 25 (1992): 103–32.

According to C, we can resist this conclusion, because in 476e–478e, Socrates does *not* talk with Glaucon. He talks with the lover of sights and sounds.[20] Socrates asks Glaucon to respond *on behalf of* the lover of sights and sounds (476e7–8). Glaucon assumes the role of the lover of sights and sounds. This change of personalities is, according to C, highly relevant to our reading of the text. Fine invokes what she calls the Dialectical Requirement: that the dialectically *better* investigation "should only use claims that are (believed to be true), and that the interlocutor accepts."[21] This criterion is formulated, according to Fine, in the *Meno* (75d). As an impersonator of the lover of sights and sounds, Glaucon understands and accepts only what this person would understand and accept. If we read the argument on this assumption, it seems that 'what is' cannot be understood as referring to Forms. Only a person trained in Plato's philosophy will catch on to this sense. As Fine suggests, the idea that knowledge is true, while belief can be true or false, no matter how philosophically significant it may be, is relatively commonsensical. Even the lover of sights and sounds who dislikes philosophy should be able to see this point. The veridical reading of the passage thus seems to be required by the standards of dialectical investigation. And the problem that T poses—that there can be no investigation that begins with belief and progresses to knowledge—disappears.

This argument fails, however, in more than one way. It is not clear that we should accept Fine's premise, namely that the dialogue follows the Dialectical Requirement. My reasons for resisting this premise are, first, that it is not clear to me whether one can unproblematically assume that such a rule carries over from one dialogue to another. Accordingly, it would seem more promising to examine the *Republic* with a view to whether something like Fine's Dialectical Requirement is at work. Independently of this and second, I find the relevant passages in the *Meno* less clear than Fine suggests. They occur in the context of Socrates' and Meno's discussions about the difference between virtue and *a* virtue, shape and *a* shape, color and *a* color. These passages are notoriously difficult, and I shall not attempt here to defend any reading of them.[22]

---

[20]T. Ebert, *Meinung und Wissen in der Philosophie Platons* (Berlin: Walter de Gruyter, 1974), 118 f.

[21]Fine, *Plato on Knowledge and Forms*, 87 f.

[22]Here is a brief sketch of why I would raise such doubts. In response to the question "What is shape?" Socrates suggests that shape is what follows color (FC) (75b–c). Meno responds with a point that Socrates dismisses: that this kind of reply is unsatisfactory, since

In short, however, I do not find it obvious that Socrates observes the Dialectical Requirement even in the very conversation in which he formulates it.

In the *Republic*, Socrates adopts a style of questioning that reflects whom he is talking to. He talks differently with Cephalus than with Thrasymachus, and many scholars think that we can detect a difference in how he talks, on the one hand, with Adeimantus, and on the other, with Glaucon. Thus a different dialectical requirement may be at work: that one should adapt one's questioning, depending on who one's interlocutor

---

we would need to know what color is. Socrates thinks that FC was correct, whether or not his interlocutor knows what color is. However, he goes on to say: If you were one of these people who fight with arguments, I would simply tell you that, if my reply is not correct, it is your task to refute it. But since Meno is not one of these eristic people, he (Socrates) ought to speak in a gentler and more dialectical fashion. He should give a correct reply, and he should only "answer through things" (i.e., only make use of notions) that his interlocutor agrees he understands. (I follow Dominic Scott here. The core idea is not that one should make use of premises that one's interlocutor understands, but that one should refer to things—or: make use of notions—that the interlocutor says he knows (*Plato's Meno* [Cambridge: Cambridge University Press 2006], 35–36). That is the way in which Socrates says he will now discuss shape with Meno. Does Meno call something *peras* (limit) and *eschaton* (the last)? Meno says yes. As long as one does not ask for a deep understanding of geometry, but merely for familiarity with these notions, it is quite plausible that Meno knows, for example, what limit is. But would it not seem that, in this sense, he also knows what color is? After some more steps, Socrates arrives at his second definition of shape: shape is what limits an area (76a). Thus shape has been explained, and Meno turns back to color. He now also wants to hear what color is. This reminds us that, in fact, Socrates thought his initial account of shape, FC, was true. If Socrates is to observe the first part of the Dialectical Requirement, that one is to give a true reply (or one that one holds to be true), why does he not stick with the account that he thinks is correct? Since it is not clear that there are several true accounts of the same thing, does Socrates violate the first half of the Dialectical Requirement? (Cf. Scott, *Plato's Meno*, 45.) Socrates gives in to Meno's request and explains color. He does so by invoking a theory about effluences, this time with even more explicit distaste for the account he is putting forward. He keeps emphasizing that Meno is so impressed with this account because the terms it uses are *familiar* to Meno. Meno *thinks* he understands it, because he has often heard his teachers speak about things of this kind. Socrates thus seems to put forward a distinction between the mere impression that one understands something, and a genuine understanding of it. Meno has only the former. Does Socrates now violate the second half of the Dialectical Requirement, which asks that one's interlocutor understands what he agrees to, not that he merely feels like he understands it? (Cf. Scott, *Plato's Meno*, 56–59.)

is.[23] This Revised Dialectical Requirement does not demand that Socrates make only assumptions that his interlocutor *shares*. Witness Thrasymachus, who is explicitly uneasy with how things progress, because he does not, at heart, agree with the ideas that Socrates extracts from the points that he has granted.[24] And it pertains importantly—and in agreement with the metaphysical epistemology of the dialogue—to the *objects* of discussion. Scholars tend to think that Glaucon is more philosophically advanced than Adeimantus, and that it is usually when things become most abstract that Socrates turns to him.[25] If one can interpret Socrates' questioning as adhering to the Revised Dialectical Requirement, then it seems he really should not talk about epistemology with the lover of sights and sounds. This is not the kind of topic such a person is interested in, nor is he up to it. If anyone is a suitable partner for this discussion, it is Glaucon.

Socrates tells Glaucon to reply in the place of the lover of sights and sounds. But it is not clear what exactly this means. Is Glaucon asked to impersonate the lover of sights and sounds? Or should he reply instead of the lover of sights and sounds? Consider the philosophical psychology of the *Republic*: it seems very unlikely that Socrates would ask a truth-loving person to impersonate someone whose soul is turned away from philosophy; such impersonation taints the soul, and must be avoided.[26] Glaucon should not do this. And he does not. In reply to Socrates' instruction, Glaucon says, '*I* will respond,' and from here on the phrasing continuously makes it clear that we are dealing with: what *seems* to be the case to Socrates (477c5) and to Glaucon (478c13); what *they* want to say (477a); what Glaucon *understands* (477c); whether *he* shares *Socrates'* notion of a power (477c9–d6); what Socrates and Glaucon can agree on (478a1–2);

---

[23]Burnyeat argues that this is how the discussion in the *Republic* proceeds, and associates the method with *Phaedrus* 271e–272b ("Culture and Society in Plato's *Republic*," *The Tanner Lectures on Human Values* 20 [Salt Lake City: University of Utah Press, 1999], 217–324, 293). There Socrates says that the power of speech is to guide souls (*psuchagōgia*), and that the rhetorician must study the different kinds of souls that his interlocutors may have, as well as kinds of speeches, and then match the appropriate kind of speech to whom he is talking to. This account is concerned with making speeches, not with the method of question and answer. However, I agree with Burnyeat's thesis that this is essentially what Socrates does in the *Republic*—he adapts his mode of discussion to whom he is talking to (and that means, to the state in which his interlocutor's soul is).

[24]Cf. for example *Republic* I, 342c10, 342e6, 346c12, 350c12–d3.

[25]Cf. Burnyeat, "Culture and Society," 293.

[26]Like the young guardians of the ideal city, Glaucon should not 'imitate' anything lowly. There is danger that imitation grows into 'being' (395b9–d1).

what Glaucon needs to consider (478b7), and so on.[27] (Further, the aim of the argument is to point out why the lover of sights and sounds can only have beliefs, not knowledge; presumably the lover of sights and sounds does not like this idea. However, nothing in *Republic* V, 476e–478e reflects that the answerer is steered into a view that he *dislikes*, a view that leaves *him* solely with belief.)[28]

Suppose that some will not be persuaded by these considerations, and hold on to the view that Fine's Dialectical Requirement applies and that Socrates' interlocutor is the lover of sights and sounds. If so, then 'what is' must mean something that at least *sounds* commonsensical, even if it has deep philosophical implications. And the claim that 'everything that we know is true' may appear to be such a claim, acceptable to nonphilosophers. Well, matters are by no means that straightforward in *Republic* V, 476e–478e. Socrates does not say things like 'whenever we know something, what we hold to be true is true.' Rather, he says things like 'knowledge is directed at what is.' And while it is possible that this claim means 'knowledge is directed at what is true,' this is not the most natural reading of the Greek; it is a sophisticated *interpretation*. Indeed, it is an

---

[27]At the end of the argument, Socrates summarizes the results, and again addresses the lover of sights and sounds. He says 'these things now being presupposed,' he should tell me whether, among the many beautiful things, there is one that is not also ugly, etc. But even though Socrates seems to directly engage with the lover of sights and sounds at this point, Glaucon again gives an answer that reflects his own perspective. Necessarily, he says, it will be somehow beautiful and somehow ugly (478e8–479b2). If he were taking the perspective of the lover of sights and sounds, the answer would have to be along the lines of 'he agreed only grudgingly that these things are beautiful and ugly.' We should not forget that the lover of sights and sounds still—*after* Book V, 476e–478e—does *not acknowledge* that there is Beauty (479a).

[28]Socrates says that the lover of sights and sounds will be mad with us if we say that he only has beliefs, and no knowledge. He suggests two ways of engaging with him: First, we could manipulate him into agreeing with our point of view, without letting him feel that he is not in his right mind. Second, we might say 'fine, so much the better if you have knowledge, we like meeting people who have knowledge.' But Socrates pursues neither of these options. He switches gears and says 'but tell us this: He who knows, does he know something or nothing?' adding 'you [Glaucon], respond in his place' (476d8–e8). This very abstract question takes up neither the manipulative strategy indicated at first, nor the second, confrontational approach. As I would suggest, Socrates changes gears because ultimately, we are not in this investigation in order to bash the lover of sights and sounds. Rather, *we* want to understand something. And if we want to understand why someone who immerses himself in the sphere of many beautiful things has only beliefs, we need a serious and difficult investigation.

interpretation that introduces the notion of truth into a passage that does not directly talk of it. The lover of sights and sounds does not engage in philosophy. Her understanding of things would have to be an unsophisticated and pretheoretical understanding. It is not clear whether there is *any* such reading of the text. What, for example, might the claim 'belief is directed at what participates in what is and what is not' mean to someone without philosophical inclinations and training? Whatever Socrates means by such expressions, his interlocutor must engage in philosophy in order to grasp it. If this is so, then Socrates must be talking to a philosopher: Glaucon.

2. *The Directedness of Knowledge and Belief*

There is thus no reason to doubt the most straightforward reading of 'what is'—that it refers to the Forms. But how is philosophical investigation possible, if belief and knowledge do not 'share' objects? For investigation to be possible, I suggest, belief must not engage with matters that, as the very same things, we can also know. Rather, we must be able to hold beliefs on questions to which we want to know the answers. This allows for the idea that, while we make progress in investigation, we on the one hand keep studying the same question (e.g., 'what is the good?')[29], but on the other hand engage with different objects (e.g., we begin by thinking about pleasurable episodes in our life and end up understanding the Form of the Good).[30] For this to be possible, belief must be able to engage deficiently with matters of understanding.

Consider the key expressions for how cognitive powers and their objects relate in *Republic* V, 476e–478e. This relationship is most explicitly

[29]Gonzalez notes that insofar as sensibles are participants, engaging with sensibles constitutes *some* engagement with Forms; "in this sense, and in this sense only, *doxa* must be about the form" ("Propositions or Objects?" 272). I agree with Gonzalez that, even within a traditional Two Worlds interpretation, these two worlds are not entirely separate; it is integral to the doctrine that they are *related*. However, my interpretation goes beyond this. I suggest that there are beliefs that are, as it were, deficiently 'turned toward' the objects of knowledge.

[30]Ebert (*Meinung und Wissen*, 139–40) thinks that the proponent of 'wisdom is the good' answers a *different question*, namely, 'what is the greatest good?' (not the question 'what is the good?'). But the point seems to be that people *understand* the question 'what is the good?' differently, not that they are actually engaging with a different question.

expressed by the verb *tassō*, used with the preposition *epi*. Grube's translation renders the relationship as 'is set over.' Knowledge is set over what is, belief is set over what is and is not.[31] Scholarly debates on the passage largely render it in this translation. This reading takes *tassō* to be used in a widespread way, a way that, however, is prevalent in military contexts: something is 'posted at a place.' In a more general sense, *tassō* can also mean 'to order.' If we translate the verb in this sense, the relationship we are interested in looks quite different. The text now says that knowledge is a cognitive power that is structured toward what is (or: 'put together' so as to be directed toward what is), and belief a cognitive power that is structured toward what is and is not.[32] The cognitive acts of understanding and believing engage with 'something' (*ti*). But the cognitive powers are, in themselves, already *directed*. This directedness is, throughout the passage, expressed through the preposition 'toward' (*epi*). Thus knowledge is described as *toward* (*epi*) what is (477b1; 478a7), and Socrates says that powers (*dunameis*) are, partly, to be described by their *direction* (by 'what they are directed toward,' *eph' hō*, 477d1). The combination of *epi* and *tassō* is used as a more elaborate formulation of this point (cf. e.g., 477d1 as compared to 477d3). At some places, these expressions are combined with *pephuke*: it is the *nature* of knowledge and belief to be structured toward their objects (477b12; 478a4–5; 478a7–8).[33]

---

[31]*Republic*, tr. G. M. A. Grube, rev. C. D. C. Reeve (Indianapolis: Hackett, 1992). Fine discusses the relevant passages in this translation, and so do her critics (see Van Eck, "Fine's Plato," and Gonzalez, "Propositions or Objects?"). Cornford renders the relationship that is expressed by '*epi*' in terms of correspondence ('knowledge corresponds to the real', etc.) and in terms of different *fields* that knowledge and belief have. He translates the clause with *tassō* as 'knowledge and belief *have different objects*' (*The Republic of Plato*, tr. Francis MacDonald Cornford [London: Oxford University Press 1945]). In their commentary on the *Republic*, Campbell and Jowett do not explain *tassō*. They only refer back to 345d; there, *tassō* and *epi* express the relationship of the art of the shepherd to his subjects, the sheep (the art is directed at its subjects). They, too, render the relationship that is expressed by '*epi*' in terms of 'A corresponds to B' (*Plato's Republic*, ed. Lewis Campbell and Benjamin Jowett, vol. 3 [New York: Garland, 1987], 258–59). Desmond Lee says that knowledge *relates* to what is, and belief *relates* to what is and is not, and that knowledge and belief each have their own 'natural field' (*Republic*, tr. Desmond Lee [New York: Penguin, 1974]).

[32]In *Republic* VII, 523a f., Plato discusses which sense perceptions lead us into theoretical thought and which do not. In this context, Plato uses *epi* and *tassō* with respect to what each sense engages with: the sense that is ordered (*tetagmenē*) toward (*epi*) the hard is necessarily also ordered *epi* the soft (524a1–2).

[33]I am grateful to Wolfgang Mann for emphasizing this point in conversation.

Socrates explains toward which kinds of things knowledge and belief are turned when they are used for that which fully fits and reflects their natures. Thus knowledge and belief have each their own kinds of objects. This does not mean that they cannot—deficiently—be directed at what they are *not* adequate for. Belief can engage with matters that it 'does not live up to,' and since people have views about all kinds of matters, this happens all the time. Similarly, knowledge could be directed at what it is not made for, and this, too, would be a deficient kind of approach. It is, according to the *Republic*, a substantive insight that we cannot, strictly speaking, know such things as whether this piece of cake is small, or, more generally speaking, particular perceptual matters.[34] The powers of belief deal adequately with such matters. As long as we have not understood this, we might direct the powers of knowledge toward believables, and try to know things that are simply not such as to be known. But once we understand the nature of knowledge and belief, we see that we do not miss anything if we have beliefs about believables; belief is exactly what we should bring to bear on such matters as whether a piece of cake is small, and so on. However, we are still interested in engaging with intelligible objects before we know them. Thus Plato must find room for the deficient application of belief to intelligible objects in a way in which he need not be concerned with the deficient application of knowledge to believables. This reading of *Republic* V, 476e–478e is traditional insofar as it takes 'what is' to refer to the Forms (T2) and ascribes their own objects to belief and knowledge. It is in disagreement with (T1) insofar as it allows for and ascribes an important role to deficient application of belief to intelligible matters.

The comparison with vision and hearing in *Republic* V, 476e–478e confirms this reading. Belief and knowledge are, as Socrates argues, different powers similar to sight and hearing. We can use the faculties of sense perception not only for what they are naturally adapted to. Though both sight and hearing are naturally adapted to specific objects (visible things; sounds), we can redirect them to some extent, and use them for what they are not made for. Suppose that we read the notation of a sonata

---

[34] A precise account of believables goes beyond the topic of this chapter—it is a difficult question how precisely we should describe the matters in the perceptual realm about which we most properly have beliefs. For the purposes of this chapter, I am thus sticking with an example that involves comparatively speaking few complications: whether a given piece of cake is small.

and get at the sound of the sonata in a less direct way than if we were to listen to it. Or suppose we train our powers of hearing so that they can take over some of the tasks in orienting ourselves in the world that are usually performed by sight. In both cases, we do not engage with the same things that the naturally fitted sense would engage with (e.g., with the notation instead of the sound of the music). But we can still aim at that which the better-fitted sense directly engages with, just as we can deficiently direct our powers of belief toward objects of understanding.

3. Beliefs with and without Knowledge

According to this reading of *Republic* V, 476e–478e, belief has its proper objects: believables, or what is and is not. Belief about believables, that is, about such matters as whether this piece of cake is small, is in some sense the standard case of belief. The powers of belief are adequate to the task of cognitively engaging with such matters. But even engagement with some of these matters leads us beyond the sphere of belief (VII, 523a–524d). Considering how something looks both small and large may make us raise questions about smallness and largeness, and so on. Even belief about believables thus need not turn the soul toward the sphere of belief.

The powers of belief can also be applied to questions about intelligible matters, questions such as 'what is the good?' or 'what is justice?'; but they do not succeed in engaging with the very object that knowledge of such matters would engage with. This conception, I think, has a great advantage over C. It captures a key feature of learning and investigation that C cannot accommodate: that while we come to better understand something, our conception of the very thing that we are studying undergoes change. In some cases, we see that we have thought about it in an entirely misguided way. For example, we might have thought that atoms are one kind of thing, and now it turns out that they are something quite different. In other cases, the object of our study becomes a more clearly defined object. There is a sense in which we only know what we are studying when we have concluded the study, and possess knowledge of the given matter. It is this process that Plato's conception of beliefs without and with knowledge elucidates.

Consider one more time the brief conversation between Socrates and Adeimantus that leads up to the similes (VI, 505a–506e). We can learn more about the deficient application of belief to intelligible matters by looking closely at Socrates' stance with respect to beliefs about the good. Socrates calls beliefs such as 'pleasure is the good' *beliefs without knowledge (aneu epistēmēs)*. For T, this notion does not make sense. If belief can only be directed toward its own objects, then no particular case of belief can be said to lack knowledge. For C, 'belief without knowledge' might either mean that a particular belief lacks justification, or that it is false. However, justifications of beliefs do not figure at all in the epistemological discussions of *Republic* V–VII; it would seem quite arbitrary to interpret Socrates' expression along these lines. And Socrates himself makes it clear that he is not referring to false belief. He elaborates on the notion of belief without knowledge by asking Adeimantus whether those who, without understanding *(aneu nou)*, believe something true *(alēthes)*, do not seem like blind people who still happen to find the way (506c6–8).

Beliefs without knowledge are beliefs about questions to which one could know the answer. Both 'pleasure is the good' and 'wisdom is the good' respond to the question 'what is the good?' As we can immediately see, they are not beliefs about the Form of the Good. One way of describing their deficiency is to say that, while they claim to say what the good is, they do not *refer* to the Good (or at least, they do not fully refer to it). That is, they do not successfully refer to the very object that one would need to know in order to answer the question adequately. Further, most holders of beliefs without knowledge do not hold their beliefs in any preliminary or hypothetical way. They are not aware of the fact that they are not referring to that which really is good. That is why they are not merely failing insofar as they do not know the Good. The fail in a deeper fashion: they are content with their beliefs.

Socrates calls beliefs without knowledge ugly. The Greek term that Socrates uses—*aischron*—is the opposite of *kalon*.[35] When Socrates calls something *aischron*, he presumably uses the word in its wide sense, a sense in which 'ugly' is close to 'shameful.' Why does Socrates use a value term in describing belief without knowledge? The beliefs of the lover of sights and sounds are ugly because they are part of a life that is ultimately miserable. The lover of sights and sounds engages only with the sphere of belief, and he is content to do so. He does not even acknowledge that

---

[35]This term is at the center of the discussion of the lover of sights and sounds. The many beautiful things that he is attracted to are beautiful (and ugly) in what we might call an aesthetic sense. But the Beautiful itself is beautiful in a broader sense, a sense that includes ethical beauty. Socrates says that both the Just and the Beautiful are also good (506a4–5).

there is Beauty, and thus cannot seek to know it. Nothing in his beliefs can steer him beyond the sphere of beliefs. A life that is confined to this sphere is 'turned away' from the objects that most deserve our love, and that are the only ones that can truly give pleasure.[36] It lacks the kind of conversion that proper education aims at, and that is integral to leading a flourishing human life. Belief without knowledge is part of a lowly, and ultimately unhappy, existence.

Socrates says that beliefs without knowledge are ugly, and that even the best of them are blind (506c).[37] This way of phrasing the claim may imply that, while even the best of them are blind, the best of them may not be ugly. Or at least: there is a way of engaging with beliefs without knowledge that would allow us to escape from their ugliness. Socrates' own beliefs about the good seem to be an example for this. Socrates says that it would take far too long to get to the point where his interlocutors could see how matters seem to him as regards the good (506e). Such advanced belief without knowledge seems different from standard cases of belief without knowledge. It is aware of its deficiency, and someone like Socrates, who desires knowledge, deals differently with beliefs without knowledge than others do. Rather than endorsing them, he uses them as stepping-stones in philosophical investigation. As parts of a life that is devoted to investigation, beliefs without knowledge can contribute to a good life. While they may, in themselves, be ugly, they need not be part of a miserable life.

However, all belief without knowledge is blind. Consider the lover of sights and sounds. According to Socrates, he lives in a dream, defined as a state in which one regards what is similar not as being similar, but as being *the very thing* that it is similar to. The philosopher, by contrast, recognizes Beauty itself as something, and he sees that which participates in Beauty as being a participant, rather than as being Beauty itself; he is awake (476c–d). Holding beliefs about something that one does not know is like trying to hit a hidden target: one takes oneself to be talking about

[36]This is the conclusion of the lengthy discussion of pleasure and pain in Books VIII and IX of the *Republic*: only the pleasures of the reasoning faculty 'satiate us.' Turning toward the objects of understanding is integral to a good life.

[37]A little later Socrates says that he would be happy to discuss the good in the way in which the interlocutors have discussed justice and the other virtues (506d6). He then suggests turning to the offspring of the good, arguing that it would take much too long to discuss the good in that manner, and that he might make a fool of himself in trying to do so (506d).

the very thing that one wants to know about, but in fact one has no idea what this thing is, and cannot even recognize that the things one engages with are only similar to it. Even the best beliefs without knowledge are blind because only when one finally understands what the matter is, is one actually referring to it. Before that, one refers to things that are merely related to the object of understanding, and one is unable to see how these are not the thing itself. (In a limited fashion one might, blindly, hit the target. One might come up with a view that indeed is true of the intelligible matter itself. For example, the view that justice has something to do with order can be held as a true belief without knowledge, a belief that one holds while not knowing the Just. In this belief, one is not, strictly speaking, referring to the Just, even though one's claim is a true claim about the Just.)

Socrates himself does not want to say what he believes about the good. It seems that he does not want to propose a belief that has, *qua* belief, the same characteristics as 'pleasure is the good', or 'wisdom is the good.' Instead, he turns to the similes. By doing so, he does not turn to knowledge. Socrates begins by saying what 'seems to him' about the sun (506e). Now, he certainly does not present a belief about the sun as part of the world of perceptible objects. Rather, he presents a belief about the sun *as* an offspring of the Good. Like the similes of the Line and the Cave, the Sun expresses beliefs about the good.

What kind of beliefs are the similes? The similes neither express knowledge nor inculcate knowledge. They provide belief, but they do not seem to be bare of understanding (*aneu nou*), and they are not ugly and blind. I would suggest that we call them beliefs with knowledge. We can see this more clearly by comparing the similes to the poetry that is part of the best city. A poet can 'make everything' (X, 596c3–597e); he can tell stories about all kinds of ordinary events. But poetry does not restrict itself to the sphere of particulars of ordinary experience (agents, shields, etc.). Rather, poetry conveys views about matters of understanding, for example about courage, or the gods. If it conveys insights about these matters (II, 377a5–6), poetry is in some sense true, even though, in a literal sense, its stories are false.[38] Poetry about the gods and similarly

---

[38]Children must at first be educated with *false* stories, but only those that pass 'censorship' (II–III, 377a–392c). Similarly, the myths that are integral to sustaining the political arrangements of the best city are 'false speeches' (III, 414–15). However, falsehood in such mimetic storytelling is different from 'true falsehood' (382b9–c2).

weighty matters is not based on knowledge. We do not know the truth about them (382d1-2).[39] And yet, by relying on core insights—such as that the gods are good—a poet may tell stories that contain some element of truth. Still, even if this is the case, his poetry falls short of providing knowledge. As Socrates says in the discussion of education, poetry makes children adopt beliefs (II, 377b7-8). Children should be raised with stories that represent the gods and humans in certain 'true' ways. When children are told such stories, they are made to engage with beliefs about intelligible things. Are these beliefs ugly and blind? It does not seem so. The beliefs that such poetry produces are beautiful insofar as they turn the souls of children toward intelligible matters. And they make the children see things as they are, even if only in an image-like way. Insofar as they have the power to turn the soul toward the objects of understanding, and provide some preliminary and deficient understanding, they are beliefs with knowledge (or perhaps: not without knowledge).

The same, it seems to me, applies to the similes. To some extent, the similes are stories, and they certainly are images. As in poetry, the physical objects and the agents (such as the puppets, or the person who leaves the cave) are not what matters most. What matters most is what the similes aim to convey about the Good. Like a poet whose work meets the standards set up in the ideal city, Socrates relates beliefs that are 'true'— true in the limited sense in which the false speech of metaphor and poetry can be true.[40] The similes do not turn us into knowers. They can only offer beliefs for us to think about. But they are neither ugly nor blind. It is good for us to engage with them, and they make us see things about the Good. In this way, the similes are beliefs with knowledge. As we might say, such belief with knowledge is belief about the Good (rather than belief about the good), but it self-consciously is not knowledge of the Good.

Books V and VI have, on the suggested reading, implications for Plato's conception of truth as related to his notion of belief. C assumes that true belief about intelligible objects is true in a straightforward, nondeficient manner. According to the interpretation that I propose, belief about

---

[39]On the lack of knowledge in traditional poetry cf. 598d8 f.

[40]Note that on this interpretation, Socrates does not have knowledge of the Good. However, his conception of it is so advanced that he can come up with images that resemble it very closely. In this way, he is like the perfect poet.

intelligible matters never is true in a full sense.[41] Belief about intelligible matters involves a misidentification. Only when one knows the Good, is one finally able use the term 'good' so as to successfully refer to the Good. Belief *with* knowledge may have the advantage of not even pretending to be knowledge about the Good. However, it is false in its own way—in the way in which even true poetry is false speech.

4. Conclusion

Plato's metaphysical epistemology in the *Republic* gives a complex picture of belief, a picture that is more multifaceted and detailed than either T or C suggests. The powers of belief can be applied to the proper objects of belief, or to intelligible objects. Both of these applications are vital to human thought. Beliefs about believables are how we deal with many of the everyday things in our lives. Beliefs about intelligible matters are integral to investigation—without them, we cannot begin to study. Beliefs about intelligible objects can explicitly acknowledge that they do not *refer* to these objects by retreating into myth or simile. Such beliefs fall short of knowledge; and yet they direct us toward the objects of understanding and have an element of deficiently acquainting us with them. They can thus legitimately be called beliefs with knowledge, or beliefs with understanding. Beliefs without knowledge, on the other hand, involve a misidentification; they take themselves to refer to the object of understanding while in fact they do not. They do not provide us with even the first glimpse of understanding. But they are indispensable as starting points of investigation. While similes make us 'see' something, they may not invite critical engagement. According to the *Republic*, philosophical investigation must engage, to an important extent, with beliefs without knowledge.

[41]This interpretation allows us to integrate *Republic* V, 476e–478e with the comparative notion of truth that Plato employs in the simile of the Line (VI, 510a9–11). While belief about intelligible matters may be true in the sense of 'blindly hitting the target,' it is not true insofar as the reference of key terms is not what the speaker takes it to be.

3

Belief and Truth in the *Theaetetus*

If one believes something, one does not know whether what one believes is true or false. In the framework of ancient philosophy, this is a truism. This truism can be taken to have a stark implication: only knowledge reaches the truth, and accordingly, beliefs are *not of two kinds*. It is not the case that there are true beliefs on the one hand and false beliefs on the other. To modern ears, this sounds far-fetched. The premise that beliefs are true or false appears to be basic to our notion of belief. I call this the Two Kinds premise. In this chapter, I ask why one might reject it. Are beliefs adequately evaluated as true or false?

Part II of the *Theaetetus* raises the question of whether there are two kinds of belief, true beliefs and false beliefs. It examines two competing intuitions. *Doxazein*, the activity of belief-formation, is generally what cognizers do when they accept something as true. But *doxa* is a deficient cognitive attitude. The Stoics embrace versions of both ideas. As they argue, the mind assents to impressions that are true or false; but beliefs are not the kind of thing that is true or false. That is, beliefs are not bearers of truth-values. Scholars tend not to notice this aspect of Stoic epistemology. As far as I can see, no one even mentions it, and there is no attempt at explaining it.[1] Given how underresearched this line of thought is, I consider it worthwhile to approach it slowly. That is, I approach it

---

[1] This applies even to publications that are immediately concerned with Stoic epistemology, such as Michael Frede, "Stoic Epistemology," in K. Algra, J. Barnes, J. Mansfeld, and M. Schofield (eds.), *The Cambridge History of Hellenistic Philosophy* (Cambridge: Cambridge University Press, 2005), 295–322. Frede writes "Now a belief will be true or false, depending on whether the impression it is an assent to is true or false" (301). In contrast to what Frede says, there are no true beliefs for the Stoics.

through a Stoic reading of Part II of the *Theaetetus*, rather than immediately turning to Stoic epistemology.[2]

I shall discuss the beginning and the end, but not the middle sections, of Part II of the *Theaetetus*. The relevance of these intermediary discussions—of the mind as wax tablet or aviary—for Stoic epistemology has long been recognized, and I do not intend to add here to the literature on these matters.[3] What interests me, instead, are underexplored passages of the text that address, as I see it, general issues about *doxa*'s relationship to truth.[4] Plato associates truth and being (section 1), and this raises the question whether indeed there are true beliefs (section 2). Does *doxa* reach being? To address this question, I insist, one must keep in mind that the notion of *doxa* carries connotations of seemingness and deficiency. For purposes of analyzing Plato's arguments, one should not think in terms of the widespread translation 'judgment' (section 3). Indeed, the final refutation of DEF II, introduced below, hangs on the intuition that *doxa* is generally deficient, no matter whether it is true or false (section

---

[2]In chapter 7, "Why Beliefs Are Never True: A Reconstruction of Stoic Epistemology," I analyze the direct evidence for the Stoic conception of belief.

[3]Cf. for example A. A. Long, "Zeno's Epistemology and Plato's *Theaetetus*," in Long, *From Epicurus to Epictetus. Studies in Hellenistic and Roman Philosophy* (Oxford: Oxford University Press, 2006), 223–35; Anna Maria Ioppolo, "Presentation and Assent: A Physical and Cognitive Problem in Early Stoicism," *Classical Quarterly* 40 (1990): 433–49.

[4]Jan Szaif locates the *Theaetetus* in a phase of Plato's philosophy in which Plato studies the way in which judgments are true or false (*Platons Begriff der Wahrheit* [Freiburg: Alber, 1996]). This is in a sense obviously true. My proposal is that, even where ostensibly Plato is concerned with the distinction between true and false belief, he doesn't consider it obvious that this is a distinction one would want to make. The topic of this chapter is one where the difference between the conceptual frameworks of different philosophical traditions are particularly pertinent. Prominent English editions of the *Theaetetus* follow Levett (Williams, Burnyeat, McDowell) and render *doxa* as judgment, thereby making it seem as if *doxa* was rather close to a modern notion of belief as truth-claim. German translations reflect the fact that there is no German philosophical term that immediately corresponds to "belief." Translations of the *Theaetetus* adapt Schleiermacher's text. *Doxa* is rendered as "Meinung," a notion that contains features both of "opinion" and of "belief"; *doxazein* is rendered as "vorstellen," which is greatly different from "judging." In German, when Socrates says that 'someone *doxazein* something,' he seems to say that someone mentally represents something as something. I shall not go into the difficult question of how the German conceptual framework lends itself to discussion of the matters in the *Theaetetus* that interest me. Note, however, that if one wanted to work closely with secondary literature written in philosophical languages from outside of the Anglo-American tradition, one would engage in several rounds of translation between different conceptual schemes.

4). And this is the thought that the Stoics pick up and develop (section 5).

1. Truth and Being

The main question of the *Theaetetus* is "what is knowledge?" The interlocutors discuss three suggestions and ultimately dismiss all three of them.

(DEF I) Knowledge is perception.

(DEF II) Knowledge is true belief.

(DEF III) Knowledge is true belief with a *logos*.[5]

Looking at these proposals and the ways in which they are examined, one may be puzzled by the absence of Plato's metaphysical epistemology.[6] DEFS I, II, and III violate the Two Worlds Doctrine (TWD). According to TWD, perception and belief engage with the realm of the perceptible and changeable, the world of Becoming. Only Being is the object of knowledge. That is, accounts of knowledge that envisage perception or belief as a component of knowledge are bound to fail. Perception and belief on the one hand and knowledge on the other hand simply do not

---

[5]"*Logos*" can be translated in a number of ways. Though this is not the place to argue for an interpretation of DEF III, I agree with Myles Burnyeat's view in "Socrates and the Jury: Paradoxes in Plato's Distinction between Knowledge and True Belief," *Proceedings of the Aristotelian Society* 54 (1980): 173–91, 180, that the relevant kind of *logos* is something like an explanatory account, not justification in the sense of contemporary JTB (justified true belief) accounts of knowledge.

[6]Interpreters are also puzzled by what they see as the refutational Socrates of earlier dialogues. They tend to accept a certain distinction that can be traced to Aristotle. According to Aristotle, the historical Socrates asked definitional questions that he himself did not know the answer to (*Soph. Ref.* 183b7). Accordingly, dialogues in which Socrates is first and foremost a questioner, and no answers are found, are seen as early dialogues. Dialogues in which Socrates formulates positive theories, however, do not present Socrates as he really was; these are the later dialogues. Sedley argues, in my view rightly, that reception of Plato's philosophy has been shaped too strongly by Aristotle's distinction (*The Midwife of Platonism* [Oxford: Oxford University Press, 2004], esp. 15). It is not clear that the Socrates of the *Theaetetus* is any more 'out of place' than, say, the Socrates of the *Philebus*, another late dialogue.

engage with the same objects. Accordingly, one might argue that DEFS I, II, and III are blatantly false and that the reader is expected to recognize this.[7]

In the wake of Burnyeat's and McDowell's influential commentaries, recent interpreters call this verdict into question.[8] Perhaps Plato is indeed quite serious about examining DEFS I, II, and III? He certainly puts great philosophical effort into doing so. The *Theaetetus*, then, should be read on its own merits, as a philosophically rich text. This reaction shares a premise with the former, more traditional approach—the premise that one knows the details of the metaphysical theory Plato is committed to in the middle dialogues, and that, accordingly, one is in a position to say that the *Theaetetus* is strangely unrelated to these metaphysical views.

Contrary to this assumption, it could be argued that several later dialogues call important aspects of earlier metaphysical proposals into question. And it could be pointed out that there is no dialogue that offers a detailed account of 'the' Theory of Forms. Instead, there are several dialogues that provide sketches. One might further observe that Plato's metaphysical concerns are rather rich and cannot be summed up in a few claims about Forms, particulars, the intelligible, and the perceptible. A wide range of questions about being, not-being, truth, the scope of the Theory of Forms, the relationship between Forms, the relationship between Forms and particulars, and so on, would have to be part of the picture. Several later dialogues are devoted to specific problems in Plato's metaphysics, epistemology, and ethics, and several of them take a critical look at ideas that were formulated earlier.[9]

---

[7]Cornford, in *Plato's Theory of Knowledge*, argues that, quite obviously, Plato must regard DEFS I, II, and III as false, because they violate TWD. For a recent discussion of arguments to similar effect, and of the wide range of contributions on this issue in the literature, cf. Gokhan Adalier, "The Case of 'Theaetetus,'" *Phronesis* 46 (2001): 1–37.

[8]*The Theaetetus of Plato*, revision of Levett's translation by Burnyeat; *Theaetetus*, tr. McDowell; Sedley, *The Midwife of Platonism*.

[9]The *Parmenides* is widely acknowledged to raise serious problems about the relationship between Forms and particulars. The *Sophist* draws attention to the fact that, if one's fundamental notion in philosophy is Being, one will also need a plausible account of not-Being, which turns out to be rather difficult. Moreover, it admits that TWD might not be able to account for the causal roles that the Forms are meant to have, which is a far-reaching problem. The *Philebus* reconsiders the account of the good from the *Republic*. As many have noted, the *Philebus* anticipates some ideas from Aristotle's *Nicomachean Ethics* and thus a way of asking "what is the good?" that situates the good in human life. Further, it is far from obvious how the metaphysics of limit/unlimited/cause/becomings relates to the metaphysics

If this is one's take on Plato, then the *Theaetetus* appears to belong to a group of late dialogues that scrutinize questions of immediate relevance to ideas that, broadly speaking, belong to Plato's metaphysics.[10] In Part II, the section of the text that interests me here, Plato takes up the question of whether, in having a belief of *something*, one has a belief of something that *is*, thus reaching being and truth. More generally speaking, he addresses the question of how thought, and belief as a variant of thought, relates to truth.[11]

Arguably, this question is right at the heart of Plato's metaphysics. The *Republic* contains a number of intriguing points on this issue, but these are not developed or subjected to any scrutiny. For example, in the simile of the Sun, knowledge and truth are closely associated. They relate to the Good, Socrates says, as light and vision relate to the sun (508e–509a): that is, knowledge and truth immediately belong together. Add to this a remark at the end of the simile of the Line. Socrates sums up what was said. There are four conditions of the soul, the higher ones counting as kinds of knowledge, the lower ones as kinds of belief. They can be ranked: each participates in clarity in proportion to the extent to which its domain participates in truth (*alētheias metechein*) (511e). Perceptibles participate in truth less than do intelligibles. Cognitive attitudes are not characterized

---

of the middle dialogues. And in particular, it is a difficult question whether the Form of the Good figures in the *Philebus* or is absent (cf. esp. the discussion toward the end, 59–65, but also the way questions about the good are initially introduced). These examples show that, in a range of late dialogues, Plato raises substantial problems for his own theories and is prepared to think through significantly altered accounts in order to address these problems.

[10]This approach has the great advantage that one need not, implausibly, assume that Plato forgot about the metaphysical issues that seem to have interested him for a long time. I agree with Sedley that this is implausible. Sedley proceeds to make a more ambitious proposal. The *Theaetetus*, he thinks, is devoted to Socrates, similarly to the way in which, say, the *Apology* is: it celebrates Socrates. In the *Theaetetus*, Sedley argues, Plato focuses on a particular side of Socrates, his maieutic art. Through his philosophizing, Socrates helps others give birth to ideas. As readers of the *Theaetetus*, Sedley proposes, we shall discover the core elements of Platonism for ourselves. In pursuing this line of thought, Sedley engages in the same kind of exercise that I engage in, though with a different focus. He in effect asks how a doctrinal Platonist can read the *Theaetetus*; I ask what a reader with skeptic-Stoic-Socratic intuitions can take away from the dialogue.

[11]The passage that is particularly relevant for my argument—the transition from Part I to Part II of the dialogue—receives almost no discussion in Burnyeat, *The Theaetetus of Plato*, or Sedley, *The Midwife of Platonism*.

in terms of truth—it is almost as if the question of what it might mean to call beliefs true or false were not envisaged. And yet it is quite implausible that Plato is unaware that such questions can be asked. More likely, Plato postpones the question of how belief relates to the truth as too far-reaching for the matters at hand in the *Republic*; he does not want to discuss it in passing.[12] Part II of the *Theaetetus* addresses this question, focusing on a metaphysical concern that was underexplored in the *Republic*.[13]

For present purposes, one aspect of the *Republic's* short remarks is particularly important. Truth is not mentioned in *Republic* V's distinctions between ignorance, belief, and knowledge (476d–479d). However, the discussion contains one intriguing sequence:

> But belief (*doxa*), we say, believes (*doxazein*). (478a10)
>
> […]
>
> But he who believes (*doxazōn*) believes (*doxazei*) some one thing (*hen ti*)?
>
> Yes. (478b10–11)

Belief is of *something*. In the *Republic*, this proposal is spelled out in the framework of a distinction between being and not-being: the domain of *doxa* is 'what participates in being and in not-being.' That is, belief is not of something that *is* in the strong sense of Platonic Being. The point that belief is 'of something' is metaphysically complicated, and Plato has good reason to return to it. Scholars have speculated that the Stoics, who take

---

[12]I take it that this attitude runs through many of Plato's dialogues. In a number of contexts, Socrates says that to pursue a given question would lead too far afield, and that the interlocutors must stay focused on the topic at hand.

[13]Add to this that, though the domain of *doxa* is described in terms of the perceptible, the *Republic* contains metaphors that suggest closeness or similarity between knowledge and perception: knowledge might be some kind of seeing, it might involve being acquainted with something and therefore being able to recognize it, and so on. Moreover, the *Meno* made some points about the knowledge-belief distinction that do not fit neatly into the *Republic's* epistemology or, at least, that Plato does not explicitly revisit there: the epistemic changeability of *doxa* (as opposed to the changeability of the domain it relates to in the *Republic*); that true belief can successfully guide action; and the idea that *reasoning* (accounts, etc.) must tie down belief because otherwise it tends to 'run away.' Surely, this means that weighty questions are left open. These questions need detailed treatment and they call for a dialogue that asks whether knowledge is perception (DEF I), whether it is true belief (DEF II), and whether it is true belief with a *logos* (DEF III).

'something' to be the highest category, have been inspired by critically engaging with Platonic discussions of this issue.[14] For the Stoics, it is one thing to say that a cognitive attitude must relate to something, and another thing to say that it relates to what is. In a sense, then, the Stoics endorse the *Republic*'s reluctance to move from 'something' to 'being' (though they reject the notion of 'what participates in what is and what is not'). For present purposes, there is no need to speculate about the specifics of Stoic engagement with this issue in Plato. It is, however, relevant to note that it seems to have been a contentious topic of discussion. This confirms the suspicion that, from the point of view of early readers in the Academy, Plato's *Theaetetus* addresses a metaphysical question left dangling in the *Republic*.

In Part II of the *Theaetetus*, discussion begins with Socrates raising the general question of what the soul does "when it engages by itself with what is (*ta onta*)" (187a5–6). It is here, he says, that knowledge must be found.[15] This—what the soul does when it engages with *ta onta*—is called *doxazein* (a7–8). This brief remark is rather complicated. For now, consider its metaphysical side. When the soul forms beliefs or believes— *doxazein*—then it engages with *what is*.[16] For the reader of the *Republic*, this is a surprising assumption. Surely, she would say, not all cognitive activity engages with what is: knowledge does, and belief does not. But

[14]Scholars have explored the idea whether the Stoics might have misread *Timeaus* 27d as if Plato suggested that 'something' was a higher genus than being and not-being, comprising both; if so, the Stoics might have taken their view about 'something' as highest genus from Plato. Cf. Jacques Brunschwig, who shows that this is an implausible reading of Stoic philosophy. "The Stoic Theory of the Supreme Genus and Platonic Ontology," in Brunschwig, *Papers in Hellenistic Philosophy* (Cambridge: Cambridge University Press, 1994), 92–157, 117–18; originally published as "La théorie stoicienne du genre supreme et l'ontologie platonicienne," in J. Barnes and M. Mignucci (eds.), *Matter and Metaphysics: Fourth Symposium Hellenisticum* (Naples: Bibliopolis, 1988), 19–127. More likely, the Stoics think it is part of a misguided metaphysical framework to think that a something must be something that *is*.

[15]According to Cicero's *Lucullus* 2.142, "Plato thought that the criterion of truth, along with truth itself, was inaccessible to opinion and the senses: he took it to belong to thought itself and the mind." (tr. Brittain, 2006). That is, Plato is associated with the view that belief does not reach the truth.

[16]Throughout these discussions, Plato goes back and forth between addressing an activity (belief-formation) and a condition or attitude in the soul (to hold a belief, to believe).

the Socrates of the *Theaetetus* develops the questions of Part II of the dialogue in this surprising framework. Consider the following exchange:

> But doesn't someone who believes, believe some one thing (*hen ti*)?
>
> Necessarily.
>
> And doesn't the person who believes some one thing (*hen ti*) believe something that is (*on ti*)? (189a7–9)

That is, instead of the *Republic*'s metaphysically cautious claim that belief engages with something (a something that falls short of being), Socrates here says that belief engages with *one thing*—or, perhaps, 'one something'—and thereby with something that *is*. The point can be rephrased in terms of truth. In believing something, the cognizer relates to what is, and thus she relates to a truth. Right at the end of Part I of the *Theaetetus*, before turning to the proposal that knowledge is true belief, Socrates formulates the relevant premise. It is not possible, he suggests, to reach truth (*alētheia*) where one does not reach being (*ousia*) (186c7).[17] Thus, two weighty premises stand at the intersection of Part I and Part II of the *Theaetetus*:

> *Belief-Being:* The believer believes something that is.
>
> *Truth-Being:* To reach being is to reach truth.

On these premises, true belief indeed must be knowledge: it would appear that there is nothing missing in a truth-claim where someone gets hold of the truth and of being. And yet, these premises make false belief impossible. If beliefs are of what is, they must all be true. The difference between knowledge and belief that 187a–c loses sight of, one might say, is that knowledge is factive and belief is not. If someone knows that p, it follows that p is true. But 187a–c says that belief-formation is of what is, and that means it is factive. Accordingly, there can be no false belief.

This is how Part II of the *Theaetetus* begins—it does not begin with a puzzle about false belief but with the question of how belief relates to the truth. That is, at least in this part of the dialogue, central metaphysical

---

[17]I return to this passage at the end of the chapter. Truth and being are also associated with knowledge.

questions are at issue, so much so that the question of why Plato's *Theaetetus* seems to be devoid of Platonic metaphysics need not arise. Of course, a reader who comes to the *Theaetetus* from the *Republic* still has much reason to be puzzled, and to wonder why DEF II should be worthy of serious consideration. And yet, the Socratically inclined reader is likely to have picked up on questions left open in the *Republic*, and she is likely to be curious when Plato returns to the idea that belief is about "something"—an idea that can be developed in different ways.

2. Two Kinds of Belief

Part II of the *Theaetetus* has a peculiar structure (187a–201c). Almost all of the discussion is devoted to the question of how, given the premises discussed above, false belief can be explained (187d–200d). Interpreters tend to think that Part II of the *Theaetetus* is a digression on false belief.[18] Contrary to this assumption, I think we should take Socrates seriously when he locates the question about false belief in an investigation that he calls "*peri doxēs*," about belief (187c7).

Moreover, it seems misguided to gloss over the fact that DEF II is not without philosophical appeal.[19] If one assumes, as interpreters often do, that there are true *doxai*, then it is by no means clear that DEF II does not formulate a serious proposal.[20] Right at the beginning of the *Theaetetus*, Socrates says that knowledge is of what is (152c).[21] I take it that this serves

[18]Sedley describes Part II as an "excursus on false belief" (*The Midwife of Platonism*, 13). As he sees it, DEF II is the "official topic" and false belief is the real topic. Sedley thinks that this fits well with the fact that Plato examines falsity in a number of dialogues (false statements, false names, false judgments, false pleasures) (*The Midwife of Platonism*, 118). Burnyeat proposes that Plato gives the reader an obviously false judgment—DEF II—that seems to imply that there are no false judgments. The beginning of Part II, he writes, is a challenge: "Spot the false judgment which makes it appear that false judgment is impossible" (*The Theaetetus of Plato*, 66).

[19]Sedley (*The Midwife of Platonism*, 149) considers it a mere "pretext" for discussion of puzzles about falsity.

[20]Burnyeat (*The Theaetetus of Plato*) is clearly committed to the premise that there are true and false *doxai*. If there are true *doxai*, then it is legitimate to ask whether they—simply because they are true—are not all we want. In wanting to attain knowledge, I take it, Plato thinks we centrally seek to attain the truth.

[21]I return to this passage in more detail below.

as a basic intuition for the dialogue as a whole. Knowledge is of what is—it is 'of' the truth. Now, if the same can be said about true *doxa*, that it 'engages with what is,' as 187a–c suggests, then arguably true *doxa* is all we want, and we should call it knowledge.[22] In suggesting that Part II examines *doxa* and its relation to the truth (rather than being a digression on false *doxa*), I am thus proposing that DEF II is not just blatantly false. I suggest that, if one takes seriously the idea that attaining the truth is what matters about knowledge, then it is indeed unclear whether true belief should not be knowledge. Though DEF II sounds misguided to anyone who approaches the *Theaetetus* with certain aspects of Platonic metaphysics in mind, it sounds attractive when one focuses on another Platonic idea: namely that to reach truth is to reach what is. Thus, if one thinks that *doxa* can be true, one will have to take DEF II seriously.[23]

Consider now the epistemic side of Socrates' gloss on what the soul does "when it engages by itself with what is" (187a5–6). It is here, he says, that knowledge must be found. But this—what the soul does when it engages with what is—is called *doxazein* (a7–8). A Socratically inclined reader would want to say, hold on, stop, this is going in the wrong direction. The way things have been set up is such that knowledge and belief are conflated. Knowledge is associated with thinking, and thinking is then described as belief-formation. This transition confuses significant matters. That is, in addition to the metaphysically suspect transition sketched above, from 'one something' to 'something that is,' there is an epistemologically suspect transition, from knowledge to thought to belief.

---

[22]Cf. *Theaetetus* 200e: Theaetetus says that making a true judgment is, at any rate, something free of mistakes, and everything that results from it is admirable and good. Other relevant passages: *Charm.* 171d2–172a6; *Meno* 97c2–10; *Republic* 477e4–478a1; *Theaetetus* 207d8–208b3.

[23]Toward the end of Part II, Theaetetus elucidates why DEF II is worth serious consideration: true *doxazein* is without error or mistakes (200e4–5). Burnyeat ("Socrates and the Jury," 174–76) refers to 200e4–5, observing that initially DEF II was a mere attempt at improving on DEF I in the light of its failure. Only at this late stage, in 200e, do we hear why DEF II might be independently plausible: because true belief does not err. Burnyeat discusses further why Theaetetus continues to say that everything resulting from it—true *doxazein*—is fine and good (e5–6); he thinks that Plato imports ideas from the *Meno* that do not really fit. On my reading, Theaetetus's remark is rather plausible: if truth was all we wanted, then true belief should count as knowledge, and then true belief must have the characteristics of knowledge.

Knowledge, then, appears to be some kind of *doxazein*.[24] But it cannot be 'all *doxa*,' says Theaetetus, because surely there is false *doxa* (187b4–5). Perhaps, then, true belief (*alēthēs doxa*) is knowledge (b5–6). This is DEF II. Socrates rephrases this proposal by emphasizing that it contains a premise about true and false *doxa*: they are, according to DEF II, two kinds of belief (c4). Notably, Socrates introduces this assumption as immediately following from DEF II (187c). If one holds that knowledge is true belief, one must hold that there are two kinds of belief, true belief and false belief. This is the Two Kinds premise.

> *Two Kinds*: There are two kinds of *doxa*, true *doxa* and false *doxa*.[25]

The fact that this premise is presented as following from DEF II should make the reader pause. Assuming that DEF II is false, its immediate implication might well also be false. And indeed, Two Kinds is in conflict with a Socratic intuition that we can call One Kind.

> *One Kind*: All belief is the same with respect to its cognitive status, because all belief falls short of knowledge, thus being, in one way or another, a deficient attitude.

One Kind is not mentioned at the outset of Part II, but it matters greatly at its end. Accordingly, Two Kinds should be recognized as contentious. It is not obvious for Plato that beliefs indeed can differ from each other in such a way as to be genuinely of two kinds. On the contrary, beliefs might differ from each other in any number of ways and yet have the standing of deficient cognitive attitudes, thus being ultimately on a par.

The lines that follow immediately in the dialogue add to the impression that one should not take Two Kinds for granted. Rephrasing the premise that there are two kinds of *doxa*, Socrates asks whether we assume that, on any given matter, there is a false belief, such that one of us has a false belief and the other a true belief (187e).

This passage is difficult in multiple ways. First, the phrasing emphasizes an ambiguity that is also otherwise present in the text. In a mix of English

---

[24]Here the *Theaetetus* may be thought to be rather close to the modern intuition that knowledge is a kind of belief.

[25] In the words of Levett/Burnyeat, "There are two forms of judgment, true and false" (187c). That seem innocuous: translation in terms of judgment hides the fact that there might be a real question.

and Greek, what Socrates says is that one of us '*doxazein* falsely,' and the other '*doxazein* truly.' The difference, then, might attach either to the activity of belief-formation or to the resulting attitude. A cognizer might fail in the way she comes to hold something to be true, thus 'believing falsely.' Or she might hold a false belief. Second, Socrates makes the rather strong claim that, for any given matter, by nature (*phusei*) someone holds a true belief and someone a false belief. This is an explicit rejection of Protagoras's relativism as discussed in Part I of the dialogue, and it is more than that. It is a far-reaching proposal. Consider that one might, contra Socrates, think that there are some matters on which no one holds a false belief, or some matters on which no one holds a true belief. I shall not pursue these matters here. All I wish to note is that Two Kinds is introduced as a contentious and far-reaching assumption rather than an obvious premise.

3. *Conflicting Intuitions about* Doxa

Following Levett, modern translators render *doxa* in the *Theaetetus* as "judgment," a choice they make in no other Platonic dialogue. According to prominent editions of the text, Socrates says in 187a that we should locate knowledge in what the soul does when it judges (*doxazein*); and he says that there are true and false judgments (*doxai*). This translation is tempting: it seems to make the text comprehensible. And yet, it disambiguates matters in philosophically misleading ways. *Doxa* is a complex notion. It can mean something like judgment, but it is also associated with various kinds of deficiency. DEF II must fail (and does fail according to the final argument in Part II of the *Theaetetus*) because *doxa* simply is not knowledge, no matter how it is qualified. This point, well hidden by the standard translation, is a point that Socrates, in another dialogue about the belief-knowledge distinction, says he would claim to know (a rare commitment for Socrates). Even though he cannot explain how true belief differs from knowledge, he is going to say that it does (*Meno* 96e1–98b5).[26] This intuition remains part of the picture—even where it is not in the foreground—when one thinks through the dialogue in terms

---

[26]Sedley (*The Midwife of Platonism*, 149) acknowledges the relevance of this point for interpreting the *Theaetetus*. Plato's Socrates is committed to only a handful of claims in this explicit fashion. Of course, we are here considering the Socrates of the *Meno*—but still, it seems worthwhile to recall it.

of *doxa*. The *Theaetetus* does not explore one intuition about *doxa*, namely that, in holding something to be true, the cognizer makes a truth-claim. It explores two conflicting intuitions, intuitions that imply Two Kinds on the one hand and One Kind on the other:

> *Doxa as truth-claim*: in forming a belief, the cognizer claims that such and such is so-and-so. (Two Kinds)
>
> *Doxa as deficient cognitive attitude*: in forming a belief, the cognizer comes to have merely a belief, or (depending on whether the deficiency is located in the attitude of *doxa* or the activity of *doxazein*) makes a deficient truth-claim.[27] (One Kind)

As a translator of the *Theaetetus*, one may aim to find a consistent way to render *doxa* and its cognates throughout the dialogue.[28] That means that one will look for a translation that can capture several connotations of these words as they matter to different parts of the discussion. As I see it, one's translation should be able to accommodate the two ideas I distinguished—*doxa* as a truth-claim, and *doxa* as a cognitive attitude that is deficient and lesser than knowledge. Throughout this chapter, and indeed throughout the book, I am translating *doxa* as belief. Like every translation, this has some disadvantages. For example, one needs to use the lengthy expression 'forming a belief' where *doxazein* refers to an activity.[29] And yet I take 'belief' to be significantly broader than 'judgment' and therefore a much better choice.

[27] The ambiguity between activity and attitude is a far-reaching topic that would deserve separate treatment. I am noting it here, but nothing in my present argument hangs on deciding the question of how Plato navigates these two aspects in the *Theaetetus*.

[28] Sedley (*The Midwife of Platonism*, 118) goes for the main part with judgment and judging but explicitly announces that he will speak in terms of belief when this appears called for.

[29] Burnyeat (*The Theaetetus of Plato*, 69) thinks that belief often stands for a "continuing state of mind or, on some philosophical views, a disposition." That is, he distinguishes between the activity of judging on the one hand, and such a continued state on the other. I proceed on the assumption that *doxa* covers an even broader range, perhaps to be captured in a threefold distinction between (1) the activity of making a truth-claim, (2) the attitude of holding something to be true, (3) a continuing state of mind in Burnyeat's sense. However, (3) strikes me as a less obvious option than (1) and (2). Plato would probably switch from talk about *doxa* to talk about memory, or what is 'stored up' in the mind, when addressing belief in a dispositional sense. Moreover, Burnyeat does not seem right when he argues that translations in terms of belief cannot capture the active side of *doxazein*. Surely, one can speak of belief-formation where Plato discusses an episode of arriving at a truth-claim.

In Part I of the dialogue, *doxa* comes to be a subject of discussion via the verb *dokein*, to seem or appear.[30] For a long section of Part I, the interlocutors do not refer to *doxa*, but to appearances.[31] When they move to talk about *doxa*, it is with the assumption that in a *doxa* something appears to be so-and-so to someone. And thus, a rather different notion of belief—one that ties belief to mere seeming—is also part of the picture in the *Theaetetus*.

In defending their translation of *doxa* as judgment, commentators tend to invoke a passage early on in Part II of the *Theaetetus*.[32] Socrates explicitly formulates the intuition that *doxa* is a truth-claim, arguably for the first time in Greek philosophy.

> [Thinking (*dianoeisthai*) is] [s]peech which the mind itself goes through with itself about whatever it's considering. [...] when the mind is thinking, it's simply carrying on a discussion, asking itself questions and answering them, and making assertions and denials. And when it has come to a decision, either slowly or in a sudden rush, and it's no longer divided, but says one single thing, we call this its *doxa*. So what I call *doxazein* is speaking (*legein*) and what I call *doxa* is speech (*logos*); but speech spoken, not aloud to someone else, but silently to oneself. [...] So whenever someone believes (*doxazein*) that one of two things is the other, he's actually saying to himself that the one is the other.[33] (*Th.* 189e–190a, tr. Levett/ McDowell with changes)[34]

The noun *doxa* is introduced via the verb *doxazein*, and the activity of *doxazein* is explained as a kind of acceptance and rejection in thought

---

[30]Plato first uses *dokein*, which perhaps is best translated as 'seeming'; Plato then switches to *phainesthai*, 'to appear,' and continues discussion in terms of sensory and non-sensory appearances.

[31]On this transition, see chapter 4 of this book.

[32]According to McDowell, 189e–190a speaks particularly clearly in favor of the translation of *doxa* as judgment: "Socrates here introduces the idea that judging should be conceived of as the making of inner assertions. Since the making of an assertion is an act rather than a state, this passage indicates the translation 'judgement' rather than 'belief' or 'opinion'" (*Theaetetus*, 205). The passage is also one of Burnyeat's primary points of reference (next to 187d–e, where Plato speaks of a *pathos*) (*The Theaetetus of Plato*, 69).

[33]Socrates then adds: I call *doxazein legein*, and *doxa logos*. Roughly: I call belief-formation 'saying,' and belief 'statement.'

[34]McDowell considers the question of whether *doxa* is to be translated as "judgment" or as "belief" as the question of whether *doxa* is an act (to judge) or a state (to hold a certain

that concludes an inner conversation. The cognizer considers a matter and eventually finds it to be so-and-so. In other words, *doxazein* is thinking that something is so-and-so. It is a particular kind of thought: thought that goes back and forth over a matter and ends with something like an assertion. The mind says that something is so-and-so, making a truth-claim. This might be rendered as 'making a judgment': one arrives at a decision, saying to oneself, yes, *this* is how I take things to be.

Socrates claims to describe all belief-formation. And yet, his account envisages what one might call a case of careful belief-formation. The cognizer does not jump to conclusions, and she does not just find herself believing things. She goes back and forth in her mind about what she should accept and what she should reject. This model had great appeal for the Stoics, who develop it further as a normative account of cautious assent to impressions. Socrates' focus on asking questions and going back and forth over a matter evokes the idea of judgment, and perhaps even of courtroom proceedings, which shall figure prominently in the final refutation of DEF II. But contra Socrates' claim in 189e–190a, one might argue that not all belief-formation is of this considered kind. Arguably, there is a difference between conceiving of *doxa* as a truth-claim and the more ambitious idea that *doxa* is a judgment that concludes a thought process where matters are looked at from different angles. This difference adds another reason to doubt whether *doxa* is translated well in terms of judgment. Insofar as this translation is based specifically on 189e–190a, it might focus too much on a certain kind of belief-formation. Translation of *doxa* as judgment, then, is far from philosophically harmless. It glosses over the derogative associations of *doxa*, and it might say more than that *doxai* are truth-claims. In a sense, then, it captures neither of the two intuitions that I take to be at issue: that *doxa* is a deficient cognitive attitude and that *doxai* are truth-claims.

---

belief). McDowell writes: "I have used the translation 'judgement,' suggesting an act, rather than 'belief' or 'opinion,' suggesting a state, because it seems to be required at 189e4–190a7. However, the Greek word (*doxa*) could equally well mean either; and in fact belief or opinion would be a better candidate to appear in a definition of knowledge than judgment. Plato shows no sign of having explicitly distinguished the act from the state" (*Theaetetus*, 193).

4. *The Final Refutation of DEF II*

DEF II cannot accommodate One Kind. Knowledge is, *pace* DEF II, the holding-to-be-true of truths. Assuming that DEF II holds, no plausible notion of belief, conceived as *one* attitude—an attitude characterized by how it falls short of knowledge—can be formulated. To accommodate DEF II, one has to give up on the idea that belief is one kind of thing. Instead, one has to take literally Socrates' proposal that, according to DEF II, there are *two kinds of belief*: true beliefs and false beliefs. Indeed, perhaps one will have to go even further. Though Socrates says that true and false belief are kinds of belief, it is not clear that these two kinds are subclasses of a larger class, belief. For, if DEF II holds, the question "what is belief?" is off the table, as indeed it is off the table in much of Part II of the dialogue, which focuses on false judgments. The question "what is belief?" is abolished because there is no such thing as belief according to DEF II: there is true belief, one kind of thing, namely knowledge; and there is false belief, another kind of thing, which turns out to be impossible to explain within the framework that DEF II provides. DEF II fails. Importantly, it does not fail because it cannot account for false belief.[35] It fails because it cannot account for belief at all. As I see it, Two Kinds should not have been granted. It denies that *doxa* is, as a whole, a different kind

---

[35]A prominent suggestion in the literature is that DEF II fails because of an implausible premise Socrates adds: one either knows something or does not know something. As I see it, that cannot be the reason. The premise that one either knows something or does not know it is, if suitably unpacked (which of course it is not in the discussion of DEF II), rather unproblematic. Sedley writes that, in his view, the dichotomy between knowing and not-knowing figures at *no* other place in Plato: "No very satisfactory account has been offered of how Plato might have arrived at this strangely extreme dichotomy, nor am I aware of any example of it in operation outside the *Theaetetus*" (*The Midwife of Platonism*, 120). However, as I see it the dichotomy is familiar from the Meno Problem (80d–e): one cannot investigate, because one either does not know the matter and thus does not know what to look for (and would not recognize it if one hit upon it), or one already knows the matter and need not investigate. As I argued in the introduction, the *Meno* offers a solution to this problem. One either knows something or not; but in another sense, belief is in between ignorance and knowledge; in a belief, one does not have knowledge (so it falls on one side of the dichotomy); but beliefs can be turned into hypotheses and employed in investigation. Surely, Plato has not forgotten that this move is available. However, this move employs a premise that cannot be accounted for within DEF II: that belief is genuinely different from knowledge, whether or not it is true.

of thing from knowledge. It is quite implausible that Plato would give up on that difference.[36]

The relevant intuition carries all the weight in the final refutation of DEF II. At the end of Part II, Socrates puts forward a seemingly simple argument against DEF II (201a–c).[37] He describes the procedures in a courtroom. A lawyer presents his case, and members of a jury come to hold a belief based on the lawyer's speech; the jurymen judge truly, but do not know what happened. According to Burnyeat and McDowell, this brief argument is by itself a sufficient and valid refutation of DEF II.[38] As they see it, there are obviously cases in which someone has a true belief that does not qualify as knowledge, and the Jury Example exemplifies this. Accordingly, "knowledge is true belief" is false.

How compelling is this reading? The general assessment—that the Jury Argument refutes DEF II—seems right. But as I see it, Plato does not argue that a true belief fails to qualify as knowledge, and thus the Jury Argument does not make a simple point to refute DEF II.[39] He proposes

[36]Burnyeat ("Socrates and the Jury") analyzes Plato's general take on *doxa* and *epistēmē* in ways that come close to my point here. His interpretation of the Jury Example, he says, ascribes to Plato views that are rather different from widespread contemporary assumptions; in particular, it ascribes to Plato a "sharp distinction between knowledge and well-founded true belief" ("Socrates and the Jury," 180).

[37]Burnyeat ("Socrates and the Jury") offers discussion of the many perplexities of the text—enough to warn anyone against thinking that the argument is straightforward.

[38]I am here referring to Burnyeat (*The Theaetetus of Plato*) and McDowell (*Theaetetus*). The Jury Example marks the transition between DEF II and DEF III. It reminds Theaetetus of something he has heard: that a true belief must come with a *logos* in order to qualify as knowledge (201c). This proposal—that knowledge is true belief with a *logos* (account, etc.)—is the topic of Part III of the dialogue. From the perspective of my reading, it fails for the same reasons as DEF II. Ancient JTB accounts are markedly different from contemporary JTB accounts of knowledge. Consider an example that fits the ancient line of argument: suppose I have the true belief that water is H_2O. I haven't studied chemistry, and in a sense I'm just repeating what others told me. If I were to study chemistry, I would come to understand a complete system. I would not *keep* the belief "water is H_2O" *and* be able to justify it. Rather, coming to know the field as a whole, I would now understand what I say when I say "water is H_2O." Accordingly, the judgment I make as a knower is a different judgment. The sentence now means something different to me. As the Stoics see it, knowledge is a *logos*. In acquiring knowledge, one replaces beliefs with pieces of knowledge, putting a whole system of knowledge in the place of changeable beliefs. This is suggested at 207c2–3: knowledge is put in place of (*anti*) belief.

[39]This is how Burnyeat puts it: to demonstrate the falsehood of DEF II "only a brief argument is required" (*The Theaetetus of Plato*, 65).

that, when someone has a mere belief, she is in no position to say whether the belief is true. Here is an outline of what I take to be the important steps in the text:

Orators (201a–b): A whole profession—oratory—refutes DEF II. The jurymen lack knowledge because the orator merely wants to persuade, rather than genuinely inform or teach.[40] The orators in courtrooms try to talk others into the belief that happens to please them at a given moment. To persuade is to produce *doxai* in others: it is to 'make' it that others come to believe (think, judge) a certain way (b5).

Jurymen (201b–c): If the jurymen have been rightly persuaded about something that only someone who has seen it—and no one else—can know, thus judging from mere hearsay, they judge while holding a true belief but having no knowledge. In such a case, assuming that the persuading was correct, they have judged well.

Conclusion (201c): If true belief and knowledge were the same in the courtroom, even the best judge wouldn't be able to believe correctly without knowledge.

Jurymen and Conclusion appear to speak for the standard interpretation: the Jury Example provides a case where someone holds a true belief without having knowledge, and accordingly DEF II is refuted. And yet it is almost ironic that this reading is widely accepted. Scholars who, with respect to most of DEF II, find it obvious that (in their terms) judgments can be false, seem to forget about this basic point when it comes to what is perhaps the archetypal case of judgment: a jury's verdict. Surely, verdicts can be false. The text asks the reader to imagine a correct verdict. But the beginning of the passage—the description of those who speak in

[40]Socrates also remarks that this is the kind of thing one only knows if one has seen it (201b). If Plato means to say that, at least in some domains, one only knows what one has seen, he could have at least two ideas in mind. On the one hand, he might be calling into question whether there is such a thing as knowledge of testimony. But this is unlikely, since it is incompatible with the framing narrative of the dialogue. The dialogue as a whole was written down by Euclides, who did not witness the original conversation, but writes up a transcript by questioning Socrates repeatedly about the conversation that took place (142d–143a). Otherwise, Plato might be suggesting that, if one's judgment relies on someone's testimony, one might judge falsely. If this is his point, then he is not concerned with an example of a true belief that does not qualify as knowledge, but instead with an example of a belief that might be true or false.

front of judges and juries—highlights that one might come to be persuaded of anything, depending on how skillful the persuaders are. Consider, then, how the Jury Argument proceeds if one shifts attention to this aspect. The orators instill whatever belief they like in those who listen. To be persuaded by an orator in court is to be persuaded by someone who may or may not describe what happened. Indeed, orators are said to 'produce' beliefs in the jurymen. This is a remarkable claim. Arguably, it involves a shift away from belief-formation as an activity of the cognizer. Beliefs, it now seems, can be created in our minds by others. Notably, the question of whether beliefs are passively acquired or actively formed was an important issue in Part I of the *Theaetetus*, and Plato seemed to side with the latter idea. Moreover, Protagoras argued that one cannot plant thoughts in the minds of others. One can only bring others into a condition where things will seem differently to them (166d–168b). Though this is Protagoras's point and not Socrates', one might think that Protagoras speaks to an intuition that runs through much of Plato: every cognizer will have to think her own thoughts.[41] Socrates' point about beliefs as products of external impact by oratory is thus surprising, at least in the given context.[42]

Socrates then says that the jury could undergo this process by being persuaded justly. In that case, the jury judges the case based on a true *doxa* without knowledge (201b7–c2). The jurymen might judge well if the persuading was done correctly (c1). That is, things can go well on both sides: the orators can take their task seriously and do things rightly (b7) and the judges can do well in response to this. But if 201c2–7 is read in conjunction with 201a–b, it is clear that the jury is in *no position to tell that their belief is true*. Though in a given case all sides may perform as they should, the jurymen are, for all they know, simply in the position of cognizers who have beliefs.

Pause here for a moment and consider why Plato might pick this particular case in order to refute DEF II. Presumably, one could come up with any number of examples where a cognizer hears about something,

---

[41]The *Republic*'s discussion of education focuses on precisely this. It is a turning around of the soul, an attempt to make children love what they should love, and so on, and that puts their minds into the condition in which they can study and learn. But they themselves will have to do the thinking. Cf. Burnyeat, "Culture and Society" and "Why Mathematics Is Good."

[42]Much could be said, of course, about Plato's discussion of rhetoric and its powers in other dialogues.

takes it to be the case, and thereby takes something to be true that actually is true, but only relies on hearsay and in that sense lacks knowledge. Why choose a juridical example? This question is too speculative to receive a firm response. And yet it is a question worth considering. For one, Socrates' reference to the fact that speakers in courtrooms only have limited time allotted links the passage to an earlier point in the conversation, the digression on philosophy. There, philosophers were contrasted with orators, and orators were, among other things, characterized as being in a hurry (172c–173b). This connection adds emphasis to the point already mentioned, namely that orators may not aim to persuade of the truth; at 172c–173b, they appear to be untrustworthy in a number of ways. Second, the courtroom might appear to be a paradigmatic locus of judgment. To form a belief, *doxazein*, was earlier analyzed as going back and forth over a matter, arriving at a decision (190a1). As I mentioned, Socrates here seems to describe a particular kind of thought, namely one where a cognizer asks herself questions and looks at things from different angles. Indeed, this kind of thought resembles the proceedings in a courtroom.[43] Earlier, it seemed that one needs to accommodate the premise that judgments can be false; surely, this should also apply to the Jury Example. If, in general, the reader is to assume that one can judge falsely, then certainly this should be part of how the final refutation of DEF II is interpreted. That is, one should not read the Jury Example as if it was obvious to the cognizer that her belief is true. Third, and most speculatively, one might say that any courtroom scene in a dialogue that, as a whole, invokes the 'early Socrates' should remind the reader of a particular case: the Athenian jury voting to put Socrates to death. For the sake of the thought experiment, let me apply the Jury Argument to this case.

In a paper on the *Apology*, Myles Burnyeat tells his readers that, when giving a certain talk about the *Apology*, he likes to have the audience vote.[44] At the beginning of his presentation, most people tend to think that Socrates is innocent. At the end, once Burnyeat has spoken about the ways in which Socrates might really be impious as far as the 'gods of the city' are concerned, his audiences tend to vote differently. Quite

---

[43]The Stoics came to extend this analogy, thinking about assent in terms of judgment, and comparing the careful assenter to the judge. Cf. Brad Inwood's discussion of this aspect of Seneca's thought in "Moral Judgement in Seneca," in Inwood, *Reading Seneca: Stoic Philosophy in Rome* (Oxford: Oxford University Press, 2005), 201–23.

[44]Burnyeat, "The Impiety of Socrates."

conceivably, Socrates is guilty as charged. Now, suppose Burnyeat argued well, and persuaded his audience rightly or correctly: that is, to the best of his knowledge, he led others to believe what, to his mind, they should believe.[45] Suppose that his audience listened well and judged well, carefully considering the points that Burnyeat raises. At the end, Socrates is judged to be guilty of the crimes of which he was accused. The audience might be said to have judged based on a true belief without knowledge. And yet, as a member of the audience—and also if one were a member of the original jury—one may insist that one really does not know whether Socrates was guilty as charged. While one arrives at a verdict, raising one's hand when asked "who votes guilty?", one might be very well aware that, though one takes oneself to have arrived at the truth, one may also have missed the truth. And thus it is more correct to say that one merely holds a belief about this matter, rather than say that one merely holds a true belief. This difference, I suggest, is important.

According to this line of thought, the refutation of DEF II does not rest in any simple fashion on identifying a case of true belief that falls short of knowledge. Plato envisages a case where everything goes as it should, and where a belief is true insofar as the judgment is correct. This assessment, however, can only be made from a third-person perspective of someone who knows what happened. It cannot be made from the perspective of a member of the jury: for all she knows, her judgment, even if arrived at with great care, might be false. My proposed reading adopts the perspective of the cognizer who forms beliefs. From a third-person point of view, her beliefs might be evaluated as true or false. If, say, the persuading was done correctly and the cognizer performed well, the judgment that she arrives at can be true in the sense that the cognizer believes something that is the case. But from the point of view of the cognizer, all beliefs are on a par. They are truth-claims: the cognizer says what she holds to be the case, whether or not it indeed is the case.

The refutation of DEF II, then, rests on the point that a true belief is not known to be true to the cognizer who has it. And thus, the final refutation of DEF II returns to the intuition that *doxa*, as a whole, is different from knowledge. For present purposes, this is the main point: the final refutation of DEF II employs an example where someone has a *doxa*—a

[45]Though Burnyeat, of course, is a philosopher, not an orator, for the purposes of his experiment with audiences standing in for juries, he might assign himself the role of speaker in front of a court.

doxa that, for all she knows, might be false. It thus employs a case where someone has a belief that, qua belief, falls short of being knowledge. The case thus returns to the intuition that I call One Kind. Beliefs are of one kind, insofar as they are deficient attitudes as compared to knowledge.

The argument Plato makes in discussing orators in court departs in even more ways from being a simple case that refutes DEF II. Plato introduces a new premise, one that did not figure earlier in Part II, namely that only someone who actually witnessed a given event can know what happened, while a jury is bound to assess things by hearsay (201b).[46] In making this point, he might be calling into question whether there is knowledge of testimony—a rather large issue to introduce at this point.[47] And yet Socrates explicitly says that only the person who has seen something, *and no one else*, knows it (b7–8). Notably, it is difficult to say what precisely Plato means to suggest about 'seeing.' Does he refer to the kind of seeing that is almost proverbially unreliable, the seeing of the eyewitness? Even though this observation may strike one as a modern one, it is related to some of Plato's discussions of sense-perception and memory in the *Theaetetus*. Or is the reader expected to recall metaphorical notions of 'seeing,' as they figure, say, in Plato's remark in *Republic* 475e5, that philosophers love to 'see' the truth? These are rather deep interpretive puzzles, and I shall not aim to resolve them here. For present purposes, it matters to note that interpreters are glossing over quite a number of difficulties when they claim that the Jury Example is a simple counterexample to DEF II. It is neither a counterexample to DEF II, nor is it at all simple.

---

[46]Burnyeat (*The Theaetetus of Plato*, 124–27) discusses the difficulties that attach to this idea and the conflicting points that Socrates makes. Still, he thinks that the Jury Argument supplies a simple counterexample to DEF II.

[47]As Burnyeat (*The Theaetetus of Plato*, 127) notes, knowledge of testimony frames the dialogue. The dialogue is reported to us as someone's testimony. Moreover, consider the question of whether Socrates knows Theaetetus by having heard things about him (144c). Given the prominence of this example at the beginning of the dialogue—who knows Theaetetus, and on account of what?—I am tempted to think that Plato indeed wants to raise questions about knowledge of testimony. But he does not seem to pursue them. Issues about knowledge of *acquaintance* frame the dialogue in rather similar ways, for there is also the suggestion that one might know someone by meeting her. I cannot here pursue the question of whether and how knowledge of acquaintance is addressed in the *Theaetetus*. Some influential contributions on related issues are John McDowell, "Identity Mistakes: Plato and the Logical Atomists," *Proceedings of the Aristotelian Society* 70 (1970): 181–96 and Gail Fine, "False Belief in the *Theaetetus*," *Phronesis* 24 (1979): 70–80.

5. Stoic Epistemology and Logic

Right at the beginning of the *Theaetetus*, Socrates says that knowledge is unerring and always true: knowledge is of what is and free from false-hood (152c).[48] The relevant intuition can be expressed in a stronger and a weaker way.

Knowledge Weak: Knowledge is always true.

Knowledge Strong: Knowledge is always true and the only cognitive atti-tude that is concerned with truth.

Consider this premise in light of the transition between Parts I and II of the *Theaetetus*. Toward the end of Part I of the dialogue, Socrates men-tions Parmenides (183e5) as a thinker he holds in great esteem. Then comes the final argument against DEF I (184b–186e), an argument that is short and notoriously difficult. This is not the place to analyze the argu-ment, or to defend a view on how Part I of the *Theaetetus* proceeds and ends. Note just one point: the final argument against DEF I states that knowledge, truth, and being belong together (186c7–e6).

If one reads this claim having just been reminded of how highly one is to think of Parmenides—what is one to make of it? Admittedly, this way of approaching the text is sketchy; but recall the present goal, namely to envis-age how philosophers in the early Academy might have engaged with it. When Parmenides is invoked, this puts a whole line of thought on the table,

---

[48]Early on in Parmenides' poem (B1.28–30), it may appear as if 'the beliefs of mortals' could be true, but lacked certainty. However, the text continues (B2.1–6): "But come, I will tell you—preserve the account when you hear it—the only roads of enquiry there are to be thought of: one, that *it is* and cannot not be, is the path of persuasion (for truth accompanies it); another, that *it is not* and must not be—this I say to you is a trail of utter ignorance." The path of belief is a path of ignorance. Interpreters sometimes employ a distinction between different ways in which "*estin*" ("is") may be used, which goes back to Charles Kahn, "The Greek Verb 'Be' and the Concept of Being," *Foundations of Language* 2 (1966): 245–65. In the spirit of this distinction, one might say the following (cf. G. S. Kirk, J. E. Raven, and M. Schofield, *Presocratic Philosophers: A Critical History with a Selection of Texts* [Cambridge: Cambridge University Press, 1983], 270): If "is not" is taken in the existential use, then the point of the passage is that one cannot know what does not exist; if "is not" is read in the veridical sense, that is, as "is not true," then the point is that knowledge of the non-true is not knowledge.

one that asks readers to take seriously a certain perspective on knowledge, being, and truth (and one that arguably reminds the reader that similar intuitions are pursued in the *Republic*). For present purposes, it suffices to say that, considered in this light, Knowledge Strong is not implausible. That is, the intuition that *doxa* is not concerned with the truth, or not in the relevant way concerned with truth, should not strike us as a remote idea. Instead, it is a rather obvious idea for Plato to take seriously.

If Knowledge Strong holds, then Two Kinds is false: there are no true beliefs. According to Knowledge Strong, only knowledge is in touch with the truth. *Doxa* does not get hold of the truth. This line of thought is without doubt radical. It moves from the premise that only the knower knows that what she holds to be true is true to the claim that beliefs do not reach the truth. There is an obvious objection: of course a belief can be true without the cognizer knowing this. And yet, one might argue that there is a rather deep difference between making a truth-claim that, unbeknownst to oneself, is true, and being 'in possession' of a truth. In the latter sense, one might argue, beliefs are never true. The Stoics make, quite plausibly via engagement with Part II of the *Theaetetus*, precisely this point. The cognizer who holds beliefs is never in possession of truth.

I examine the Stoic conception of *doxa* in the final chapter of this book. For now, let me just sketch briefly how the story continues. The Stoics think that Plato rightly takes seriously two intuitions about belief but that he fails to integrate them with each other: the intuitions that beliefs are deficient and that all truth-claims have the same structure. According to DEF II, every instance of holding-to-be-true is an inner assertion, and it can be described in terms of judgment. From the point of view of the Stoics, something important is being captured here. This proposal is perhaps one of the greatest achievements of the *Theaetetus*. It is developed further by the Hellenistic philosophers, engaged with by early modern philosophy, and arguably influences how we still conceive of belief-formation. Thought and judgment are envisaged as a kind of conversation that the mind has with itself, a conversation that ends with settling on an answer to a question that one was considering. The mind comes to a decision. No longer going back and forth, it "says one thing"—this inner statement is a *doxa* (189e). Belief-formation is the acceptance of some content as true.

This idea is central to Stoic logic. According to the Stoics, philosophy of language and logic deal with the way in which the mind accepts, as they put it, impressions (*phantasiai*). The impressions of human beings are thoughts, and they have linguistic entities corresponding to them, the so-called *lekta* or sayables. Those *lekta* that can be asserted—complete *lekta*, rather than incomplete *lekta* such as predicates—are called assertibles (*axiomata*). They are, according to the Stoics, the bearers of truth-values. Assertibles are defined as that which is true or false (DL 7.85). Strictly speaking, only assertibles are the bearers of truth-values.[49] That is, the Stoics propose that the truth-predicates are to be assigned to entities that resemble our propositions, not to beliefs.

Logic, understood as the field that studies *lekta*, is not concerned with evaluative and normative issues. It leaves open questions that then need to be tackled in normative epistemology, in particular, the distinction between belief as a deficient and knowledge as a superior kind of judgment and attitude. And yet the very line of thought in Plato that invites one to think of truth-claims as having the structure of assent to impressions also opens the door to a particular kind of normative concern. As I noted, one can consider a matter more or less carefully before settling on a view. Normative epistemology discusses how we should judge, when we should assent, which judgments to revise, and so on.[50] If the relevant epistemic norms (a main topic of Stoic epistemology) are consistently applied, one will come to acquire knowledge.

The Stoics distinguish between *the true* in the sense of true assertibles and *truth* as a state of mind.[51] Only a knower—that is, only someone

---

[49]Impressions (*phantasiai*) are true or false in a derivative sense: a true impression is an impression of which a true predication (*katēgoria*) can be made (SE, M 7.242–46, LS 39G). Early research on Stoic logic in the 1980s was enthusiastic about the fact that the Stoics develop a propositional logic, and the Greek term *axiōma* was often translated as 'proposition.' However, it is important to keep in mind that the Stoics assign truth-predicates to particular utterances, that is, to utterances made by a specific person, in a specific context, and at a specific time. For example, "it is raining" is true when uttered by someone who is at a place where it is now raining. Importantly, while assertibles are true or false, more strictly speaking, assertibles that are *said* by someone are true or false. "Assertibles are those things saying which we either speak true or speak false" (SE, M 8.73).

[50]The Stoic divisions into philosophical disciplines do not map onto ours. Epistemology is included in what they call logic. However, within logic broadly construed, different kinds of study are conducted, some of them normative (how to assent, how to acquire knowledge), and some of them resembling what we today call logic.

[51]Truth and the true differ in three respects (SE, PH 2.80–84). (1) In what they are: the true, i.e., a true *axioma*, is incorporeal; truth as a state of the soul is corporeal. (2) In composition: the true is simple in the sense that individual *axiomata* are the bearers of truth-values; truth is constituted by the knowledge of many truths. (3) In their modalities: it is possible to say something true by chance, not having the relevant knowledge; truth is tied necessarily to knowledge.

whose rational soul is structured and made firm by a system of knowl-edge—possesses truth. Someone who holds a belief is never, even if the corresponding assertible is true, in possession of truth. The upshot of this line of reasoning is that truth-predicates should only be used in charac-terizing assertibles, not in characterizing beliefs. The Stoics advance a thesis on the question of which entities are truth-evaluable. These must be entities that can be true *or* false. Neither pieces of knowledge nor beliefs are plausible candidates: pieces of knowledge cannot be false, and beliefs are not true in the normatively relevant way—the believer is not, as the Stoics would put it, in possession of truth. The bearers of truth-values must be found outside of the field of normative epistemology; they are part of the subject matter of logic and the philosophy of language.

While we ordinarily call beliefs true and false, we might agree with the Stoics that, strictly speaking, propositions (or their Stoic cousin, com-plete *lekta*) are the bearers of truth-values. At the outset of this chapter, I said that it might appear foreign to us that beliefs should not be evalu-ated as true or false. In the light of where the Stoics take this thought, however, it might appear plausible: we tend to agree with the Stoics, that strictly speaking something other than beliefs—assertions, propositions, and so on—are bearers of truth-values. In conclusion, then, I want to recommend the proposed Stoic reading of Part II of the *Theaetetus* as one that establishes rather good reasons for separating the normative assess-ment of belief from the study of the bearers of truth-values.

4

The Nature of Disagreement: Ancient Relativism and Skepticism

Suppose you and I decide to go to that new place across the street and have tea with honey. Taking a sip, you find you cannot drink your tea. "The honey is bitter," you say. I'm also taking a sip—it tastes lovely. "The honey is sweet," I say. Ancient relativism, as construed by Plato in the *Theaetetus*, says that both of us are right, and seeks a metaphysical explanation of this presumed fact.[1] Aenesidemus's Pyrrhonism takes the opposite perspective, suspecting that we are both wrong, and asks what the world must be like for this to be possible.[2] The skepticism of Sextus Empiricus is a rejection of these earlier metaphysical analyses of disagreement.[3] Sextus's skepticism reinvigorates a Socratic intuition: if there are conflicting appearances, or if one cannot figure something out, one should continue to investigate. From this point of view, relativism and earlier Pyrrhonism appear dogmatic. They say that the world must be such and such for there to be conflicting appearances. Sextus's version of skepticism suggests these philosophies misrepresent phenomena of disagreement—phenomena of conflicting appearances or conflicting views on a given question. Disagreement does not immediately raise

[1] I am greatly indebted to some publications on Plato's *Theaetetus*, more than I can acknowledge at particular points of the chapter: Burnyeat, *The Theaetetus of Plato*; McDowell, *Theaetetus*; Sedley, *The Midwife of Platonism*.

[2] Cf. Richard Bett, *Pyrrho, His Antecedents, and His Legacy* (Oxford: Oxford University Press, 2000); for a different view, see Luca Castagnoli, "Self-Bracketing Pyrrhonism," *Oxford Studies in Ancient Philosophy* 18 (2000): 263–328.

[3] Mi-Kyoung Lee discusses some related issues in *Epistemology after Protagoras: Responses to Relativism in Plato, Aristotle, and Democritus* (Oxford: Oxford University Press, 2005).

the question of what the world must be like to accommodate it; more plausibly, it raises the question of how one should think about the disputed question. The parties to a disagreement are not locked into their positions. To encounter disagreement is disturbing, and it is a reason to reconsider one's views.

These issues are hard to address by studying exclusively the writings of Sextus. Indeed, I shall propose that they are usefully approached from a different angle—via a close reading of arguments in Part I of Plato's *Theaetetus* that are likely to have figured importantly in Hellenistic discussions. Though Sextus does not explicitly reference the *Theaetetus*, it is obvious that many of its arguments loom large in Pyrrhonian skepticism. While scholars have long assumed that Stoics and skeptics read the *Theaetetus* very closely, there is astonishingly little literature on the details of how we can imagine this engagement. The lack of testimony partly explains this fact: it is impossible to say with any certainty who read which passage in which way. At the same time, the philosophies of the early skeptics and the Stoics certainly provide us with a lens. The exercise that I suggest is that we try to read the *Theaetetus* from their point of view—we know enough about their arguments and preoccupations to do so. As a result of this exercise, I argue, it becomes clearer why Sextus thinks of skepticism as an improvement upon relativism. I will begin by looking at the relevant kinds of disagreement (section 1), discuss Plato's analysis of the epistemology and metaphysics of relativism (sections 2 to 4), and end with a sketch of how these debates relate to the Pyrrhonism of Pyrrho and Aenesidemus (section 5) and to Sextus Empiricus's skepticism (section 6).

1. Some Examples of Disagreement

All extant versions of ancient skepticism, as well as the most fully formulated version of ancient relativism, are *global*: they are intended to apply to all domains of judgment.[4] This does not mean that ancient skeptics recognized no differences between domains of judgment. Rather, dis-

---

[4]Contemporary philosophers tend to assume that these matters are naturally discussed in domain-specific ways. Cf. for example John MacFarlane, "Relativism and Disagreement," *Philosophical Studies* 132 (2007): 17–31; Crispin Wright, "Intuitionism, Realism, Relativism, and Rhubarb," in P. Greenough and M. P. Lynch (eds.), *Truth and Realism* (Oxford: Oxford University Press, 2006), 77–99.

agreement is thought to invite similar responses whether it occurs in the domain of evaluative-normative judgments, perceptual judgments, or theoretical judgments. Moreover, a range of locutions is relevant to the phenomena I refer to as 'disagreement': conflicting appearances, disagreements between views held by different people, conflicting thoughts entertained by the same person, and so on. Consider first an example from the evaluative-normative domain.

Funeral: Members of one culture (Funeral 1) burn their dead parents and consider it terrible to eat the dead bodies of their parents. Members of another culture (Funeral 2) eat the bodies of their dead parents and consider it terrible to burn them.

Herodotus, the earliest anthropologist-cum-historiographer, discusses this case.[5] His *Histories* contain many such examples: similar conflicts occur with respect to marriage, family, religious festivities, birth, and so on. These cases share the following features. (1) One's own values and practices appear right, and one is attached to them. The values and practices of others not only appear wrong; they appear to be terrible. (2) There is a shared background assumption: a domain of life is considered important enough to deserve cultural practices and regulations. The two practices are not just *different*; they constitute a *disagreement* in the sense that there is something—say, how to conduct a funeral—about which people disagree. Notably, this is not the only way to describe the relevant kind of phenomenon: one might also think of different cultures as incommensurable systems, or as living in different worlds.[6] On that proposal, an evaluative judgment counts as true or false within a given system. The judgments are assumed to differ without being in conflict: the conceptual

---

[5]The two cultures are the Greeks and the Callatiae (3.38). Lee (*Epistemology after Protagoras*, 8) also cites this passage. It is famous, in part because Herodotus takes himself to interpret the dictum "law is king" by the eminent poet Pindar. Though the Sophists are associated with discussions about law and nature, it is hard to find similarly helpful passages. The closeness of Herodotus and sophistic thought about the role of law and custom is underexplored. I discussed this issue with several classicists, all of whom agreed with my basic assessment, but none of whom could point me to scholarship on the issue. On the question of whether the Sophists should in general be considered relativists, cf. Richard Bett, "The Sophists and Relativism," *Phronesis* 34.1 (1989): 139–69, esp. 141–45.

[6]A classic formulation can be found in Bernard Williams's "The Truth in Relativism," *Proceedings of the Aristotelian Society* 75 (1974–75): 215–28.

schemes operative in different cultures are seen as not translatable into each other. Accordingly, there appears to be no genuine disagreement. Plato conceives of a version of this, asking whether it makes sense to assume that each cognizer refers to 'her world.' But the kind of value relativism that thinks of different cultures as incommensurable systems does not seem to figure in early Greek philosophy.[7] Examples follow the pattern of Herodotus's accounts: for every disagreement, there is some shared background assumption.[8] (3) Practices differ deeply. The contrast is meant to draw attention to the enormous powers of custom, and to raise the question of whether we are mistaken in the assumption that there is a right way to conduct funerals.

Consider next two cases of perceptual disagreement, cases that derive from the pre-Socratic atomists: Lucretius's Sea, and Democritus's Honey.

Sea: The sea sometimes looks white and sometimes blue.

Honey: Honey tastes sweet to healthy people, and bitter to people with certain diseases.

Sea and Honey differ from Funeral with respect to (1). 'Disagreement' means, here, simply that the appearances *differ* from each other, and in

___

[7]A version of it may figure in Greek literature. Arguably, Odysseus's travels lead him into incommensurable worlds. The world of war, in which Odysseus spent ten years, and the world of peace, to which he means to return, are far apart. To transition from one to the other is almost impossible. It involves a detour through even stranger worlds, worlds that are literally incommensurable with any ordinary way of leading a human life. As James S. Romm discusses, the shoreline of Polyphemus's island is referred to as the 'boundary of the earth' (*peirata gaiēs*; 9.284) (*The Edges of the Earth in Ancient Thought: Geography, Exploration, and Fiction* [Princeton, N.J.: Princeton University Press, 1992]).

[8]In comparing different religions, Herodotus implicitly assumes that there is *one* divine reality. Herodotus lists the names that different cultures give to, as he sees it, Zeus (culture A calls Zeus "X," culture B calls him "Y"). Religions differ in giving different names to the gods; these names attach to interpretations of who these gods are and what their powers are, and reflect different cults, rites, and so on. Accordingly, disagreement in religion is like disagreement in value questions. In describing the disagreement, Herodotus assumes that there is *one thing* that people disagree about. Xenophanes' well-known claims that human beings imagine the gods according to the way they look and dress, so that different cultures have different ideas of what the gods look like, can be construed along similar lines. Different cultures imagine the same reality—divinity—according to their own ways of life (DK 21B14, B15, B16).

that sense—in the sense that there is a difference—they do not agree with each other. It does not mean that those who disagree—which might also be one cognizer at different times—are in any way *opposed* to each other's views. Sea and Honey come to be described as cases of disagreement by the skeptics. Early Greek philosophers refer to such cases simply as involving different appearances. For example, the early atomists seem to have speculated that honey atoms interact differently with cognizer atoms, depending on the state of the cognizer.

Sea and Honey share feature (2) with Funeral. Different cognizers, or the same cognizer at different times, are thought to refer to something in reality (for example, honey atoms) that, though it appears differently, is one thing. In this sense, there is genuine disagreement, not only difference: there is in fact one thing (the honey atoms) that appears differently. Sea and Honey are also like Funeral with respect to (3): in both domains, phenomena of disagreement give rise to the question of whether there is a determinate reality.[9] That honey tastes differently under different conditions, that the sea looks differently colored at different times, and that different cultures have different funerary practices, each suggest that there may not be a fact of the matter of how honey *really* tastes, what color the sea *really* has, or how funerals *really* should be conducted. Disagreement indicates that reality might be underdetermined or indeterminate.[10]

Finally, consider a case of a theoretical disagreement, one that can be associated with the Sophists, Socrates, and Plato.

Virtue: Is virtue teachable? One interlocutor says yes; the other interlocutor says no.

Theoretical disagreements may or may not come with the kind of attachment to one's perspective we saw in Funeral (1). They resemble Funeral

[9]Along these lines, Lucretius argues that, if the sea's atoms were really blue, they could not undergo change and look white (DRN 2.774–5). That is, he assumes that the atoms cannot have the property blue, for otherwise they could not appear to have the property white. The appearance of blue and of white can be produced by something that is neither blue nor white, but not by something that is blue or white. Cf. Sylvia Berryman, "Democritus," first published 2004, substantive revision 2010, in Edward N. Zalta (ed.), *Stanford Encyclopedia of Philosophy*, http://plato.stanford.edu/entries/democritus/.

[10]As Lee (*Epistemology after Protagoras*) argues, Democritus's philosophy can be seen as a response to Protagorean relativism.

and Honey/Sea in being genuine disagreements in the sense mentioned above: there is *one* question about which people disagree (2). They may or may not be discussed with the presumption that, in principle, the issue is resolvable (3).

In setting out the examples, I stipulated a distinction between three domains: values/norms/practices, perception, and theory. The fact-value distinction that is central to today's discussions is alien to ancient conceptual frameworks. This is not because all ancient philosophers were 'naturalists about value' in any contemporary sense. There is a complex set of other reasons, including a core intuition of pre-Socratic philosophers—one that Plato takes on board and that lives on in skeptical arguments—namely that there is a fundamental distinction between the perceptual realm on the one hand, and the realm of thought or theory on the other. According to this distinction, questions about values do not form their own class.[11] Some fall into a broadly construed domain of perception: for example, certain practices strike one as disgraceful, acts of kindness strike one as precious, and so on. Others fall into the realm of theory, for example, the question of whether virtue is teachable. This is the inherited framework of skeptical engagement with disagreement.[12]

2. Global Relativism in the Theaetetus

In the *Theaetetus*, Plato develops one of the most thorough analyses of relativism of which I am aware, including contemporary analyses. Rather than pertaining to any particular domain, relativism, as Plato formulates it, applies globally. Plato associates relativism with Protagoras, and thus with a Sophist, as well as with Heraclitus, a pre-Socratic philosopher. I shall not ask whether Protagoras or Heraclitus really held the views that Plato ascribes to them. This would be hard to establish given that Plato's reconstructions of their philosophies have been extremely influential and

---

[11]Similarly, practical judgments (in the sense of judgments involved in action, deliberation, etc.) do not form their own class. The perception-theory distinction predates distinctions between theoretical and practical reasoning, and remains central to discussions about skepticism. The Aristotelian distinction between theoretical and practical reasoning, however, does not become part of these debates.

[12]Plato specifically discusses the nature of value disagreement in *Euthyphro* 7a–8b and *Phaedrus* 263a–c. However, both passages discuss problems not immediately relevant to my present topic.

shape other ancient reports. It also does not matter for present purposes. What matters is that Plato offers a detailed analysis of the scope, epistemology, and metaphysics of relativism. Discussion begins with Theaetetus's proposed account of knowledge:

[K]nowledge (*epistēmē*) is perception (*aisthēsis*). (151e3)

Socrates rephrases this as follows:

Perception, you say, is knowledge. (151e6–7)

But Socrates' reformulation is a different claim. It prepares the ground for the idea that, when something appears to be such and such, it is such and such: when one sees something, one knows it, and that entails that what one sees is the case.[13] This idea is ascribed to Protagoras:

Man is the measure of all things, of things which are, that they are, and of the things which are not, that they are not [...]. (152a2–5; this is a quote from Protagoras's book *Truth* [*Alētheia*]; cf. SE, M 7.60)

[A]s each thing appears to me (*emoi phainetai*), so it is for me (*estin emoi*), and as it appears to you, so it is for you. (152a7–9)

Protagoras's Measure Formula does not refer to any particular domain of judgment, and eventually, as the discussion progresses, Plato interprets it as global—as referring to all domains of judgment. In a first step, however, Plato begins with the analysis of a perceptual example. He considers a case where the same wind blows, and A freezes and B does not (152b2–3). The wind is a cold wind for A but not for B (152b5–7).

Thus it [the wind] appears (*phainetai*) to each of them? [...]

And this 'appears' (*phainetai*) is the perceiving (*aisthanesthai*)? [...]

Impression (*phantasia*) and perception (*aithēsis*) is then the same with respect to what is warm and everything of that sort? (152b9–c2)

---

[13]Theaetetus's initial formulation, "knowledge is perception," could be taken quite differently. One could argue that to know something involves a perception-like acquaintance, an idea that is not foreign to Plato (say, in knowing the Form of the Good the cognizer in some sense 'sees' it).

Phantasia is, as it were, the bridge between *aisthēsis* and *phainetai*: sensing the wind as cold, one has a perception and an impression, and this impression is a case of something appearing so-and-so. At this point, it seems as if we were exclusively concerned with the limited domain of properties like warm and cold. But in discussing the implications of Protagoras's view, Socrates construes 'perception' broadly, so as to include pleasure, pain, desires (or pursuits), and fears (or avoidances):

> [S]ight, hearing, smelling, feeling cold and feeling hot, and pleasures and pains and desires and fears are also called such, and others, countless unnamed ones, and many that have names. (156b4–7)

The next step toward global relativism is taken when Protagoras defends his position. Protagoras speaks—as it were in character, given that he is a Sophist—of value judgments, which he introduces through a parallel with gustatory taste. Some things taste better to the sick person but not to the healthy person. The doctor aims to change the overall condition of the patient, so that things shall no longer taste bitter to her. In other words, the doctor does not aim to change how things taste to the sick person; rather, he aims to cure her, and as a consequence, things shall no longer taste bitter (166e–167d). This is precisely what the Sophist does in teaching people. No one has ever brought anyone who held false beliefs to hold true beliefs simply through speeches (167a5–7). Why? Because it is not *possible* to believe what, for the cognizer, is not:

> For neither is it possible to believe that which is not, nor to believe otherwise than one is affected; and this is always true. (167a7–167b1)

Accordingly, the Sophist tries to change someone's overall condition or state of mind. As a consequence, she will have different beliefs.[14] The Sophist's wisdom fits together with the Measure Doctrine in the following way:

> I do say that things are in truth as I wrote, that each of us is the measure of what is and what is not; but one of us shall differ a thousand times from the

---

[14]Protagoras dismisses the idea that one view is true and the other false; but one view can be *better* than another view. With respect to the truth, 'better' and 'worse' are on a par (167b). What appears just and noble in each given (political) state, is just and noble for this state. There is no point trying to change people's views. Rather, the wise person brings it about that the beneficial will seem just and noble to a state, instead of the pernicious.

other, precisely because one thing is (*esti*) for him and appears to him (*phainetai*), and something else to someone else. And I am far from saying that there is no wisdom or no wise man; instead I call him wise who, when to one of us bad things appear and are, can set off a change, so that good things appear and are to him. (166d1–8)

Depending on the condition one is in, something appears good and something bad. Lectures and explanations will not lead one to change one's mind; instead, one needs to be brought into a different condition to see things differently. This position might initially sound extreme. I think, however, that Plato takes very seriously a significant part of it—although not the claim that there are no false value judgments. In the terminology of the *Republic*, education must 'turn around the soul,' so that the person loves the good and is attached to the good.[15] Only if she is in this overall condition will things strike her the right way, and only in this state can she come up with the right value judgments by herself.

At this point in the dialogue, the "man is the measure" formula seems to pertain to perceptual and value judgments. The next formulation relevant to our purposes extends the domain of appearances further. Instead of speaking in terms of *phantasia* and *phainesthai*, terms that were introduced as intuitively close to perception, Socrates now uses another verb for 'to appear,' *dokein*. This verb is the root of *doxa*, belief; it covers all cases of appearing, perceptual and nonperceptual:

What seems (*to dokoun*) to each, he [Protagoras] says, that is (*einai*) also as it seems to him (*hō dokei*). (170a3–4; this also appears to be a quote from Protagoras's book *Truth*)

This passage is sometimes seen as evidence for one of two interpretations of the Measure Doctrine. The Measure Doctrine says that "man is the measure." This dictum might mean that things are either as they appear to human beings, or as they appear to each individual human being. Interpreters take 170a3–4 to indicate that Protagoras speaks about individual persons and their beliefs. For the purposes of the skeptical reception of his ideas, however, the ambiguity is best left unresolved. As we shall see, the skeptics put into opposition not only how things appear to

---

[15]The 'turning around' (*peritropē*) of the soul is the topic of Books II–III on education. Cf. Burnyeat, "Culture and Society."

different persons, but also how things appear to human beings on the one hand, and to other animals on the other. Privileging human cognizers looks just as arbitrary as privileging one particular human cognizer, a point that Socrates also raises in the *Theaetetus* (see below).

From 170a3–4 onwards, Protagoras's Measure Doctrine counts as an example of something that, since it appears to someone, namely to Protagoras, is true. That is, we are now considering neither a perceptual case nor a value case but a theoretical case: a certain theory or doctrine appears to someone and is true for someone. Discussion proceeds in terms of *doxa*, belief or judgment, and *doxazein*, belief-formation or judging (170b–c). (However, *phainesthai* and its cognates are not fully discarded. Indeed, there is a use of *phainesthai* that covers perceptual and nonperceptual appearances, just as *dokein* does.) Relativism, according to Plato, implies a certain account of belief. On this account, beliefs are *passively* acquired. As Michael Frede puts this idea, beliefs "grow on us."[16] In all cases in which something appears to be so-and-so, the cognizer is *affected* a certain way: things seem to her a certain way, rather than her actively forming a judgment.[17]

A series of reformulations, then, has led Plato from the discussion of perceptual judgments to value judgments to theoretical judgments.[18] It

---

[16]Michael Frede argues that Protagoras is committed to an account of belief (how something seems-to-someone and what she, accordingly, believes) according to which belief is passive. "The Protagorean view, on the other hand, and the other views alluded to in the beginning, which are like it, assume that beliefs normally are something we just find ourselves with, which have grown on us, which we have just come by by being struck by things in a certain way" ("Observations on Perception in Plato's Later Dialogues," in Fine, *Plato*, 377–83, 383). The Pyrrhonists are greatly interested in the question of whether belief is passively acquired or actively formed. In saying that they do not have beliefs, they assume—*pace* Plato—that all beliefs involve judgments. However, in saying that they find themselves, passively, with something like a cousin to beliefs, they invoke the idea that beliefs 'grow on us.' Lee (*Epistemology after Protagoras*, chapter 7) examines Aristotle's discussions of the account of thinking as a passive affection he sees as implied in Protagoras philosophy.

[17]Plato's final argument against relativism turns against this notion of belief (186b–c). Plato distinguishes between passive affections (*pathēmata*) and active reasoning. Belief-formation is an activity of the soul.

[18]In discussing Protagoras's doctrine Plato rejects the view that all judgments are on a par (171d–172c; 177c–179c). Protagoras's doctrine is found to be true for present-tense judgments about perceptual qualities. Statements about future perceptual properties can be false. For example, an expert can predict whether the season's wine will turn out sweet, while the nonexpert would not get it right. There is also a sense in which what states declare

led from sense-perception to appearance in the sense-perceptual realm to appearance in the domain of value, and to beliefs on all kinds of matters, including theoretical issues. Relativism, as developed in Plato's *Theaetetus*, is accordingly global; it is not restricted to particular domains of discourse or to particular kinds of properties. This feature of the *Theaetetus* often goes unnoticed. Interpreters tend to turn immediately to Plato's more explicit arguments against relativism. However, if the sequence of steps I outlined is meant to be an argument for the view that relativism, if held in one domain—say, the domain of values—is tied to relativism in all other domains, then the very scope of relativism might constitute an argument against it.[19] Those who have relativist intuitions might have started out by thinking about disagreement of values. Perhaps they were aiming to capture the nature of disagreement precisely in this domain. If they find themselves committed to global relativism, they might rethink their position.

3. Skeptical Arguments in the Theaetetus

The *Theaetetus* contains some further arguments (arguably subsidiary to the main steps in the discussion outlined above) by which the range of relevant appearances is extended. These arguments have a distinctively skeptical flavor, and I shall refer to them as skeptical arguments.

First, the range of judgments to which the Measure Doctrine applies might include what appears to animals and gods (161c–162e). Socrates raises the objection that, in declaring *man* to be the measure, Protagoras makes an unwarranted assumption. Why not say that the pig or the

---

to be just is just. But this is a limited, and conventional, sense of the just. Insofar as laws intend to lay down what will be beneficial for the state, there can be error. Plato introduces the notion of a criterion (*kriterion*) (178b). With respect to the white, heavy, etc., people have the *kriterion* in themselves: the cognizer experiences something that is for her. But we do not have a criterion in ourselves (or do not ourselves constitute the criterion) for future states of ourselves; for example, people make false predications on whether they will have a fever or whether this year's wine will be good (178b–c).

[19]A more detailed interpretation of the *Theaetetus* would be needed to make this point. For current purposes, I am making a weaker claim: that *if* the dialogue can be read as an argument against the option of being a domain-specific relativist, then this constitutes in itself a challenge of relativism.

monkey is the measure (161c)?[20] Similarly, why exclude the gods?[21] These questions resonate with thinkers who discuss skepticism in later, theologically framed philosophy.[22] Though the skeptics suspend judgment on the existence of gods, thus not integrating reference to gods into their skeptical arguments, reference to other animals—to whom the world is likely to appear differently—becomes a stock element of Pyrrhonism (PH 1.40–78).

Second, at different times and under different conditions, things appear differently to individual cognizers. The Measure Doctrine might initially sound as if every person had *her* truth in a relatively robust sense (say, her view on a given issue). But this is a naive understanding of the doctrine. An appearance is a momentary event, and individual cognizers will over time disagree with themselves. These kinds of disagreement arise in particular when the person comes to be in a significantly different state, say, in dreams, illness, and madness (157c–160e). The relativist, as Plato depicts him, is prepared to bite the bullet. For the relativist, there is no criterion by which we could give priority to one of these states over the other. Dreaming and waking occupy more or less the same amount of time in our lives; to privilege the waking state seems arbitrary. With respect to madness and illness, there certainly seems to be a temporal prevalence of nonmad and healthy states. As the relativist sees it, however, to

[20] According to Protagoras, the thought that human beings are not superior to other animals should not be considered frightful (162d). However, Protagoras dislikes the point about animals. He says that Socrates acts like a pig in bringing up pigs and monkeys in discussing the Measure Doctrine. We might speculate that, for him, relativism aims to explain the world *as it is for human beings*. If this is the goal, then it is beside the point that, obviously, the world is different for other animals.

[21] Protagoras's response is that Socrates should leave the gods alone. Since he, Protagoras, leaves it open whether the gods even exist, he is not willing to consider them as cognizers (162d). This passage and its history is underexplored; in early modern skepticism, the idea that the world looks different from a divine perspective assumes great importance. To some later thinkers, the idea that the gods might be just another group of cognizers might be offensive. The ancient relativists and skeptics, however, do not dismiss it because it is blasphemous. Their reaction is, from a religious perspective, even worse: they consider it quite possible that there are no gods.

[22] Arguably, early modern philosophers are not hostile to the thought that, in some sense, 'God is the measure': that is, reality *really* is as it is for the perfect cognizer God. In the *Laws*, Plato explores a different (though not unrelated idea): that God is most of all the measure *of all things*, where this means we should aim to be as much like God as we can (4.716c–d). Perhaps the *homoiōsis* digression in the *Theaetetus* can be taken to lead up to this kind of proposal.

decide the question of truth by appeal to how much time one spends in each state would be absurd. Dreaming, madness, and illness do not provide obvious examples of false perceptions. The skeptics adopt the relativist's perspective insofar as they do not dismiss these states as obviously fraught with error. Dreams, illness, and madness furnish them with yet another set of examples about ways in which the world can appear differently.[23]

4. The Metaphysics of Relativism

Turn now to the metaphysics of relativism. Consider again the wind example:

> Would not sometimes, with the same wind blowing, one of us freeze while the other does not? (152b2–3)

The wind appears differently to A and B, and it is true for A that it is cold, and true for B that it is not cold (152b). A and B make different claims about the wind, but their claims only appear to be a disagreement. In fact, A and B do not disagree. As we saw in Funeral, Sea/Honey, and Virtue, for there to be genuine disagreement, there must be something—in this case, the wind—to which both parties refer and with respect to which they judge differently. This is how the example is initially phrased: there is one wind, two perceivers, and two truths. Relativism initially just seems to imply the *relativization of truth.* "The wind is cold" is true for A, and "the wind is warm" is true for B.

But since both A and B are right, each party must refer to a *different* reality. For A and B each to make a true judgment, there cannot be *one* wind: there must be a wind-for-A, and a wind-for-B.[24] These are, respectively,

---

[23]There is also a third skeptical argument, which, however, is not immediately relevant to our present topic, an argument that envisages a kind of memory skepticism (163d–164b). According to Socrates' interpretation of the Measure Doctrine, understood as an interpretation of "perception is knowledge," one knows what one perceives, at the moment of perception. This means that, when the moment of vision has passed, the knowledge is lost. This is incompatible with the phenomenon that we remember things.

[24]I am here putting things in terms of the Cold Wind Example. Plato introduces further examples as he goes along to develop these ideas, such as the examples of a stone or human being in 157b–c.

what A's and B's judgments are about. Accordingly, relativism must also imply the *relativization of objects-cum-properties* ("cold-wind-for-A").[25] Relativism thus does not envisage A and B as genuinely disagreeing: there is no conflict between what they say. They each speak about the world they happen to inhabit, a world that constitutes itself in their acts of perception. As someone perceives (*aisthanetai*), thus it will be for him (152c2–c3).

The notion of a "cold-wind-for-A" leads Plato to discuss perception. The cold-wind-for-A must be the product of an interaction between A's cognitive activities and some physical processes outside of A, a product that is constituted at the moment of the perception. Accordingly, there are not even temporally stable objects-for-A or objects-for-B. For such objects to exist, there would have to be, for example, a "wind-for-A" that persists over time. But that is impossible. The "cold-wind-for-A" is a momentary product, constituted through the interaction between cognitive activity and outside world at a given time. This is the metaphysics of radical flux, a view that Plato ascribes to Heraclitus: the world dissolves. There are no stable objects or properties.

Relativism thus implies a highly revisionist metaphysics, a metaphysics that is so incredible that it may refute relativism. If we have to accept radical flux in order to be relativists, we should probably give up on relativism. In what is arguably the final blow for radical flux, Socrates shows that, on this metaphysics, there could be no language. Language *refers* to objects and properties that have some temporal stability (179c–184b). A language that would be adequate to the metaphysics of relativism still needs to be invented. Two expressions are discussed as coming close to capturing a world in flux, but they are only approximations. We might use the expression *ou mallon* (no more this than that) (182e), saying for example that something is no more red than not red. On the other hand, we might use the expression *oud' houtōs*: something is 'not at all thus' instead of 'so-and-so' (183b). But even these ways of speaking imply that there are objects for us to refer to. According to radical flux everything is motion (179c–182a) and thus language is impossible.[26]

---

[25]Plato's discussions of the metaphysics of relativism have had tremendous influence in the history of philosophy. Indeed, they might set the premises for a long-standing assumption, namely that relativism, though it is often initially formulated as a position about values, is ultimately a *metaphysical* position.

[26]David Sedley argues that traditional interpretations that consider the 'collapse of language' as an argument against relativism miss out on the fact that Heracliteans *themselves*

5. Pyrrho and Aenesidemus on Disagreement

Consider again Funeral. Feature (1) noted above—namely, that members of each culture find the practices of the other culture horrible—might be misleading. Presumably, the members of Funeral 1 and Funeral 2 are not themselves travelers, and do not know of each other's customs.[27] Those who encounter disagreement—say, because they travel, or because smaller matters are at issue, observable within a given culture—can respond in a number of ways. Obviously, they can simply be horrified. They might insist on their point of view, and refuse to engage with any other perspective. Alternatively, they can react like Herodotus, the Sophists, Socrates, and to some extent all Greek philosophers in the Socratic tradition: they might call into question their own attachment to local values. They may not actually give up on the views they acquired earlier in life, but they might consider it likely that, given that everyone seems to find the values natural that they grow up with, *everyone* needs to rethink her stance.

Arguably, Plato misrepresents sophistic relativism in claiming that, according to relativism, what seems to A is true for A, and what seems to B is true for B. Encountering other laws and customs, the Sophists *distance* themselves from the initial attachment to cultural values they may have had. To borrow a phrase from Bernard Williams, it is either too early or too late for relativism: "too early if two groups have never heard of one another, too late if they encounter one another."[28] Phenomena of disagreement give the Sophists pause. They call for a response other than simply holding on to one's claims; for example, one might enter into some kind of dialogue, or one might wonder how it is possible for people to

---

proposed major revisions of ordinary language. "What Socrates is seeking to do, then, in this final phase of his argument against the Protagorean-Heraclitean theory is not to confront the Heracliteans with unexpected and embarrassing implications for the use of language, but to find out exactly how self-denying about language they must themselves be setting out to be in order to maintain their position" ("The Collapse of Language? *Theaetetus* 179c–183c," *Plato* 3 [2003], http://gramata.univ-paris1.fr/Plato/article38.html). For present purposes, we need not pursue this question (in my view, it might well be the case that Plato is discussing Heraclitean views that, at the same time, he considers reasons to reject relativism).

[27]Those who do not travel are likely to imagine others doing what they do, at least in those domains where they take themselves to be doing what is obviously and naturally right. For example, in the *Iliad*, composed from the perspective of Greek culture, the Greeks *and* the Trojans burn their dead according to Greek customs.

[28]"Relativism, History, and the Existence of Values," in Joseph Raz, *The Practice of Value*, ed. Jay Wallace (Oxford: Oxford University Press, 2005), 106–20.

hold such different views. Unqualified commitment to one's values appears naive to the Sophists, and indeed to most travelers who encounter different ways of life and values. Arguably, disagreement is in itself almost as disturbing as the particular foreign custom one observes. It raises the question of how the relevant phenomena of disagreement can be understood, and whether the disputed issues can even be settled.

Pyrrhonism pursues these questions. Although Pyrrho is the 'founder of Pyrrhonism', he is not a skeptic. Pyrrho held instead a metaphysical position, namely that reality is indeterminate and unstable.[29] According to his student Timon, Pyrrho says that "things are equally indifferent and unstable and indeterminate (*adiaphora kai astathmēta kai anepikrita*); for this reason, neither our perceptions nor our beliefs either tell the truth or lie (*adoxastous kai aklineis kai akradantous*)." Accordingly, we should abstain from beliefs. That is, we should not have beliefs, because a belief affirms that something is so-and-so. Since there are no determinate states, all judgments are false.

> For this reason, then, we should not trust them [our perceptions and beliefs], but should be without beliefs and without inclinations and without wavering, saying about each single thing that it no more is than is not, or both is and is not, or neither is nor is not.

This is obviously an alternative to relativism.[30] Rather than claim that all parties to a disagreement are *right* and construct a suitable metaphysics

---

[29]This has appeared unthinkable to scholars because this means that Pyrrho is not a skeptic. However, I think that Bett has argued the case successfully, and I shall not take it up again. Cf. Bett, *Pyrrho*, 29–37. The core piece of testimony comes from Pyrrho's student Timon. "Pyrrho of Elis [...] himself has left nothing in writing; his pupil Timon, however, says that the person who is to be happy must look to these three points: first, what are things like by nature? second, in what way ought we to be disposed towards them? and finally, what will be the result for those who are so disposed? He [Timon] says that he [Pyrrho] reveals that things are equally indifferent and unstable and indeterminate (*adiaphora kai astathmēta kai anepikrita*); for this reason, neither our perceptions nor our beliefs tell the truth or lie (*adoxastous kai aklineis kai akradantous*). For this reason, then, we should not trust them, but should be without beliefs and without inclinations and without wavering, saying about each single thing that it no more is than is not, or both is and is not, or neither is nor is not (*ou mallon estin ē ouk estin ē kai esti kai ouk estin ē oute estin oute ouk estin*)." Aristocles in Eusebius PE 14.18.1–5 = DC53; tr. Bett, *Pyrrho*, with changes.

[30]For a recent summary of scholarship on the pre-Socratic precursors of Greek skepticism, see Mitzi Lee, "Antecedents in Early Greek Philosophy," in Bett, *Ancient Greek Scepticism*, 13–35.

around this claim, Pyrrho suggests that everyone involved in a disagreement is at *fault*. This claim comes with a metaphysics of indeterminacy. While the assessment is metaphysical, it also leads beyond metaphysics and toward normative epistemology. One odd feature of relativism, after all, is that it imagines people as not *responding* to the realization that others do not share their views—other than, say, as responding with hostility. Relativism imagines that people simply hold on to their views. Pyrrho proposes that one must understand why there is disagreement: we disagree because of the indeterminate nature of reality. Understanding this, one must change one's doxastic attitudes: one must stop holding beliefs.

Like Plato, Pyrrho addresses the question of what a given metaphysics implies for our ability to refer to the world and speak about it. He picks up the expression *ou mallon*, which originally derives from pre-Socratic atomism (PH 1.213), and which Plato mentioned as a mere approximation for reference to a world in flux. For Pyrrho's indeterminate reality, "no more" is the right kind of expression. Presumably, there is a reality to which to refer—a kind of background reality, which gives rise to varying perceptions. Thus, in saying that "A is no more this than that" one might successfully refer to some aspect of reality, describing its indeterminate nature. "*Ou mallon*" thus becomes a stock expression of Pyrrhonism, one of the so-called formulae (*phōnai*). These are expressions that presumably figure in every Pyrrhonian utterance—explicitly or as implied qualifiers—and thereby contribute to the various linguistic methods that the skeptics invent in order to counteract the assertive nature of ordinary statements (PH 1.187–209).

Several generations later, Pyrrho is an inspiration for Aenesidemus, a philosopher in Plato's Academy, at the time when the Academy is already skeptical. Aenesidemus is discontent with Academic skepticism, leaves the Academy, and develops his own version of skepticism. Contrary to Academic skepticism, he picks up on the strand of Greek philosophy that focuses on disagreement and appearances. Aenesidemus formulates ten forms of argument (the so-called "Ten Modes" or "Modes of Aenesidemus").[31] The skeptic employs these modes so as to

---

[31]The Ten Modes are preserved in Diogenes Laertius (9.78–88), Philo of Alexandria (*On Drunkenness* 169–202), and Sextus. Sextus gives extensive illustrations, and integrates the Ten Modes into his general account of Pyrrhonism (PH 1.36–163; cf. M 7.345 for ascription of the Ten Modes to Aenesidemus; cf. J. Annas and J. Barnes, *The Modes of*

construct oppositions between appearances and theoretical claims, in any possible combination.[32]

Theoretical claims play a relatively minor role in the Ten Modes, although they are present. Any philosophical thesis can figure in an opposition with a thesis or with an appearance; the same holds for views about the right laws, or views on other evaluative-normative issues. In a striking analogy to the *Theaetetus*, Aenesidemus's Ten Modes construe perception in broad terms: perception includes sense-perception, aesthetic taste, the pleasant and unpleasant, as well as the useful and harmful. Pursuit and avoidance are considered as reactions to perception. Moreover, there are mixed phenomena. For example, something appears more precious or more admirable if it is perceived only rarely. The good and bad are thus largely integrated into a broad domain of quasi-perceptual judgments: things seem good and bad to us insofar as we like or dislike them, take pleasure or displeasure in them, see them as useful or harmful, appreciate them as precious or less precious, and so on. Accordingly, no clearly demarcated domain of values and norms exists, much along the lines of the *Theaetetus*. Most evaluative matters are associated with perception; others come with theoretical views, say, on what virtue is.[33] Apparently in agreement with Pyrrho (we have no testimony on Aenesidemus's metaphysical views), Aenesidemus thinks that, if there is disagreement on whether X is F or F*, then X is *neither* F nor F*.

Pyrrho and Aenesidemus thus both *resurrect disagreement*. Recall that, in the Cold Wind Example, A and B do not genuinely disagree

---

Scepticism [Cambridge: Cambridge University Press, 1985]; R. J. Hankinson, *The Sceptics* [London: Routledge, 1995], 268). Among these, Sextus's report is known best. However, Sextus adjusts the Ten Tropes (as they are called) so as to fit into his skeptical philosophy. In Sextus's report, disagreement leads to suspension of judgment: we cannot determine how things really are, and thus we should suspend judgment.

[32]Sextus's claim that Pyrrhonism is the ability to put appearances and theses into opposition (PH 1.8) is likely to derive from Aenesidemus's version of Pyrrhonism.

[33]Pyrrhonian discussions of ethical questions testify to an awareness that such questions can trouble us particularly, and give rise to shock and disgust when we encounter practices that differ deeply from our own. Cf. Bett's discussions of *Against the Ethicists*, which, though written by Sextus, seems to contain many traces of Aenesidemus' philosophy. Cf. also Bett, *Ancient Greek Scepticism*, on ethical discussions in skepticism. On Sextus's lengthy contrasts between cultural practices, which evoke Herodotus, the tragedians, and in general everything in Greek literature that contains examples that might strike one as crass and disgusting, see K. Vogt, *Law, Reason, and the Cosmic City: Political Philosophy in the Early Stoa* (New York: Oxford University Press, 2008), chapter 1.

because neither refers to the same thing; they each refer to 'their wind.' Everyday experience, however, tells us that people disagree, and it is precisely the very phenomenon of disagreement that led to relativism. If the upshot of relativism is that, in fact, no disagreement ever exists, then relativism is a theory that rejects the phenomenon it sets out to explain. Early Pyrrhonism aims to fare better in this respect: for Pyrrho and Aenesidemus, there is something that appears differently to different cognizers. The world may be indeterminate, but there is a world that appears in one way or another to different people.

6. Disagreement in Sextus's Skepticism

Pyrrho's and Aenesidemus' Pyrrhonism, however, may have an obvious problem. The inference from disagreement on a given issue to the claim that there is no fact of the matter regarding this issue is too hasty. Consider again Funeral. Perhaps Funeral 1 gets it right, or Funeral 2, or some other culture(s), or no culture. Perhaps there is a right way to conduct funerals; or perhaps there is not. Given that all these options are conceivable, the metaphysics of indeterminacy seems unfounded. As it stands, phenomena of disagreement such as Funeral or Sea/Honey or Virtue do not imply *any* metaphysical theory. Instead, they may lead toward an epistemic norm: one should suspend judgment, both on the question at hand and the question of whether it could be settled.

This is, I think, Sextus's line of thought. Sextus devotes chapters of *Outlines of Pyrrhonism* to the question of how his skepticism differs from Protagoras's Measure Doctrine (PH 1.216–219), from Heraclitean philosophy (PH 1.210–212), and from Democritus's atomism (PH 1.213–214). In all these cases, he distances himself from the metaphysical assumptions of the other positions—that the world is in flux, that things can have opposite properties, that perceptual properties like "sweet" are not part of a determinate reality, that in reality there are "only atoms," and so on.[34] He presents his skepticism as a philosophy that improves upon earlier analyses of disagreement.

---

[34]This appears to be a conventional grouping of kinds of views. In *Met.* G.5, Aristotle considers a similar triad: the view that everything is characterized by opposites, Protagoras' Measure Doctrine, and radical flux.

According to Sextus's skepticism, suspension has a double nature: if X appears F and F* to different cognizers (cognizers in different states, etc.), one should suspend judgment both on whether X is F or F* and on whether the issue could be settled. At some points, Sextus might appear to presuppose a commonsense metaphysics—as if we should suspend judgment on the issue under discussion because the issue, presumably capable of being settled, has not yet been settled. But Sextus is not committed to such a metaphysics.[35] The double nature of suspension is reflected in a crucial term: as Sextus puts it, one suspends judgment given that the disagreement is *anepikriton* (e.g., *PH* 1.165). This term can mean either 'unresolved' or 'unresolvable.' In Sextus's argumentation, it is primarily employed in the former way: a given disagreement is as of yet unresolved, and the skeptic continues to investigate.[36] In other words, suspension of judgment does not indicate that there can be no decision, but it also does not indicate that the issue is in principle resolvable— perhaps it is, perhaps it is not. Suspension of judgment reflects no more than the fact that the issue has not yet been settled, and that the skeptic shall investigate further (*PH* 1.1).

What does this mean for our initial question, namely, whether an analysis of disagreement can preserve the phenomenon of disagreement? Does Sextus presuppose that there is 'one thing' about which people disagree, so that there is genuine disagreement? In other words, does Sextus assume that, although various kinds of properties (value properties, gustatory properties, etc.) may or may not be real features of the world, at least there are objects, the bearers of such properties?[37] For example, does he assume that there is such a thing as honey, suspension of judgment applying only to the question of whether it is sweet?

Although this may appear to be Sextus's implicit assumption, it is not. Insofar as the texts may give this impression, this merely reflects the piecemeal nature of skeptical investigation. At any given point, one

---

[35]Cf. G. Fine, "Sextus and External World Scepticism," *Oxford Studies in Ancient Philosophy* 23 (2003): 341–85.

[36]Cf. Jonathan Barnes, *The Toils of Scepticism* (Cambridge: Cambridge University Press, 1990).

[37]Cf. Fine, "External World Scepticism," who calls this type of view "property skepticism." This kind of view is not an option for Sextus. In particular, he is likely to be aware of metaphysical positions according to which objects are explained in terms of properties (an object being a set of properties); on such views, the notion of property skepticism makes no sense.

particular issue is investigated. Right now, the skeptic may ask whether the honey is sweet ('the honey' referring to a given bit of honey, enough for two people to taste it, as opposed to honey in general). But at other times, the skeptic investigates whether there is, for example, matter. The skeptic suspends on a wide range of questions about the physical world (PH 3.1–167 and M 9–10). Taken together, these suspensions certainly call into question whether there are any physical entities, including honey. However, it is a distinctive feature of Pyrrhonism that this kind of 'adding up' never takes place. In investigating one question, the Pyrrhonist hypothetically stipulates that the rest of the world remains in place. For example, when the honey tastes differently to people, one inquires only about whether it is sweet, not whether reality is such that there is anything corporeal or material.

Notably, Sextus uses the technical term for disagreement—*diaphōnia*—only when discussing theoretical disputes.[38] He assumes in such discussions that disagreement is genuine in the sense of being about one particular matter: namely, about a given question. This assumption, however, does not come with any weighty metaphysical commitment: it implies no more than the commonsensical idea that, if two people address a question, they both in fact address the same question, although they may understand it differently. But when it comes to perceptual or normative-evaluative issues, suspension of judgment includes the question of whether the parties who apparently disagree *really* disagree (both speaking about the same thing and ascribing different properties to it), or whether they simply say different things. This is one of the metaphysical issues on which the skeptic suspends judgment.

7. Conclusion

Recent discussions of relativism assume that relativism arises as a response to disagreement. Recent discussions of skepticism, however, do not take disagreement as their starting point. Instead, they begin from radical but hard-to-dismiss skeptical scenarios, and construct paradoxes from, on the one hand, the skeptical conclusion, and, on the other hand,

---

[38]Disagreement (*diaphōnia*) is the first of the Five Modes (or Modes of Agrippa), forms of skeptical argument that are used in examining dogmatic theories. Sextus uses the mode extensively throughout his writings.

some ordinary knowledge-claim. In ancient discussions, phenomena of disagreement are the starting point *both* for relativism and for skepticism, and metaphysical discussions accordingly provide an important background for skepticism. This becomes particularly clear when we look at the earliest Greek discussions of disagreement, and their culmination in a *tour de force* on the issue—Part I of Plato's *Theaetetus*.

According to Sextus, when we encounter disagreement, we should suspend judgment on the disputed issue *and* on the question of whether it is decidable. That is, we should step back from holding any views, and we should suspend judgment on whether there is a fact of the matter that could in principle be discovered. This norm for suspension of judgment reflects awareness of a complex metaphysical discussion, a discussion on whether disagreement indicates that there are several realities, no reality, or an indeterminate reality. As I hope to have shown, Sextus's skepticism aims to supersede these metaphysical positions, and is—though abstaining from any metaphysical views—metaphysically sophisticated.

5

The Aims of Skeptical Investigation

Investigation, it has been claimed, must aim at the discovery of truths. I shall call this the Discovery Premise: investigation is only genuine investigation if it aims at the discovery of truths. As I shall argue, the Discovery Premise rests on too simple a notion of investigation. Instead, we should adopt the Truth Premise: investigation must be guided by epistemic norms that respond to the value of truth. The Truth Premise makes room for a broader and more compelling conception of investigation.

Adherents of the Discovery Premise raise an objection against Pyrrhonian skepticism.[1] They formulate the Tranquility Charge: skeptical investigation aims at tranquility, rather than at the discovery of truths; therefore it cannot count as genuine investigation. The Pyrrhonian skeptics describe themselves as investigators (PH 1.1–2). If the skeptic's activity is not investigation, she is not a skeptic and her philosophy collapses.[2] Admittedly, tranquility is, with some qualifications, the end of skepticism (PH 1.25). But the skeptics aim at tranquility *as skeptics*, that is, as investigators. Their activities thus cannot simply be unrelated to truth.

---

[1] I am exclusively concerned with the version of Pyrrhonian skepticism that Sextus presents. For some earlier skeptics, Sextus reports, suspension of judgment is, in addition to tranquility, the end of investigation (PH 1.30). However, Sextus does not incorporate this view into his own account of the skeptic's end.

[2] For a forceful version of the Tranquility Charge see G. Striker, "Scepticism as a Kind of Philosophy," *Archiv für Geschichte der Philosophie* 83 (2001): 113–29. See also J. Palmer, "Skeptical Investigation," *Ancient Philosophy* 20 (2000): 351–73, and Casey Perin, "Pyrrhonian Scepticism and the Search for Truth," *Oxford Studies in Ancient Philosophy* 30(2006): 337–60. The Tranquility Charge is not among the standard ancient antiskeptical moves. It is a modern complaint against Pyrrhonism. Perin considers PH 2.1–12 an ancient instance of the objection ("Pyrrhonian Scepticism," 338 n.2). But PH 2.1–12 raises a different problem (cf. M 8.337–336a): the skeptic cannot investigate without mastering concepts and thereby, inconsistently, holding some assumptions. Cf. Jacques Brunschwig,

They aim at tranquility in matters on which one *could* have beliefs, and on which they would form beliefs, if they did not employ their skeptical methods of investigation. The Tranquility Charge fails because the Discovery Premise is too limited. First, the idea that investigation aims at the discovery of truths may not adequately capture the many ways of doing philosophy that we and the ancients are familiar with.[3] Some might even find the idea that we as philosophers aim at the discovery of truths naive. They might not expect to resolve any philosophical questions. But their ways of doing philosophy might still be guided by the value of truth. Second, we should distinguish between the motivational source of philosophical investigation and its aim. Suppose I feel restless if I am not exercising my mind by thinking about complex theoretical questions, or that I find philosophy pleasurable, even though I do not see much point in the whole endeavor. The Discovery Premise overlooks the possibility that someone could be motivated to engage in philosophy, but not seriously try to achieve anything by doing so. Third, it is a commonplace that the value of truth is associated with two aims rather than one: the acceptance of truths, and the avoidance of falsehoods. The relationship between these aims can be construed in several ways. Accordingly, there must be several different modes of investigation. Insofar as the avoidance of falsehoods reflects valuation of the truth, investigation that aims at the avoidance of the false should count as genuine investigation.[4]

"Sextus Empiricus on the κριτήριον: The Sceptic as Conceptual Legatee," in Brunschwig, *Papers in Hellenistic Philosophy*, 230–43; my "Skeptische Untersuchung und das Verstehen von Begriffen," in Ch. Rapp and T. Wagner (eds.), *Wissen und Bildung in der antiken Philosophie* (Stuttgart: Metzler, 2006), 325–39, and its successor, chapter 6 in this book, "Skepticism and Concepts: Can the Skeptic Think?"; and Filip Grgic, "Sextus Empiricus on the Possibility of Inquiry," *Pacific Philosophical Quarterly* 89 (2008): 436–59. Perin accepts the Discovery Premise and argues that the skeptic aims at two values: truth and tranquility. Palmer argues that skeptical investigation is second-order investigation: the skeptic does not search for the truth, but investigates the theories of the dogmatists. This way of untying the connection between investigation and truth does not seem compelling: what would be the point of investigating dogmatic theories? Even though different theories are critically explored, skeptical investigation must be concerned with thinking about the questions at issue, and thus must have some relationship to the truth.

[3]Striker, "Scepticism," points out that the philosophizing of an Academic skeptic is much like what many of us do today as philosophers.

[4]I shall assume that truth is plausibly considered the epistemically fundamental value, in the sense that it explains other epistemic values. Cf. for example Ernest Sosa, *A Virtue Epistemology: Apt Belief and Reflective Knowledge* (New York: Oxford University Press, 2007), 54.

Pyrrhonian investigation, as I shall argue, needs to be construed with all three considerations in mind. First, it inherits a rather complex conception of investigation, shaped by Socrates and Plato, whose philosophizing does not always immediately aim at the discovery of truths (section 1). Second, it has a motivational source—the unsettling discrepancy between conflicting thoughts—that is distinct from any particular aim one might have (section 2). Third, the value of truth figures importantly in Pyrrhonian investigation, though Pyrrhonian investigation is more immediately concerned with avoidance of the false than with discovery of the true (sections 3 to 5). Investigation must respond to the value of truth. The Truth Premise is crucial for any activity that claims to be a kind of investigation. But contrary to the Discovery Premise, the Truth Premise leaves room for different modes of investigation, among them Pyrrhonian investigation.

1. Socratic Investigation

Sextus draws on a complex conception of philosophy, developed most significantly in the Socratic tradition.[5] He describes phases of Plato's Academy by reference to how Plato and Socrates have been interpreted, thus showing that he is aware of a range of different approaches to philosophy within this tradition (PH 1.220–35). Some, according to Sextus, focus on the dogmatic side of Plato (including Socrates as main speaker), taking him to put forward theories about the Forms, the soul, recollection, and so on. Others focus on *aporia*—dialogues ending without any response to the question at hand. They see that Socrates is sometimes playing with people, and that at other times he is in a contest with Sophists. These interpreters claim that such dialogues are concerned with a kind of training. Furthermore, Sextus is aware of Socratic schools outside of the Academy, such as the Cyrenaics (PH 1.215), who interpret Socrates' investigations in yet a different fashion.

---

[5] I cannot explore all facets of the conception of philosophy that Sextus engages with. For example, Pyrrhonism seems in various ways inspired by pre-Socratic philosophizing, where central ideas are often expressed in enigmatic, dense, and almost obscure ways. This mode of formulating one's ideas influences the so-called skeptical formulae, such as "no more," "I determine nothing," and so on (PH 1.187–209). However, for the present purposes, the Socratic-Platonic tradition seems most important.

Arcesilaus, who according to Sextus begins a new phase of the Academy (PH 1.220), is inspired by Socrates' commitment to investigation. Arguably, Arcesilaus does not turn to Socrates by turning away from Plato. Rather, Arcesilaus is likely to have interpreted Plato (not just Socrates) as less dogmatic than other members of the Academy took him to be. Even in middle and later dialogues, which do not focus on *aporia* and refutation, Plato can be seen to investigate in a manner that speaks to the skeptics. For example, one might argue that Plato never fully formulates a version of the Theory of Recollection, or the Theory of Forms, that he puts forward as his considered view. Rather, he explores different versions of these theories, thinking through their implications, including the difficulties attached to them.

Sextus is acquainted as much as we are with the many sides of Platonic and Socratic investigation. A wide range of activities figures in Plato's dialogues. Socrates can be seen to refute a series of proposals put forward by his interlocutor (for example, in the *Euthyphro*). He interrogates others who claim to have knowledge, arriving at the conclusion that they do not know what they think they know (for example, in the *Apology*). He examines with an interlocutor a range of ideas this person already had or was familiar with, seeing that all of them are problematic (for example, Meno's ideas about virtue in the *Meno*). He and his interlocutor present arguments for and against a given thesis, with no apparent resolution at the end of the conversation (for example, regarding the question of whether virtue is teachable in the *Protagoras*). At times, Socrates and his interlocutor jointly develop some theories, even if none of them is presented as fully compelling (for example, accounts of the immortality of the soul in the *Phaedo*, where even the final account is considered merely hypothetical). At other times, Socrates appears to emerge unchanged from a conversation, while his interlocutor has genuinely made progress (for example, the examination of Meno's accounts of virtue in the first part of the *Meno*). Socratic investigation here seems to be concerned with the insights of an interlocutor, not with Socrates' own insights. But nevertheless, philosophical investigation seems to be a joint, dialogical enterprise: both Socrates and his interlocutor investigate together.

These various kinds of Socratic discussions are usually considered to be philosophical investigations. Scholars also agree in ascribing to Socrates a deep concern with the truth. Socratic investigations thus seem to meet the criteria that the Truth Premise sets up. But they may not meet the criteria of the Discovery Premise. It is not obvious how Socratic concern for the truth translates into the aim of discovering truths within a given investigation. For students of Platonic dialogues, it seems possible that philosophers spend years clearing away preconceived ideas and thinking through competing theories. Note that the clearing away of ideas that an interlocutor finds herself with need not and usually does not involve discovery of the truth that they are false. Socrates and his interlocutors often dismiss ideas because their proponent cannot adequately defend them. A better philosopher might be able to argue convincingly in favor of a claim that a beginner, who holds an unexamined view, is unable to explicate. Accordingly, the fact that a given idea is dismissed does not mean that one discovered that it is false.

When asking whether the Pyrrhonian skeptics engage in genuine investigation, I think we should have this multifaceted picture in mind. We should hesitate to level a charge against the skeptics that we would not level against Socrates—that investigation that does not aim immediately at the discovery of truths cannot qualify as investigation. It appears obvious that Socratic and Platonic investigations meet the Truth Premise: they are inspired and guided by the value of truth. But it is a complicated question how precisely Socrates and Plato respond to the value of truth. Surely, different answers would have to be given for different dialogues, and these answers would involve difficult interpretive concerns. This consideration should warn us against stipulating too straightforward an account of investigation when asking whether the Pyrrhonian is a genuine investigator.

2. The Motivational Source: Anomaly

Pyrrhonian investigation begins with the realization (*to nomizein*) that discovery has not yet taken place (PH 2.11). This realization comes with the experience of anomalies. The skeptic is disturbed by the conflicting impressions she has on a given issue. In PH 1.25–29, Sextus describes this turmoil and tells the story of the skeptic's conversion to skepticism.[6]

Up to now we say the aim of the skeptic is tranquility in matters of belief (*kata doxan*) and moderation of feeling in matters forced upon us. For the

[6]I am adopting the term 'conversion story' from Gisela Striker, "Scepticism." The term must, of course, be taken with some caution. It nicely captures that the skeptic undergoes a life-changing experience when she first becomes a skeptic. However, we need to keep in mind that skepticism is not a state of mind acquired once and for all. The skeptic must continually produce her skepticism through a life of investigation.

skeptic began to do philosophy in order to decide among appearances and to apprehend which are true and which are false, so as to become tranquil; but he came upon equipollent dispute, and being unable to decide this he suspended judgment. And when he suspended judgment, tranquility in matters of belief followed fortuitously. For those who believe that things are good or bad by nature are perpetually troubled. When they lack what they believe to be good, they take themselves to be persecuted by things naturally bad and they pursue what (so they think) is good. And when they have acquired these things, they experience more troubles; for they are elated beyond reason and measure, and in fear of change they do anything so as not to lose what they believe to be good. But those who make no determination about what is good and bad by nature neither avoid nor pursue anything with intensity; and hence they are tranquil. [...] So, too, the skeptics were hoping to acquire tranquility by deciding the anomalies in what appears and is thought of, and being unable to do this they suspended judgment. But when they suspended judgment, tranquility followed as it were fortuitously, as a shadow follows a body. (PH 1.25–29, tr. Annas and Barnes with changes)[7]

Preskeptical investigation aims at settling what is true and what is false. The investigator looks at her views (how things appear to her, i.e., her impressions), with the aim of settling which of them are true and which are false, and in turn puts herself in a state of turmoil. Why is that? Consider two explanations.

(1) Eudaimonism. Sextus says that those who think that something is good or bad by nature are perpetually troubled. If they consider something good, they worry about getting it, or losing it. If they consider something bad, they worry about avoiding it, or getting rid of it. This worry can be called 'eudaimonist'; it has something to do with the role of good and bad things in a well-going life, and with the desire for happiness. More specifically, the worry is characteristic of a certain kind of eudaimonism, the kind that focuses on the instability of human life. Even

---

[7] I differ from Annas and Barnes in translating *doxa* and cognates in terms of belief rather than opinion (Sextus Empiricus, *Outlines of Scepticism*, tr. J. Annas and J. Barnes [Cambridge: Cambridge University Press, 1994]. All translations throughout this chapter, even though they are largely my own, are indebted to Annas and Barnes, as well as to Bett (Sextus Empiricus, *Against the Ethicists*, tr. Richard Bett [Oxford: Clarendon Press, 2000]; first published 1997; citations are to the 2000 edition) and Bury (*Sextus Empiricus*, tr. R.G.Bury, Loeb Classical Library [Cambridge, Mass.: Harvard University Press, 1933–49]).

if I knew that having X is good, and even if I had X, I would be tormented by the thought that X can be lost. This is a long-standing Greek preoccupation, already prevalent in Herodotus's *Histories*. Human life is unstable, and the so-called goods of fortune are characterized by the fact that they are not under our control. Children die, health is lost, houses burn to the ground. Whatever I consider good (family, health, wealth), and whatever I consider bad (illness, death, poverty), I shall be in turmoil. In a parallel passage in M 11, Sextus says that all disturbance comes from intensely pursuing and avoiding things, and pursuit and avoidance comes with value judgments (M 11.112–13). Stoic and Epicurean ethics capture versions of this traditional concern. Most importantly, they do so by arguing that what is truly good cannot be lost (virtue, according to the Stoics), or is available even under adverse conditions (the kind of pleasure that turns out to be good in Epicurean ethics).

While this kind of worry figures widely in Greek thought, it is ultimately not particularly relevant to the Pyrrhonism of the *Outlines*. Sextus may mention the eudaimonist concerns because they are likely to resonate with his interlocutors. The idea that human life is unstable and that all pursuit of goods comes with turmoil is intuitive for many contemporaries of the skeptic. But with respect to a general account of Pyrrhonism, the reference to eudaimonist concerns is misleading. The skeptic investigates all kinds of questions, not only questions of value. Further, it is not clear why, if one is given to the worry that one might lead one's life in a way that brings misery, one should be better off suspending judgment.[8] In leading her life, the Pyrrhonian skeptic adheres to appearances, that is, to custom, tradition, and the ordinary ways of life (PH 1.21–24). If the

[8]In M 11.110–167, a major part of one of Sextus's treatises on ethics, it appears as if skepticism were actually confined to ethics. Sextus invokes the dogmatic idea that happiness consists of having good things. Based on this premise, it is essential to the good life to know what is good and what is bad (110). Now add the premise that all unhappiness is disturbance, and that all disturbance comes from intense pursuit or avoidance of that which is deemed good or bad (112–13). The combination of these premises implies that life is inevitably miserable (at least as long as it is assumed that good and bad things can be lost). Perhaps this state of affairs could lead one to a kind of value-skepticism; only the absence of value judgments can prevent the turmoil of intense pursuit and avoidance. But as Bett argues, this is a distinctively different, and probably earlier strand of Pyrrhonism from the skepticism of the *Outlines*, which is the skepticism that we are most immediately concerned with here (Bett, *Against the Ethicists*, 128–81). Perin too notes that PH 1.25–29 does not fit well into Sextus's skepticism ("Pyrrhonian Scepticism," 342; cf. 352).

worry regarding value beliefs is that they might be wrong, the same worry should arise for an agent who adheres to appearances. There is no presumption that conventions and customs get things right. One is likely to fare better with views that have stood the test of time, or views that are otherwise explained or plausible, even if one still does not know that they are true. The kind of disturbance we should ascribe to Sextus's skeptic must be different—it cannot be rooted in the idea that, if one's value beliefs are false one is likely to act in ways that bring misery.[9]

(2) Anomaly. In PH 1.29, Sextus says that the skeptic, prior to her conversion, investigates in order to resolve the anomaly (*anōmalia*) between different appearances and thoughts. This is the core of the disturbance that sets off skeptical investigation. Inconsistencies (or discrepancies and tensions) between the impressions available to the investigator cause disruption: one is confused because the views one holds or is acquainted with do not fit together. Pyrrhonian turmoil comes from the conflicts between several truth-claims. Anomaly arises in all domains, not only the domain of value. The skeptic can be confused with respect to all kinds of questions, if only several ways of seeing things are available to her. This is an important point. The eudaimonist reading fails in part because it cannot account for the generality of Pyrrhonian investigation. The skeptic is confused not only with respect to questions of value, but with respect to any given question that arises for her. This account is also given in PH 1.12, a chapter entitled "The Source of Skepticism."[10]

---

[9]M. McPherran argues that the physiology of belief causes disturbance. He argues that the Stoics view the mind as actively in motion when it assents, and that the skeptics invoke this idea. Furthermore, he suggests that this goal-directed motion creates the disturbing experience of belief. Suspension resolves the disturbance and generates a smooth movement. "*Ataraxia* and *Eudaimonia* in Ancient Pyrrhonism: Is the Sceptic Really Happy?*" Proceedings of the Boston Area Colloquium in Ancient Philosophy* 5 (1989): 135–71, esp. 158. McPherran seems right to me in emphasizing the physiology of thought. However, the disruption seems to come with conflict or *anomalia*, not with a particular cognitive activity like assent.

[10]Annas and Barnes (*Outlines of Scepticism*) and Perin ("Pyrrhonian Scepticism," 343) translate "*archē*" as 'causal principle.' This translation suggests that the driving force behind skeptical investigation is causal, rather than rational. However, our translation should not prejudge this question. The Greek *archē* can mean 'source' or 'origin.' In Hellenistic epistemology, where dogmatists think of the mind as physiological, any cognitive process can be described in causal terms, and Sextus's ways of putting things are often parasitic on this framework. However, this does not imply that such movements of the mind could not be described as rational.

Men of talent, who were perturbed (*tarassomenoi*) by the anomalies in things (*en tois pragmasin anōmalian*) and in confusion as to which of them they should rather assent to, came to investigate what in things is true and what is false, so that by deciding these issues they would become tranquil. (PH 1.12, tr. Annas and Barnes with changes)

The skeptic's mind is upset—it is pulled into different directions, because conflicting views or appearances induce her to assent. This is what puzzlement or confusion consists of: it is a state of being epistemically moved. Trains of thought are set in motion, and the subject experiences the tensions among the various views she is attracted to.[11]

Both Stoics and Epicureans, that is, both main interlocutors of the skeptics, conceive of the soul as a physical entity. Thoughts are physical movements in the bodily soul.[12] Sextus, of course, does not hold any dogmatic theory of the mind. But he exploits this picture insofar as he speaks about the way in which impressions *affect* the mind (this being a point that can be reported as an experience, rather than dogmatically stated). According to the picture that is thus invoked (though not defended), the motions that disturb one's peace of mind are conflicting thoughts.

When thoughts do not fit together, the mind is stirred up. Even though the confusion is rational (it is a confusion among several thoughts), this is a causal event in the bodily mind—the thoughts are physiological alterations of the soul. One way or another, we need to react to this movement. If we are, for example, like some interlocutors in early Platonic dialogues, we run away from the immediate source of confusion (Socrates), divert ourselves with other activities, and let it run its course until it dies out. New impressions or perceptions create fresher movements in the soul, and the alterations that were our earlier impressions wear off. However, if we do not run away from the cause of confusion, we need to do something else with the motion it creates. In this case, we need to respond

[11]Sextus says that the experience that appearances are in conflict is not just the experience of the skeptics, or of philosophers. It is the experience of all of mankind (PH 1.210).

[12]The Stoics define impressions as imprints or alterations of a physical soul; rational impressions (i.e., the impressions of adult human beings) are a subclass of impressions; they are thought processes (DL 7.49–51 = SVF 2.52, 55, 61 = LS 39A). Impression, impulse, and assent are movements of the soul (Plutarch, *Against Colotes* 1122A–F = LS 69A); cf. Stobaeus 2.86, 17–87, 6 (= SVF 3.169, part = LS 53Q). Epicurus conceives of the soul as a fine-structured body, and of thought processes as occurring in this body (*Letter to Herodotus* 63–67 = LS 14A).

rationally and try to clear up the confusion by thinking things through. That is, if we want to set the turmoil to rest in a rational fashion, we need to work through the confusing thoughts. The skeptic is committed to rationality in this sense. She needs to sort out the confusion. Anomaly is—causally and rationally—the driving force of skepticism. Anomaly responds to a basic concern with the truth; if truth were not an end or value, then conflicting thoughts might not be disruptive. That is, whatever we go on to say about skeptical investigation, its motivational source reflects the value of truth.

3. The Truth-Directedness of Pyrrhonian Investigation

Anomaly thus is the motivational source of skepticism. Tranquility appears as a plausible correlate of the motivational origin of investigation. If one is moved to investigate because one is in turmoil, then this endeavor will be directed toward the quieting of turmoil. But by itself, this cannot yet account for the complex investigative activities of the skeptic.

Preconversion, the skeptic wanted to resolve instances of anomaly by settling which of her impressions were true and which were false. But anomaly is not just the initial starting point of investigation; it is also investigation's ongoing source. That is, being struck by anomaly, the skeptic is again and again caught in the attempt to settle what is true and what is false. She investigates conflicting positions with a view to their truth and falsity. She works her way through the individual theses, arguments, and so on, that together make up theories. If it came to the point that she found a given claim to be true, she would accept it.[13] That is, with a view to the examination of every given impression, and with a view to accepting or rejecting it or suspending judgment on it, the skeptic's activity is *truth-directed*.

---

[13]With a view to particular impressions, the skeptic engages in something like belief-formation, but gets stuck. Suppose that belief is an attitude to a proposition that is truth-directed: to believe a proposition is to accept it with the aim of thereby accepting a truth. (This is a formulation discussed by David Velleman, "On the Aim of Belief," chapter 11 in Velleman, *The Possibility of Practical Reason* [Oxford: Oxford University Press, 2000], 251.) The skeptic never arrives at the point of actually accepting an impression. However, her attitude in examining theses and arguments is still truth-directed in the sense in which belief is truth-directed.

Suspension of judgment follows for the skeptic from the equipollence of several positions, and it enables the skeptic not to accept or reject anything (PH 1.8–10). In describing equipollence (*isostheneia*), Sextus speaks about several accounts being equal as far as belief and disbelief are concerned—*kata pistin kai apistian*. Neither of several positions is 'more believable' (*pistoteron*) than the other (PH 1.10). These expressions are difficult to translate, and it might seem that, in order to properly mark the difference between *pistis* and *doxa*, we should not translate in terms of belief. Annas and Barnes render the relevant phrases as "equality with regard to being convincing or unconvincing," and "more convincing."[14] This translation, however, suggests that Sextus invokes a category that is at least in part psychological: a position could be convincing in the sense of looking attractive; or it could be convincing because something about it speaks to one. But Sextus refers to a property that impressions are seen to have when assessed in terms of truth and falsity. The skeptic examines competing *logoi* (PH 1.10), arguments or accounts. Doing so, she assesses impressions with respect to their truth or falsity, that is, with respect to whether she should accept or reject them, or whether she should believe them.[15] But admittedly, 'believability' is an awkward term, and there is a legitimate concern with keeping *pistis* and *doxa* apart. We might rephrase Sextus's point in terms of credibility: several positions fare equally in terms of their credibility, and neither is more credible than the other.

Accordingly, there is an important sense in which Pyrrhonian investigation is truth-directed, thus meeting at least in part the criteria that the Truth Premise sets up. But proponents of the Tranquility Charge might point to what could appear to be an unrealistic feature of Sextus's account of suspension of judgment. Why should several positions on a given question appear *equally* credible to the skeptic?[16] Suppose there is an issue for which there are two different, but seemingly quite plausible

---

[14]This translation is an improvement over Bury, who translates in terms of probability.

[15]Paul Horwich writes: "there is no substantial difference between identifying a proposition as false and disbelieving it. So, refusing to believe what we identify as false is just refusing to believe what we *dis*believe" ("The Value of Truth," *Nous* 40.2 [2006]: 347–60, 354). I think that something like this is the core of how Sextus relates believability to truth and 'disbelievability' to falsehood.

[16]I am grateful for feedback on this point to Nandi Theunissen, who raised some related concerns.

positions. While there are arguments on both sides, one side may still strike one as more credible. And since there are some strengths and some weaknesses in each position, one may find oneself drifting toward a new position, which aims to combine the views one has studied. Why should the skeptic end up with a standstill of thought (*stasis dianoias*; PH 1.10), as Sextus calls it, resting between competing positions that are each equally credible, and thus suspending judgment?

Some familiar points can be made in response. The skeptic does not only investigate positions that already exist, as fully formulated positions. New positions, which combine strong points from several other theories, are also among the theories that are investigated. That is, we should think of standstill of the mind as provisional and temporary. The skeptic suspends with a view to a couple of theories; but then she finds herself drifting toward a new option, and investigation resumes; now she will explore the weaknesses of the newly conceived theory, or several revised theories; and so on. Sextus says that, even if the skeptic cannot come up with a counterargument to a given thesis right now, she is aware that other arguments were once not yet formulated, and later were put forward (PH 1.34). Thus, even if the skeptic should not be able to produce an objection on the spot, she would be inclined to expect that there is an objection. However, this point may seem to give further weight to the aforementioned objection. Is the skeptic realistically stuck between two equally credible ideas when, say, there are weighty objections on the one side, and merely the expectation of a future objection on the other side?

In order to address this question we must say more about the difference between the skeptic's experience of anomaly and the restful state of suspension. In both states, different appearances on a given issue are on the skeptic's mind. Why is one of these states a resolution of the other? The answer, I suggest, is that anomaly involves a mix of psychological and rational factors, while suspension is an attitude that arises when one is immersed into *argument*.

Consider an example drawn from a difficult philosophical problem, such as freedom and determinism. Suppose we are intuitively strongly committed to seeing our actions as originating in our deliberations, thinking that it is in some important sense up to us whether we choose one course of action or another. Insofar as we focus on our intuitions, we might never get to the point where several positions seem equally credible. However strong the arguments for determinism, we still conceive of our actions as we used to do. But insofar as we focus on the arguments that can be adduced for both sides (or rather, for multiple competing theories), we might arrive at a different attitude. We might genuinely get to the point where we see the strengths and weaknesses in several accounts, and find ourselves surveying them in a noncommittal state of mind.[17] It is only through the focus on argument, and immersion into argument, that the skeptic can arrive at this balanced state of mind.[18]

Prior to investigation, we are drawn to particular positions because they happen to speak to us; they are persuasive in a psychological, rather than an argumentative way. This kind of imbalance can be remedied by close study of the arguments. The skeptic investigates things '*hoson epi tō logo*' (PH 1.20). That is, in investigation, the skeptic looks at opposite positions *from the point of view of argument*. When she eventually suspends judgment on them, she does so with a view to the arguments she considered. Through the transition from confusion to suspension, the skeptic is no longer subject to the psychological pull of various positions that differ in strength (and which would, if investigation did not prevent this, eventually lead her to assent to the view that looks most attractive).

This proposal involves the interpretation of a much-debated expression: *hoson epi tō logō*. Scholars often take this formula to address the question of whether the skeptic has any beliefs, or beliefs of any kind. Michael Frede argues that, when Sextus says that the skeptic does not dispute that honey appears sweet to her, but investigates whether it actually is sweet *hoson epi tō logō* (PH 1.20), this means that Sextus only bans a dogmatic kind of belief from the skeptic's life. He translates the tag as

---

[17]Compare this to contemporary discussions about skepticism, which often proceed by setting out so-called skeptical paradoxa. That is, it is assumed that, on the one hand, we are committed to, for example, thinking that there are other minds, and on the other hand, there is a skeptical argument to the effect that there are no other minds. The argument looks valid, and thus we find ourselves in a paradox. We can only sustain this state of mind (of finding ourselves in a paradox) by focusing on the skeptic argument. Once we turn away and back into our ordinary lives and other concerns, it loses its grip on us, and we easily accept the thought that there are other minds.

[18]Hume makes a version of this observation with respect to the arguments concerning skepticism. He thinks that, once we stop focusing on these arguments, they lose their grip on us and we fall back into our ordinary knowledge claims. In some sense, this is lucky, since—according to Hume—all life would otherwise perish. But "[n]ature is always too strong for principle." *Enquiry concerning Human Understanding* XII.ii (Oxford: Oxford University Press, 1999).

"to the extent that this is a question for reason."[19] According to his interpretation, Sextus is here distancing the skeptic from beliefs that are based on reason in a certain emphatic, dogmatic sense. However, Sextus uses the expression in order to paraphrase a distinction: in his investigations, the skeptic does not investigate that things appear a certain way; he investigates *what is being said* (*ho legetai*) about appearances. That is, the skeptic investigates statements, theses, accounts, arguments, and so on.[20] Sextus sometimes uses a longer version of the clause: *hoson epi tō logō tōn dogmatikōn*, which Bury translates as "as far as what the dogmatists say is concerned." This longer expression might appear to confirm Frede's reading, insofar as it might suggest that Sextus distances himself from a dogmatic kind of reasoning. But I think that it works even better with the interpretation I suggest. The skeptic investigates things with respect to the arguments that are put forward about them. These arguments, of course, are often formulated by dogmatists. The skeptic thinks through the arguments that different theorists offer, also formulating critical arguments of her own, making sure to arrive at suspension with respect to any particular position.

Sextus's skeptic does not move away from the use of reason. The skeptic is a reasoner, and she must be a reasoner. In her investigations, she thinks through the arguments that can be adduced for various sides of an issue. If she did not do this, she would not be testing these views in terms of their believability, assessing them for truth and falsity. As a reasoner—or, as an investigator who studies arguments—the skeptic arrives at suspension of judgment, in a way that reflects the value of truth. If she arrived at it in any other fashion, her suspension would be willful, rather than rational.

---

[19]"Des Skeptikers Meinungen," *Neue Hefte für Philosophie* 15–16 (1979): 102–29, reprinted as "The Sceptic's Beliefs," in M. Frede and M. Burnyeat (eds.), *The Original Sceptics: A Controversy* (Indianapolis: Hackett, 1998), 1–24. Bury translates "in its essence" and "as far as what the dogmatists say is concerned." Perin compares the expression to qualifiers like "as of yet" (*achri nun*) ("Pyrrhonian Scepticism," 349), suggesting that the skeptic 'only' suspends as far as the arguments are concerned. But that seems misleading—it is not as if the skeptic, in some other respect, did not suspend. Suspension is not qualified by relating to arguments. Rather, it is generated by focus on the arguments.

[20]For a similar interpretation of the expression, cf. Brunschwig, "La formule *hoson epi tō logō* chez Sextus Empiricus," in Brunschwig, *Etudes sur les philosophies Hellenistiques* (Paris: Presses Universitaires de France, 1995), 321–41. Annas and Barnes translate "as far as the argument goes."

4. *Epistemic Preferences and Injunctions*

However, it is a difficult question how the truth-directedness that characterizes the skeptic's attitude to particular impressions relates to the more complex practices of her investigation. Also, it is not clear how the two aims of attaining truths and avoiding falsehoods are reflected in Pyrrhonian investigation. If one wanted only to accept as many truths as possible, one could just accept all impressions. If one wanted only to avoid falsehoods, one could just reject all impressions. But valuation of the truth must consist in a combination of both aims.

Even on the Discovery Premise, investigation does not aim at the acceptance of as many truths as possible. There are too many trivial truths for this to be a sensible goal. More plausibly, we aim to accept all the truths that are worth accepting (for practical purposes of ordinary life, or for purposes of understanding the world, or for making progress in a given field of study). A further aim of investigation (either taking the place of the aim to attain worthwhile truths, or combined with this aim) might be the best possible proportion of true as compared to false beliefs.[21]

However, if one aims for the best possible proportion of true versus false beliefs, one accepts that one will come to hold some falsehoods. That is, one proceeds on the assumption that, if one wants any beliefs at all, one cannot avoid that some of them shall be false. But this assumption might appear problematic. Why should one accept that one's practices of belief-formation will provide one with some false beliefs, mixed in with a greater number of true beliefs? Perhaps this is a plausible picture of belief-formation, at least in some domains of everyday life. But it is not obvious that, as investigators, we should be content with investigative practices that lead one to a favorable ratio of true versus false beliefs. One might devise strategies that reflect different epistemic values: values according to which, for any given question, it is preferable to acquire no view at all as compared to acquiring a view that could turn out to be false.

Sextus's skepticism builds on this intuition. Of course, unlike Stoic or Epicurean epistemologists, the Pyrrhonian skeptic cannot argue for a particular set of epistemic values. However, skepticism develops in

---

[21] These options are taken (roughly) from Velleman, "Aim of Belief," 251.

conversation with Stoic and Epicurean philosophy. In these exchanges, the skeptics dialectically engage with a range of ideas about the value of truth. Consider for example the famous debates between Academic skeptics and early Stoics.[22] The Stoics put forward an ambitious criterion of truth, the cognitive impression. A cognitive impression arises from what is, and is stamped and impressed exactly in accordance with what is, thus being clear and distinct.[23] The Stoics formulate the epistemic norm that one should only assent if one has a cognitive impression.[24] Otherwise one should suspend. That is, the Stoics think that to adequately respond to the value of truth is to withhold judgment in every case where an impression could turn out to be false. The Stoic attitude is radical: for any given impression, suspension is better than assent that comes with only the slightest risk of accepting a false impression. Every such assent, however slim the risk would be, is considered rash. From the point of view of the Academics, this means that the Stoics should end up as skeptics: they should always suspend their judgments.

Consider further the Epicurean claim that all sense perceptions are true, and the skeptic engagement with this view. This thesis is notoriously difficult to interpret. Roughly, it means that all sense perceptions are physiological events; as such, they are facts.[25] For example, a tower looks round from a distance and square from nearby. In the first case, the atomic image (emitted by the object and traveling toward the perceiver) is affected by its travel through the air; accordingly, the edges are eroded. But this does not mean that the former impression is false and the latter

---

[22]The main arguments in this debate can be found in the following texts. Phase 1 (Arcesilaus): 7.46, 54; Cicero, *Acad.* 1.40–1 and 2.77–8; SE, M 7.247–52; SE, M 7.402–10. Phase 2 (Carneades): DL 1.177; Cicero, *Acad.* 2.57 and 2.83–85; SE, M 7.253. Many of the relevant passages are collected in chapter 40 in LS. Cf. my "Ancient Skepticism," in Edward N. Zalta (ed.), *Stanford Encyclopedia of Philosophy* (2010), http://plato.stanford.edu/entries/skepticism-ancient/.

[23]DL 7.46 (= SVF 2.53, part = LS 40C); Cicero, *Acad.* 1.40–41 (= SVF 1.55, 61, 60, part = LS 40B).

[24]Cicero, *Acad.* 2.77–78 (= LS 40D).

[25]One line of argument says: all sense perceptions are true because nothing can refute them (the senses cannot refute each other, no particular sense perception can refute another sense perception, reason cannot refute the senses because reason has its starting point in the senses) (Lucretius 4.469–521 = LS 16A and DL 10.31–32 = LS 16B). Another line of argument is the one I am focusing on above—it ultimately seems more promising to me: every sense perception is true insofar as sense perception does not yet involve judgment; perceptions are facts, just like pain, and in this sense true (DL 10.31–32).

true. To expect otherwise is as if one thought that, when hearing a bell ring, one would hear its actual or true tone only from inside of the bell. Perceptions differ, but they are not in conflict: the differences between them can be accounted for by physics (SE, M 7.206–9). Accordingly, there is no falsity on the level of perception. Falsity comes with judgment: "[W]e judge some things correctly, but some incorrectly, either by adding and appending something to our impressions or by subtracting something from them, and in general falsifying arational sensation" (SE, M 7.210).[26] Note that perception here is characterized as arational, which means that it does not involve any active cognitive stance. Sense perceptions are not yet beliefs.

Epicurean epistemology focuses on the methods by which we should arrive at our judgments, and on the evidence we have for and against them. True beliefs are those that are attested (and that means, attested by what is evident), and those that are uncontested by self-evidence. False beliefs are those that are contested and those that are unattested by self-evidence (SE, M 7.211–16). In order to arrive at true beliefs, we must on the one hand aim to adhere to the evidence of the senses, rather than doing what we are prone to do: add to or subtract from perceptions while we make our judgments. On the other hand, we must keep an open mind when the evidence is not conclusive. At times, we must list several possible explanations, rather than settle for one.[27] The Epicureans thus put forward a thought that greatly interests the skeptics: that falsity is introduced by judgment, and that prior to judgment, we have available to ourselves some mental content—the perception—to which our own cognitive activities have not yet added anything.

---

[26]When Epicureans explain the details of this conception, it is clear that they talk to skeptics, and with skeptical examples in mind (things taste differently to different people, the tower that looks round from a distance and square from nearby, and so on). Schofield suggests that there is an exchange of arguments between Epicurean epistemology and Aenesidemus's skepticism ("Aenesidemus: Pyrrhonist and 'Heraclitean,'" in A. M. Ioppolo and D. Sedley [eds.], *Pyrrhonists, Patricians, Platonizers: Hellenistic Philosophy in the Period 155–86 BC. Tenth Symposium Hellenisticum* [Naples: Bibliopolis, 2007], 269–338). While I cannot argue for this view here, I think that Pyrrhonian engagement with Epicurean epistemology is much underrated, and runs through several strands of Pyrrhonism. Skeptical arguments often target a philosophy that does not declare cognitive impressions to be criteria of truth, but more radically, sense perception—that is, they address themselves toward philosophers with Epicurean views.

[27]Epicurus, *Letter to Pythocles* 85–88 (= LS 18C) and Lucretius 6.703–11 (= LS 18E).

Based on these and other debates with dogmatic philosophers, the skeptics develop what I shall call their own epistemic preferences and injunctions. A Pyrrhonian skeptic cannot argue for any epistemic values and norms. But at the same time, it is clear that no one would turn into a skeptic if she did not deeply care about avoiding falsehoods. Indeed, it seems that the immediate interlocutors of the skeptics are all committed to epistemic norms geared toward the avoidance of falsehoods. As one interlocutor among them, the skeptic seems to be part of this project. If the skeptic did not greatly prefer not to accept any falsehoods, she would cease to be a skeptic.[28]

Sextus picks up, as an injunction that captures the skeptic commitment to avoiding falsehoods, one of the Stoics' central epistemic norms; he continuously warns against precipitate assent.[29] Similarly, Sextus can cite Epicurean epistemic norms, without endorsing them, or offering his own arguments for them. Sextus employs the Epicurean distinction between the evident and the nonevident.[30] He says repeatedly that the skeptic investigates the nonevident, and does not call into question the evident. What is evident, in Sextus, are the skeptic's affections.[31] The skeptic can invoke the Epicurean thesis that everything that is added to or subtracted from the experienced is a potentially falsifying alteration. The skeptic leaves intact that which she passively suffers—she does not subtract anything (does not deny it), but also does not add anything (does not affirm it or formulate it in any way that goes beyond a report of the experience; PH 1.4, 19–20, 22). Similarly, the Epicurean instruction not to settle for any theory if several theories are equally well (or badly)

---

[28]Horwich mentions (but does not endorse) a rationale for considering the value of avoiding falsehoods prior to the value of pursuing truth that seems rather similar to the skeptic preference: "once someone has decided to investigate a certain question—whatever it may be—then his not getting the answer right would surely be subject to criticism. But are we really obligated to investigate *all* questions—to believe every single truth?" ("The Value of Truth," 348). Also, an unqualified 'pursue truth' norm might be less plausible than an unqualified 'avoid falsity' norm.

[29]The idea that one should avoid rashness comes up in a number of contexts, for example PH 1.205, 236–37, 3.235.

[30]This distinction is of course employed by different philosophers and schools. It would take up too much space and lead too far away from my topic to explore whether Sextus invokes, as I think he does, the Epicurean distinction. However, not much in my present argument hangs on this point.

[31]When the skeptic 'is coldened' or 'sweetened,' he shall not say that he is not (PH 1.13). Such passive experiences are, in Sextus, the realm of the evident.

attested by the evidence fits the skeptic's argumentative techniques (PH 1.181). Citing other skeptics (not dogmatic philosophers), Sextus also invokes the injunction to oppose an equally weighty argument to every argument.[32] Sextus says that the skeptic might be in danger of giving up skeptic inquiry, and might need to be reminded that she should oppose each argument with an argument—otherwise, she will fall back into dogmatism (PH 1.205).

5. The Modes

But over and above the less formalized strategies, Pyrrhonian investigation employs so-called modes of argument. These are forms of argument that the skeptic can apply to different questions, thus leading herself or her interlocutor into suspension of judgment. The Ten Modes (Modes of Aenesidemus) provide her with a number of ways of setting appearances and thoughts into opposition (PH 1.36–163). For example, she can keep herself from assenting to "the honey is sweet" by reminding herself of the different physiology of different animals, which is likely to affect taste-experience; she can recall how it tasted differently when she was sick; and so on. The Five Modes help the skeptic investigate any thesis or theory put forward on a given issue (PH 1.164–77). She can ask whether some premises are not accounted for; whether the argument is circular; and so on. Or consider the modes employed against causal explanations (PH 1.180–86). For example, if a medical theory said that such and such symptoms are caused by such and such hidden processes in the body, the skeptic can point out that the theory explains matters in its own conceptual framework; that it neglects alternative explanations; that it postulates nonevident substances and events; and so on. With these and similar techniques, the skeptic can produce suspension of judgment on any given matter (or at least, this is the aim). The Tranquility Charge—that the skeptic is not an investigator, because she aims at tranquility rather than at the discovery of truths—may appear particularly forceful when we

---

[32]"To every argument an equal (equally weighty) argument is opposed" is one of the skeptic's formulae. Sextus does not trace this to any dogmatic theories. However, if asked whether this kind of norm is a piece of dogmatism, he certainly could. It has a long ancestry in Socratic and Sophistic disputations, as well as in Peripatetic practices of training in argument.

consider the modes. The skeptic's argumentative practice might seem mechanical and exclusively geared toward suspension.

However, by now we have prepared the ground for the skeptic's response to this charge. For anyone with the epistemic preferences of the skeptic—as well as her dogmatic interlocutors—the modes may be just what she needs. Yes it is true that the skeptic has an arsenal of argumentative techniques, designed to produce suspension of judgment. But that is rationally called for, and from the point of view of the skeptics, the dogmatists might implicitly be committed to adopting such techniques too. Impressions have the power to move us toward assent, and we need to constantly work against this if we want to make sure that we only assent when we should. Given that one is likely to have weak moments, where one is not sufficiently on one's guard, it is best to devise routine strategies—methods that can be applied when needed in a mechanical fashion.

The Tranquility Charge finds fault with something that is utterly needed: a reliable technique of critically examining any given impression. The Tranquility Charge says that to apply this technique is to lack genuine commitment to the truth. But this is a misguided objection. For the skeptic's modes seek to draw attention to every problem that might lurk in a given theory. If one prefers not to assent to impressions that could turn out to be false, such modes are quite appropriate. The skeptic would happily recommend her methods to her dogmatic interlocutors, and it is not clear that her contemporaries would find this advice as unattractive as we would. The Tranquility Charge was not raised by the skeptic's contemporaries. Many of them share the skeptic's intuition that all must be done in order to avoid falsehood, even if this means that one will not form any beliefs at all.

6. Conclusion

The Hellenistic intuition that the false is seductive—that the mind assents easily when it should not, or adds and subtracts falsifying assumptions to the evident if we do not guard ourselves against this—resonates with the skeptics. One needs to work actively against these tendencies. Dogmatism is not a specific kind of theorizing, engaged in by some particularly confident thinkers, while others find it easy to keep an open mind.

Dogmatizing is like swimming with the current. It is, in Sextus's characterization, the default mode of the mind: if the skeptic became lazy and forgot to investigate, she would turn into a dogmatist (PH 1.205). If one does not make a systematic effort, the movements of one's mind will lead one to accept falsehoods. So far, the Hellenistic interlocutors agree. The skeptic's techniques of steering away from assent go further than those of her dogmatic contemporaries. But they are inspired by the same intuitions.

Pyrrhonian investigation meets the criteria set up by the Truth Premise. Its motivational source—anomaly—arises due to the role that truth plays in thought. The skeptic's attitude toward particular appearances is truth-directed. Her epistemic preferences respond to the value of truth, and her epistemic injunctions are geared toward avoiding falsehoods. The modes of argument are an even more elaborate technique, designed with this aim in mind. Though Pyrrhonian investigators do not expect to discover that anything is true or false, they engage in a kind of investigation that reflects the value of truth.

6

Skepticism and Concepts: Can the Skeptic Think?

Suppose you read a Platonic dialogue that addresses some of its core questions through myths.[1] You wonder whether Plato would claim to have established a given theory through myth, or what the status of the ideas presented in such a fashion might be. Thinking about the dialogue as a whole, you may be tempted to say that some of what you have been reading is more like a poem than like a proof, or that some of it is too much like a poem to plausibly come across as a proof. In making this observation, you employ a vague idea of what proofs are. Perhaps you are not able to explain precisely what you take proofs to be. But you can say that a poem is not a proof.

The skeptics scrutinize the theories and arguments of nonskeptical philosophers. In doing so, they do what you just did as a reader of Plato: they invoke some kind of conception of what things are. Ancient opponents of the skeptics claim that this very activity is problematic. The skeptics employ concepts—the concepts of proof, truth, virtue, time, and so on—and are arguably committed to some assumptions about what a

[1] I am grateful to Jens Haas for his help in translating and substantially reorganizing this chapter from Vogt, "Skeptische Suche und das Verstehen von Begriffen," in Rapp and Wagner, *Wissen und Bildung*. My position, however, is unchanged. I cut down on footnotes, but added one or two references. I should acknowledge that, as a consequence, I am not engaging with Gail Fine, "Sceptical Enquiry," in D. Charles (ed.), *Definition in Greek Philosophy* (Oxford: Clarendon Press, 2010). Apart from many details, Fine's approach differs from my approach insofar as she does not consider M 8, and insofar as she takes Sextus's claim that, according to the Stoics, one needs cognition (*katalēpsis*) in order to investigate, at face value (as I see it, Sextus's move is utterly polemic; Sextus knows full well that the Stoics are not committed to this self-defeating claim).

proof is, what truth is, what virtue is, what time is, and so on. However, the skeptics claim to suspend judgment on these matters.

I shall call this line of thought the Concept Charge. Put somewhat crudely, the problem is that thought involves concepts, and that concepts might involve beliefs. Consider an example from the *Meno*, a hypothetical investigation of the question "is virtue teachable?" (86c–96c). In such an investigation, all kinds of beliefs about virtue—say, that it belongs to the soul (87b)—can be turned into hypotheses. Doing so, the investigator avoids *doxa*. But what about ideas that attach immediately to the concept of virtue? One of Socrates' hypotheses is that virtue is a good thing (87d1–2). Here one might wonder whether the move to hypotheses is insincere. Is it possible to ask "is virtue teachable?" and not to believe that virtue is a good thing? This might amount to not understanding what one is even talking about. Virtue, *aretē*, means 'best-ness.' This is the charge turned against the skeptics: in investigating, you use concepts, and in using concepts, you are committed to some beliefs about the matters under consideration, beliefs that you claim not to have. As I see it, this antiskeptical objection goes to the heart of Socratic epistemology. It calls into question whether one can investigate philosophical questions without holding beliefs about the very things that one aims to investigate.

The Concept Charge figures importantly in ancient discussions, but goes almost unnoticed by modern scholars. Sextus begrudgingly acknowledges the Concept Charge as a forceful threat to skeptical philosophy. I suspect he realizes that this is a particularly devastating charge, and also one that is difficult to refute. Though it is a long-standing principle of interpretation that one should not ascribe intentions to authors, it is hard not to feel that Sextus hides the Concept Charge as well as he possibly can. He does not explicitly refer to it in *Outlines of Skepticism* (PH) 1, mentioning it only in less prominent sections of his writings (PH 2.1–11 and M 8.337–336a).[2] In PH 2, Sextus develops a promising strategy in response to the Concept Charge—but, as I see it, only after he failed to address it properly in M 8.

If the Concept Charge is as important as I think it is, then it might seem that it *ought* to play some role in PH 1, Sextus's general account of skepticism. As I hope to show, it does, though not in an overt fashion. In responding to the Apraxia Charge (the charge that, without assent, the

---

[2] The pagination is faulty. §336 comes *after* §337.

skeptic may not be able to live and act), Sextus explains the skeptics' adherence to appearances (PH 1.21–24). Before turning to actions in the ordinary sense, Sextus says that the skeptic is able to perceive and think through the guidance of nature. This brief remark makes sense in the context of Sextus's response to the Concept Charge. Sextus is well aware that, if he wants to explain skeptical activity, he must first of all explain skeptical thought.

1. The Concept Charge

Sextus begins his *Outlines of Skepticism* (PH) by distinguishing between those who investigate something and end up finding it, those who deny that it can be found and declare it incomprehensible, and those who continue to investigate. The third option describes skepticism (PH 1.1). Skepticism, according to Sextus, is a capacity for investigation: it is the ability to set appearances (*phainomena*) and thoughts (*noumena*) into opposition (PH 1.8 f. and 131 f.). The balance (*isostheneia*) that the skeptic creates between various theses and appearances leads her to suspension of judgment (*epochē*) and thus to tranquility (*ataraxia*) (PH 1.8–10 and 25–28).

Sextus distinguishes between general and specific skeptical arguments (PH 1.5–6). The general arguments are the ones that give an outline account of skepticism. More specifically, they serve four purposes. They describe the skeptical position, distinguish it from other philosophical schools, list and illustrate the skeptical Modes, and explain the skeptic formulae (*phōnai*). The entire first book of the *Outlines* is devoted to these general arguments. Books 2 and 3 of the *Outlines* and all eleven books of the *Adversus Mathematicos* (M) contain special arguments. Here the various skeptical modes are employed in the investigation of particular philosophical questions. PH 2–3 and M thus showcase the activity of skeptical investigation. They provide a quasi record of what the skeptic does: the skeptic explores questions by examining potential responses, eventually coming to suspend judgment on any given issue.

In many ways, this kind of investigative activity might be unproblematic. First, the skeptics often argue that, given the dogmatists' own premises, such-and-such a proposal of theirs fails. Suppose a dogmatic argument appears to fall short of being a proof for somewhat more technical reasons than the ones in my initial example (the relevant series of sentences fails in less obvious ways than by including myths). In pointing this out, the skeptics need not refer to whatever assumptions might be implicit in *their* notion of a proof. Instead, they can refer to more technical assumptions the dogmatists make about the nature of proof.

Second, skeptical philosophy develops in a dialectical exchange with other philosophies. As a result, much of what the skeptics say about themselves is cast in the conceptual framework of their interlocutors. For example, the skeptical notion of 'suspension of judgment' arises in conversation with the Stoics. According to the Stoics, human beings have rational impressions (*phantasiai*) that they assent to, reject, or suspend judgment on.[3] The skeptics describe their philosophy by reference to these options.[4] This kind of indebtedness to a dogmatic conceptual scheme is far-reaching. But it does not put skeptical consistency at risk. The skeptics' way of speaking about suspension of judgment tends to remain less specific than real adherence to the Stoic theory would demand. For example, it fits equally well for conversations with Epicureans, who do not share the Stoics' epistemological views, but agree on the most basic idea, namely that belief-formation involves judgment or acceptance. Sextus's account of skeptical philosophy can be read as addressed to the dogmatists. In this dialectical setup, the skeptics are within their rights when they explain their philosophy in the terms of their interlocutors.

Third, the skeptic is free to employ dogmatic terms in a loose, nontechnical way. For example, Sextus adds a caveat to his description of skepticism as the ability (*dunamis*) to put appearances and thoughts into opposition in every possible way. The skeptic, Sextus says, does not use the term 'ability' in any specific or philosophically sophisticated way (*periergon*), but simply (*haplōs*) in the sense of 'being able to do something' (PH 1.9). Sextus provides several paraphrases for 'in every possible way'; for example, this phrase is intended to convey that the skeptic uses 'appearances' and 'thoughts' in a nontechnical way (*haplōs*).

[3]Cf. DL 7.49–51.

[4]Cf. P. Couissin, "Le stoicisme de la nouvelle Académie," *Revue d'histoire de la Philosophie* 3 (1929): 241–76; A. M. Ioppolo, *Opinione e Scienza: Il dibattito tra Stoizi e Academici nel III e nel II a. C.* (Naples: Bibliopolis, 1986), 57 f.; Vogt, *Skepsis und Lebenspraxis: Das pyrrhonische Leben ohne Meinungen* (Freiburg: Alber, 1998), 36 f.

In other words, the skeptic avoids making any claims about the ways in which appearances appear, and in which thoughts are thought (PH 1.9–10).[5]

How, then, does the Concept Charge arise? Consider the question of what time is. Suppose a given philosopher said that the notion of time can be explained via the notion of movement; the skeptic could argue against this by pointing out that the notion of movement is as controversial as the notion of time. So far so good. But in assessing more deeply what certain proposals amount to, the skeptics would inevitably draw on their *own* comprehension of the term 'time'; for example, they might bring to bear the assumption that, in one way or another, there is a past, a present, and a future. Suppose that someone who can employ the concept 'time' in an everyday context makes these assumptions, and that, in employing the concept, one is invoking them and committing oneself to them. These assumptions are rather imprecise, and they are nontheoretical. And yet they are claims about the way things are. Accordingly, they are a potentially problematic feature of skeptical thought.

A similar point can be made when we ask what it takes to be able to formulate a question. Suppose a skeptic examines someone's theory of justice, and asks whether, on this account, there could be cases in which it is bad to be just. In raising this question, the skeptic would invoke the assumptions that justice is a virtue and that for something to be a virtue it must be good. The skeptic appears to be trapped. She must make some assumptions about what virtue, time, proof, the criterion, and so on, are, or otherwise she cannot even phrase genuine questions, and she cannot examine dogmatic theories on these issues in any meaningful way. The problem can be described in terms of a distinction between preliminary and more advanced—and eventually scientific—concepts. One does not need a scientific concept of proof (virtue, time, etc.) in order to scrutinize the proposals of others on matters pertaining to proof (virtue, time, etc.). One does need, however, some kind of minimal notion of what proof (virtue, time, etc.) is supposed to be.

---

[5]Another related move on the part of the skeptics is to employ phrases katachrestically (contrary to ordinary usage); cf. for example PH 1.195 on the skeptics' usage of "perhaps." The katachrestic use of expressions aims to avoid the assertoric force that these expressions ordinarily have.

2. Preconceptions

Both Epicureans and Stoics—two of the main opponents of the skeptics—distinguish between preliminary concepts (so-called preconceptions, *prolēpseis*) and more advanced concepts. According to Epicurus, preconceptions are a criterion of truth.[6] Things strike us as evident, and these experiences are as it were mentally stored, which results in preconceptions.[7] Preconceptions develop in a nature-guided process that importantly involves passive perception of the world; they arise without any active contribution from the cognizer. Hence they cannot be flawed, and they can function as criteria. We can assess potential explanations of phenomena, and quite generally theories, by asking whether they are in agreement with our preconceptions.[8] According to the Stoics, we acquire reason—with preconceptions as an essential part of reason—through experience and by learning to engage with the world around us. Preconceptions arise out of impressions that are stored in memory. They 'furnish' the rational soul with content.[9] Preconceptions play a lesser role in the Stoic account of the criterion of truth than in Epicurus's philosophy. However, as in Epicurean philosophy, preconceptions are a starting point of investigation for the Stoics, and a criterial point of reference.

Preconceptions can be seen as an attempt to solve the problem (or a version of the problem) that Plato describes as the eristic argument in the *Meno*. According to the Meno Problem, investigation is impossible, because we need not look for something we already know, and cannot look for something we do not know; we would not know what to look for, nor would we recognize it if we found it (80d–e). The Meno Problem focuses on two crucial aspects of investigation: the ability to begin investigation, say, by formulating a question; and the ability to test possible findings as one goes along.

---

[6]DL 10.31 (LS 17A). Cf. Brunschwig, "Sextus Empiricus on the κριτήριον," on Stoic and Epicurean criteria of truth, and Gisela Striker, "κριτηριον της αληθειας," *Nachrichten der Akademie der Wissenschaften in Göttingen, Phil.-hist. Kl.* 1974, 47–110) on the Stoic theory.

[7]DL 10.33 (LS 17E); Epicurus, *Ep. Hdt.* 37–38 (LS 17C); Cicero, *De nat. deorum* 1.43; cf.Brunschwig, "Sextus Empiricus on the κριτήριον," 226.

[8]Cf. the passages in chapter 18 in LS.

[9]Aetius 4.11.1–4 (LS 39 E). Cf. Michael Frede, "The Stoic Conception of Reason," in K.J.Boudouris (ed.), *Hellenistic Philosophy*, vol. 2 (Athens: International Center for Greek Philosophy, 1994), 50–61.

Consider an example. Suppose I ask whether wolves are an endangered species. In order to ask this question, I need not be able to say any of the things a biologist might say about wolves; but I must have some idea of what wolves are, and how they live. Similarly, I must have a vague notion of species, and a vague notion of what it means to describe a species as endangered. If I were to pursue my question, I might discover that different contributors to the debate hold different views, and make different predictions about the near future of the species wolf. In trying to assess their views, I can employ my preconceptions as criteria.[10] For example, if someone were to say that there is no danger at all to the life of wolves because wolves are nothing but dogs, and it is obvious that there are plenty of dogs, I would be in a position to dismiss this view, insisting on the difference between wolves and dogs. While I could not state in any precise way what distinguishes wolves and dogs, my handle on these notions is sufficient to assess the presumed expert's opinion as questionable. This is the way in which preconceptions, according to both Stoics and Epicureans, enable us to think. They enable us to phrase questions, and to pursue these questions. They provide us with points of reference for the assessment of competing theories. However minimal these points of reference may be (and in my example they surely are minimal), they are quite powerful. In our everyday ways of thinking about contested questions, we often dismiss views as misguided because they are in conflict with rather minimal notions of what something is.

The framework of Hellenistic thought about concepts supplies some indication of how we should understand the Concept Charge. Importantly, we should resist phrasing it in terms of conceptual knowledge, though this might be a language we are familiar with. The dogmatic interlocutors of the skeptics do not claim that mastering or employing concepts involves *knowing* what they mean. Instead, they claim that there is a metaphysical link between preconceptions and the world, with perception of the world being integral to the acquisition of preconceptions. We would not end up with a given preconception if things were not as the preconception presents them to be. For example, we would not have a

---

[10]In a well-known debate about the nature of god, the Stoics argue that Epicurean theology destroys the preconception of divinity. According to this preconception, god is not just blessed and immortal, but also well-meaning, caring, and beneficial. That is, the Stoics invoke what they consider the preconception of god in order to assess someone else's theology. Cf. Plutarch, *On Common Conceptions* 1075 (SVF 2.1126; LS 54K).

notion of 'wolf' if there were no wolves. We can form more complicated notions (say, 'werewolf'), which do not have this kind of metaphysical import. But we can only form these more complicated notions once we already have a basic conceptual scheme. The core of the Concept Charge is, accordingly, that being a competent user of concepts comes with implicit commitments to the effect that such-and-such *exists* and has such-and-such *traits*.

The Hellenistic theories give a developmental account of how one becomes a reasoner. They do not aim to provide us with criteria to determine whether a given concept we use has been naturally acquired, or is more advanced. Similarly, it is no easy task to state what the implicit commitments of a given preconception are; we implicitly invoke them, but may not be able to formulate them in any precise fashion.[11] There can also be cultural variation. For some people, the notion 'wolf' is naturally acquired, for others, it is a notion learned by putting together naturally acquired notions of 'wild,' 'dangerous,' 'living in a pack,' and so on. For present purposes, the important point is that the distinction between preconceptions and more advanced concepts offers a developmental account of how a human being grows up—as part of a natural process—to be a reasoner.

3. The PH 2 Version of the Concept Charge

Sextus discusses the Concept Charge twice, at the beginning of PH 2.1–11 and in M 8.337–336a. Though not as prominent as anything in PH 1, PH 2.1–10 is a relatively conspicuous place within Sextus's writings. It marks a transition. Sextus has completed his account of skepticism, and turns now to the investigation of particular dogmatic theories. His response to the Concept Charge serves—rightly—as an introduction to these specific discussions. Without a response to the Concept Charge, it would not be clear how the skeptic can engage in these discussions. Notably, Sextus identifies the Concept Charge as a standard objection to Pyrrhonism:

[11]Cf. Vogt, "The Good Is Benefit: On the Stoic Definition of the Good," *Proceedings of the Boston Area Colloquium in Ancient Philosophy* 2008, 155–74. The attempt to provide an explicit formulation of what a preconception says is already part of investigation, and it is already open to error.

Since we reached our investigation of dogmatism, let us inspect, concisely
and in outline, each of the parts of what they call philosophy, having first
answered those who persistently allege that skeptics can neither investigate
nor, more generally, think about the items on which they hold beliefs. They
say that skeptics either grasp (*katalambanein*) what the dogmatists talk
about or do not grasp it. If they grasp it, how can they be puzzled about
what they say they grasp? If they do not grasp it, they do not even know
how to talk about what they do not grasp. (PH 2.1–2, tr. Annas/Barnes
with changes)

Sextus's response to the charge (PH 2.4–11) begins with the remark that
all depends on whether 'to grasp' is understood as being able to think
about something (*to noein haplōs*), where that would not imply that the
object really exists, or whether it is understood in the technical sense of
the Stoics. Notably, the verb I translated as 'grasping' is a technical Stoic
term, central to Stoic epistemology. According to the Stoics, the person
who grasps something has a cognitive impression, that is, an impression
that presents things precisely as they are.[12] To grasp something in this
way does not only mean that one is able to think about it. It means that
one grasps that the matter is really such-and-such; one grasps the matter
precisely as it is. Sextus now asks what the Concept Charge amounts to if
'grasping' is thought of along the lines of Stoic cognition: read in this way,
the Concept Charge says that, without prior cognition as the Stoics conceive of it, the skeptic is unable to investigate.

This version of the charge is easy to refute. Indeed, it is obviously self-
defeating. Sextus presents two arguments to this effect. (1) If the dogmatist indeed assumed that one either cognizes something in the technical
sense or is not even in a position to understand what others say about it,
then a Stoic would not be able to criticize an Epicurean; she would either,
in case she grasps what the Epicurean says, immediately agree with her,
or she would not be able to enter the conversation. (2) Dogmatic investigation is about, and here Sextus invokes an Epicurean distinction, the
nonevident (*adēlon*). Presumably, that which is evident (*dēlon*) need not
be investigated. But how can the dogmatists begin investigation of something nonevident? Certainly not by starting from a cognition: whatever is
accessible to cognition without investigation qualifies as evident, not as

---

[12]On cognition, cf. DL 7.46 (SVF 2.53; LS 40C; FDS 33); SE, M 7.251 (SVF 2.65; LS 40E;
FDS 333).

nonevident. If, on the other hand, the dogmatists claim to move *toward* cognition via investigation, they cannot hold on to their antiskeptic argument, according to which one needs cognition prior to investigation. In both cases, dogmatic philosophy turns out to be impossible. The position of the skeptic survives (PH 2.6 and 9).

If, on the other hand, 'to grasp' means only that one can think, then the skeptic is able to understand the things that the dogmatists are talking about. However, we should not immediately turn to this second option. The setup of the problem in PH 2 should arouse our suspicion. Why does Sextus formulate the Concept Charge in terms of Stoic cognition? To do so is highly polemical. Surely, no Stoic claimed that one needs cognition in order to investigate (and Sextus knows Stoic epistemology well enough to be aware of this); this would be an obviously self-defeating claim. The first half of Sextus's response is thus quite worthless: no one is likely to have challenged the skeptic by claiming that the skeptics cannot investigate because they have no cognition of the relevant matters.

Sextus does not mention the distinction between preconceptions and full-fledged concepts. In a fair representation of the Concept Charge, it is likely that this distinction would play a role. Before we turn to the rest of the text in PH 2.1–12, we should ask whether Sextus presents a more plausible version of the objection at another point in his writings. The version in PH 2.1–12 misrepresents Stoic epistemology, and it disregards the role of preconceptions in an all too obvious fashion.

4. M 8.337–336a: Preconceptions and Skeptical Thought

In M 8.337–336a, Sextus renders the Concept Charge in a significantly different fashion. He identifies the Epicureans as core proponents of the charge. Accordingly, the Stoic notion of cognition (*katalēpsis*), which— though misrepresented—is central to PH 2.1–12, does not come up. Instead, Sextus is now immediately concerned with concepts.[13]

[13]The context of this passage differs from the context in PH 2 (where Sextus marks the transition to the special arguments). In M 8, he addresses the Concept Charge in the course of asking whether 'there is proof,' and more specifically, whether the notion of proof implies that there is such a thing as a proof.

Either you understand (*noeite*) what proof is, or you do not understand it.
And if you understand it, and have a notion (*ennoian*) of it, then there is
proof. But if you do not understand it, how then are you investigating what
is entirely incomprehensible to you? (M 8.337)

Having presented the Concept Charge in these terms, Sextus sees himself
compelled to make some concessions. Sextus refers to a presumed consensus, according to which a notion or preconception must precede any
investigation (331a). He cites a reason that is familiar from Plato's *Meno*:
otherwise, the investigator would not be able to recognize whether she
'hits' or 'misses' what she is looking for (331a). Having conceded the criterial role of preconceptions, Sextus switches from defense to attack
mode. The skeptic, Sextus says, has preconceptions; indeed, he has several preconceptions for anything he investigates, not one (332a). Sextus
admits what he did not grant in the *Outlines*: to have a vague notion of
something already comes with some assumptions about what it is, and
that it is. If the skeptic had precisely *one* preconception of something, he
would believe that this one thing existed and was as it is presented in this
unified concept (333a). Having *several* preconceptions, however, dissolves this link between concept and reality, a link that threatens skeptical
consistency. A subject that has several notions of something is not committed to the assumptions associated with either one of these notions.

What should we make of this move? Brunschwig, as far as I can see the
only scholar who has given real consideration to it, finds it utterly weak.
As he sees it, the best we can do for Sextus is to assume that he is joking.[14]
Contrary to this rather negative assessment, Sextus's idea strikes me as
having genuine potential. At least for a certain range of questions, it is
quite possible to conceive of investigation as guided by several preconceptions. Consider an example. Stoics and Epicureans differ on what they
think our preconception of god is. The Stoics emphasize goodness, thus
arguing that it is impossible to think that god does not care about the
details of what happens to a human being. The Stoic god is caring. The
Epicureans say that the preconception of divinity is mostly about greatness, and argue accordingly that it would be pathetic for god to concern
himself with the minute details of our lives. When growing up in a given
culture and acquiring a preconception of god, could not this preconception be sufficiently fuzzy to be well characterized as, in the end, consist-

---

[14]Brunschwig, "Sextus Empiricus on the κριτήριον," 226.

ing of several preconceptions? Could not the skeptic be able to reference a preconception of god that emphasizes goodness, picked up in one kind of context of religious life, and another preconception of god that emphasizes greatness, picked up in another context? Why should investigation not be informed by such a set of preconceptions?

However, Sextus does not pursue this line.[15] The idea that the skeptic has several preconceptions appears thoroughly ad hoc. It is not integrated with Sextus's general account of skepticism. Neither in PH nor in M does Sextus describe skepticism as engaging with conflicting preconceptions; rather, his focus is on conflicting appearances and thoughts. Moreover, the move to multiple preconceptions does not even fit into the immediate context of M 8.337–336a. Sextus initially admitted that there is no investigation without a preconception as its starting point. Though there is no explicit focus on "a preconception" meaning "one preconception," Sextus takes himself to refer to a widely held view. This is likely to be the view his interlocutors hold, and they think that one has *one* preconception of what something is. Presumably, if one were not looking for *one* thing, then no particular finding could be identified as the finding one set out to discover.

Sextus could try to reformulate the Meno Problem's conditions for investigation—that one must have an idea of what one is looking for, otherwise one cannot look for it and cannot assess potential findings—in terms of multiple preconceptions. But he does not do so. The move to multiple preconceptions appears halfhearted; Sextus does not develop this line of thought in any serious way. Instead, he is digging the skeptic's grave by making further ad hoc moves, moves that are badly integrated with each other. In M 8.334a–336a, Sextus changes his strategy and says that a preconception implies nothing about the existence of the relevant matter.[16] Accordingly, there should have been no problem in admitting that the skeptic has a preconception of what she investigates in the first

---

[15]Sextus at times contrasts different dogmatic notions. For example, he makes a list of different accounts of god, as corporeal, incorporeal, anthropomorphic, and so on (PH 3.2–5; cf. PH 3.13 on the notion of a cause). However, this kind of strategy is different from arguing from several preconceptions.

[16]At this point, Sextus mixes Stoic vocabulary into his engagement with an Epicurean objection. He argues that having a preconception is not the same as having cognition (*katalēpsis*), precisely because a preconception does not entail the reality of the matter at issue.

place. It is hard not to find Sextus's overall argument in M 8.337–336a somewhat desperate. Sextus does not have a consistent strategy. The *Outlines* are traditionally considered earlier than M.[17] Recently, however, some scholars compared versions of particular discussions in PH and in M, and found the arguments in PH to be of greater philosophical sophistication. These findings suggest that the *Outlines* might be the later, more mature, and ultimately superior work.[18] PH 2.1–12 and M 8.377–336a constitute a nicely complicated example for the question of relative chronology. Sextus clearly wins the argument in PH 2. But the version of the Concept Charge he formulates misrepresents—at least in its first interpretation—dogmatic theory. The version of the Concept Charge in M 8 seems to do greater justice to Sextus's opponents. And yet Sextus's faithfulness in representing the charge is untimely. In terms of winning the argument, it is unfortunate to present one's opponents' view in the strongest terms if one has not yet thought of a good reply.

Ideally, Sextus would offer an adequate formulation of the Concept Charge and a promising reply to the charge so understood. An adequate formulation of the charge would be in agreement with core premises of Stoic and Epicurean epistemology. In a promising reply, then, the skeptic would have to point out to the dogmatists that the use of concepts entails, according to their own views, nothing but the capacity for linguistic and conceptual thought. According to the dogmatists, the skeptic could argue, preconceptions are about the way things are; they are not formed in a process of active belief-formation, and thus they do not represent truth-claims about the world. Once preconceptions are acquired, any thinker can come up with more advanced notions, without thereby committing herself to any claims about the reality of things.

5. The Skeptics' Ability to Think

Turn now to the second option in PH 2.1–12. If the point of the Concept Charge is that, in order to investigate, one simply must be able to think through the proposals that others put forward, then the skeptic is surely able to investigate:

---

[17]Cf. Karl Janaçek, *Prolegomena to Sextus Empiricus* (Olomouc: N.p., 1948), and "Skeptische Zweitropenlehre und Sextus Empiricus," *Eirene* 8 (1970): 47–55.

[18]Cf. Bett, *Pyrrho*, xxiv and appendices A and C.

If they say they mean that it is not cognition of this sort but rather mere thought which ought to precede investigation, then investigation is not impossible for those who suspend judgment about the reality of the non-evident. For a skeptic is not, I think, barred from having thoughts, if they arise through reason (*logō*) itself as a result of what passively impresses him as evident appearance, and does not at all imply the reality of what is being thought of—for we can think, as they say, not only of real things but also of unreal things. Hence someone who suspends judgment maintains his skeptical condition while investigating and thinking; for it has been made clear that he assents to any impression given by way of a passive appearance insofar as it appears to him. (PH 2.10, tr. Annas/Barnes with changes)

PH 2.1–12 is arguably incomprehensible on its own. Sextus uses the phrase 'mere thought' (*noēsis de haplōs*), saying that no more is needed for investigation, and that this is available to the skeptic. Mere thought, Sextus says, simply comes from reason (*logō*), which passively receives impressions and takes in appearances. What does this mean? With the exception of Bury, commentators tend to emend *logō*.[19] Some manuscripts have *logōn*; accordingly, Mates renders the text as if it was about *discussions*, during which some things that interlocutors say strike the skeptic as evident. Hossenfelder reads the sentence along similar lines. But this way of reconstructing the passage is implausible. Sextus keeps emphasizing throughout the *Outlines* that the things others say do *not* appear to the skeptic in an evident manner. Indeed, the skeptic scrutinizes the various things others say. Annas and Barnes translate in the spirit of my proposal above, albeit without reference to reason, and based on the assumption that *logō* (or *logōn*) is to be omitted.[20]

Surely, Sextus does not suggest that all skeptic thoughts are a product of reason in the sense that they simply arise, without any activity on the part of the thinker. Consider some of the complicated arguments (many of them employing skeptical modes) Sextus makes when investigating dogmatic theories. It is highly implausible that the relevant thoughts just come to mind, generated as it were by reason. Sextus's remark that simple

---

[19]Sextus Empiricus, *Grundriß der pyrrhonischen Skepsis*, Malte Hossenfelder (tr.) (Frankfurt am Main: Suhrkamp, 1985); *The Sceptic Way. Sextus Empiricus's Outlines of Pyrrhonism*, with introduction and commentary by Benson Mates (New York: Oxford, 1996); Annas and Barnes, *Outlines of Scepticism*; Bury, *Sextus Empiricus*.

[20]Annas and Barnes, *Outlines of Scepticism*, 13.

thoughts just arise through reason is plausible, however, if we take it to invoke dogmatic theories of preconceptions.[21] On this reading, the word that commentators tend to emend, *logō*, makes sense. Sextus is plausibly talking about the way reason is constituted, and thus about the way in which reason enables the skeptic to think.

Once preconceptions are acquired, a subject can arrive at more complicated notions.[22] Accordingly, the skeptic can not only think (and comprehend) that which is but also that which is not (PH 2.10). By themselves, preconceptions have a metaphysical dimension. Since they are formed in a passively undergone process that crucially involves perception, they are a link to how things are. But once we begin to combine aspects of preconceptions, formulate analogous notions, and so on, this metaphysical dimension is diluted (say, when we imagine a child raised by wolves) and eventually dissolved (say, when we imagine a werewolf).

If this is the core of Sextus's response to the Concept Charge, then it refers to a crucial, but comparatively obscure and badly understood, passage in PH 1, namely Sextus's brief account in PH 1.24 of how it is that the skeptics are thinkers (*noētikoi*). In response to the Apraxia Charge, Sextus explains that the skeptics adhere to appearance in a fourfold way:

> By nature's guidance we are naturally capable of perceiving and thinking. By the necessitation of affections, hunger conducts us to food and thirst to drink. By the handing down of customs and laws, we regard piety as good and impiety as bad in a practical, everyday kind of way. Through instruction in skills we are not inactive in those kinds of expertise which we adopt. (PH 1.24, tr. Annas/Barnes with changes)

Though the details of how we should understand them are controversial, the second, third, and fourth point are relatively clear. The first point,

---

[21]Sextus does not actually use the terminological notions for 'preconceptions' (*prolēpseis*) as compared to full-fledged concepts. However, in substance he is referencing precisely the relevant ideas.

[22]In M 8.58–60, Sextus describes some of the operations that lead to more complicated concepts (diminution, composition, etc.). He does so in the context of a dialectical argument against theories that cast sense-perception in a negative light. Employing what sounds like a mix of Stoic and Epicurean ideas, Sextus calls such theories into question by exploring how more complicated concepts draw on less complicated ones; less complicated concepts, he argues, are preceded by sense perception. If sense perception was abolished, he goes on to say, then all thought is done away with.

however, that the skeptics can perceive and think through the guidance of nature, is genuinely hard to make sense of.[23] Indeed, I think that as long as the Concept Charge is not recognized as a central antiskeptical objection, PH 1.23–24 makes no sense. Why would Sextus's first move in refuting the Apraxia Charge be to address the skeptics' abilities to perceive and to think? The stipulation that, in some sense, thinking and perceiving are activities does not provide a sufficient explanation. Ancient versions of the Apraxia Charge target activities of a more ordinary kind, activities that have something to do with setting oneself in motion by thinking that one should do such and such (drink, administer a medication, attend a religious festival, and so on).

The skeptics' abilities to perceive and to think are crucial to one of their core activities: the activity to investigate. The skeptics are, literally, 'investigators' (this is what 'skeptic' means), and investigation is what they spend their lives doing. Surely, then, the skeptics must be able to investigate if they are to be skeptics. Most basically, this means that they must be able to think. For the skeptics' opponents, however, the ability to think is not something that just comes with being born with a human brain. It is an acquired ability. Reason must be furnished with acquired concepts for a human subject to be able to perceive the world conceptually (say, to see *a horse*) and to think. That is, the skeptics' opponents advance a *substantive* notion of reason, according to which an account must be given of how a human being grows up to be a perceiver and reasoner. Accordingly, there is a question of whether this process involves anything that is in conflict with skeptical suspension of judgment. The skeptic must explain how she can employ concepts without making any claims about the way things are. This explanation is a crucial part of the skeptic's response to the Apraxia Charge, simply because investigation is the very activity that makes the skeptic a skeptic.

---

[23]Jonathan Barnes and Martha Nussbaum think that the passage invokes skeptical reliance on commemorative signs (Barnes, "The Beliefs of a Pyrrhonist," *Proceedings of the Cambridge Philological Society* 28 [1982]: 1–29, 16–17; Nussbaum, "Skeptic Purgatives: Disturbance and the Life Without Belief," in Nussbaum, *The Therapy of Desire: Theory and Practice in Hellenistic Ethics* [Princeton, N.J.: Princeton University Press, 1994], 280–315, 293 f.). Julia Annas argues that it does not make sense to invoke nature's guidance only for one aspect of the skeptic's adherence to appearances; as she sees it, the skeptic is generally active in a *natural* way (*The Morality of Happiness* [New York: Oxford University Press, 1993], 207–13). For critical discussion of these views, cf. Vogt, *Skepsis und Lebenspraxis*, 157–65.

Sextus's account of the skeptic's ability to think is not yet an account of the skeptic's ability to investigate. Further questions have to be addressed. An account of skeptical thought, however, is a necessary first step. Without it, the skeptic cannot explain her skeptical activities. Sextus invokes a nature-guided process in order to account for the skeptics' abilities to perceive and think. Doing so, he makes a move that is, in the dialectical context of his engagement with his critics, entirely obvious. This is precisely what the dogmatists say about anyone's ability to perceive and think: this ability is acquired as part of a natural process.

6. Conclusion

In PH 2.1–12 and M 8.337–336a, Sextus addresses a question that scholars writing on skepticism largely ignore: can the skeptic think? The Hellenistic interlocutors of the skeptics explain reasoning in substantive terms; to be a thinker is to be able to employ concepts. They account for concept-acquisition as a natural process of growing into a perceptible world. The competent use of concepts thus arguably invokes assumptions about the way the world is: wolves are dangerous, trees grow in soil, and so on. Are these assumptions in violation of skeptical suspension of judgment? As I argued, Sextus can show that they are not. These assumptions do not qualify as beliefs in the relevant sense. They are not formed through active assent. Instead, they are naturally acquired.

The proposed reading of PH 2.1.12 has several advantages. It adds an intriguing charge to the list of interesting antiskeptical objections, the charge that the skeptic may not be able to think. Once this challenge is formulated, the beginning of PH 2—after all a quite prominently placed text—turns out to be a central piece of the *Outlines*, much more so than scholars have recognized. Moreover, the first part of the skeptics' fourfold adherence to appearances—the idea that nature enables the skeptic to perceive and think—shows itself to be a crucial aspect of PH 1. Indeed, Sextus is right to explain the skeptic's ability to perceive and think *before* he addresses anything else about the skeptic's life. If the skeptic did not have these rational capacities, skepticism would be doomed. These capacities are relevant to action and other aspects Sextus addresses in response to the Apraxia Charge. More than that, they are crucial to the endeavor to lead a life of investigation.

Moreover, the proposed reading has the advantage of seeing Sextus not merely as a compiler of skeptical arguments, but as a sophisticated philosopher. Though I cannot argue for this in general terms here, I think it is obvious for anyone who spends significant time reading Sextus that he is genuinely a major thinker. Traditional biographies emphasize that Sextus is a medical doctor; his writings are seen merely as containers for a rich reservoir of skeptical strategies. But this is quite implausible. How could anyone write so extensively, and on such a high level, without actually devoting much of his or her life to thinking through the issues? Though Sextus is also a source for arguments from various phases of skepticism, he is a philosopher who tries to formulate *compelling* versions of arguments he inherits. My interpretation ascribes to Sextus a continued effort to come to grips with a deep challenge to his philosophy, the question of how one can think if one does not form beliefs. With respect to the relative chronology of PH 2 and M 8, I take Sextus's engagement with the Concept Charge to indicate that M 8 represents an earlier stage of Sextus's thought. When Sextus writes the *Outlines*, he has a worked-out strategy of how to view the Concept Charge, and how to respond to it.

Sextus does not showcase the Concept Charge, for reasons that, as I see it, are best described in terms of not waking up sleeping dogs. Most people who argue against the skeptics probably never thought of the problem. But some of the more sophisticated opponents considered it, apparently so much so that they kept talking about it. Once discovered, this objection is likely to capture one's imagination. It has the potential to stop the skeptic in his tracks: if the skeptic cannot think, then surely there are no skeptics. Accordingly, Sextus needs a reply, and one that goes to the heart of the skeptic's endeavor. Quite adequately, this reply is already part of PH 1.23–24, Sextus's account of the skeptic's life. However, it is rather well hidden. The reader who does not know that there is yet another antiskeptical objection that Sextus needs to respond to can get through PH 1 without noticing that Sextus is gearing up for an explanation of skeptic thought.

7

Why Beliefs Are Never True:
A Reconstruction of Stoic
Epistemology

Today, most epistemologists hold that knowledge entails belief.[1] If some-one knows that p, she also believes that p. "To believe that p" is under-stood as referring to the attitude of holding p to be true. We have a unified notion of holding-to-be-true: every case of unqualified holding-to-be-true counts as the same *kind* of propositional attitude, namely belief. When we characterize an attitude as a belief, we do not mean to express a value judgment. We assume that everyone has beliefs. Further, we con-sider it obvious that there are true and false beliefs.

These assumptions seem natural to us, and it is hard to appreciate how deeply an epistemological theory differs from contemporary views if it does not share these or similar ideas. In particular, it is hard to see how one might hold the following claims:

(1) In aiming for knowledge, we should aim to have no beliefs.
(2) Beliefs are a kind of ignorance, and therefore bad.
(3) Beliefs are not bearers of truth-values.

These claims are central to Stoic epistemology, and they have been up to now largely unappreciated. Indeed, though (3) is particularly striking, it

---

[1]Of course, not everyone shares this premise. For example, an externalist about knowl-edge can argue that there are things S knows, but does not believe. However, as far as I can see, the externalist way of divorcing knowledge from belief is motivated in a way that is quite foreign to all major ancient theories.

has up to now not even been noticed.[2] The plan for this chapter is to explain these claims, and to show that, in spite of their initial strangeness, they have much speaking in their favor.

1. Beliefs as Weak Assents

The Stoics define beliefs—*doxai*—as weak and changeable assents. Before I turn to the details of the Stoic conception of belief, a brief note on the relevant Greek term, *doxa*. As with respect to other theories discussed in this book, it is a difficult decision whether one wants to translate *doxa* as belief or as opinion. In reconstructing Stoic texts, scholars often choose "opinion," which has the obvious advantage that the derogative sense of *doxa* that is central to Stoic philosophy is well captured. However, this translation also has a serious disadvantage. "Opinion" sounds to modern ears like a subclass of belief. There could be a theory according to which all instances of holding-to-be-true are beliefs, while some of them are merely opinions. In such a theory, opinions could be badly supported beliefs, beliefs that, for example, involve prejudice, intellectual laziness, or a shallow engagement with the issues. This is not how the Stoics think of *doxai*. The full force of the Stoic theory only comes out when we draw attention to the fact that, for the Stoics, *doxa* is generally, and not only under particular conditions, a bad mode of holding something to be true. For this reason, I shall speak of belief, not of opinion.

Core characteristics of the Stoic notion of belief can be gathered from the following three texts:

> 1. The Stoics say there are three things that are linked together, knowledge (*epistēmē*), belief (*doxa*) and cognition (*katalēpsis*) stationed between them [1a]. Knowledge is cognition that is secure and firm and unchangeable by reason. Belief is weak (*asthenē*) [1b] and false assent [1c]. Cognition in between these is assent belonging to a cognitive impression [1a]; and a cognitive impression, so they claim, is one which is true and of such a kind

[2]Cf. for example Michael Frede's chapter "Stoic Epistemology." Frede writes, "Now a belief will be true or false, depending on whether the impression it is an assent to is true or false" (301); however, there are no true beliefs for the Stoics.

that it could not turn out false. (M 7.151–52 = LS 41C, part; tr. LS with changes)

2. They [the Stoics] say that, due to his not forming beliefs (*doxazein*) and his being ignorant of nothing [2a], the wise man never supposes (*hupolambanein*) anything false [2b], and that he does not assent at all to anything noncognitive. For ignorance is changeable and weak (*asthenē*) assent [2a]. But the wise man supposes nothing weakly (*hupolambanein asthenōs*), but rather, securely and firmly; and so he does not hold beliefs (*doxazein*) either [2b].[3] For beliefs are of two kinds, assent to the noncognitive, and weak supposition (*hupolēpsis asthenē*) [2c], and these are alien to the wise man's disposition. So precipitancy and assent in advance of cognition are attributes of the precipitate and inferior man [2d], whereas they do not befall the man who is well-natured and perfect and virtuous. (Stobaeus 2.111, 18–112, 8 = LS 41G = SVF 3.548, part; tr. LS with changes)

3. We say that the wise man's absence of belief (*mē doxazein*) is accompanied by such characteristics as, first of all, nothing seeming to him so-and-so (*to mē dokein autō mēden*); for such 'seeming' (*dokēsis*) is noncognitive belief (*doxa*) [3a]. (Anonymous Stoic treatise (Herculaneum papyrus 1020), col. 4, col. 1 = LS 41D = SVF 2.131, part; tr. LS with changes)

I have inserted number-letter designations at the points in the texts that I address below in my comments.

Weak assent (1b)

Belief is characterized by the kind of assent by which a subject accepts an impression (*phantasia*) when she forms a belief. Her assent is *weak*, which reflects the overall state of mind of the subject. The Stoics envisage a subject who holds a whole body of beliefs, rather than a body of knowledge.[4] Her beliefs do not stand in the logical relationships that pieces of knowledge stand in, relationships that 'root' individual pieces of knowledge, making them firm and stable. Beliefs lack this kind of anchoring. They are issued from a weak state of mind, and become part of this weak state of mind. Note that the person who forms a belief fully accepts an impression. Her assent is not weak in the sense of being tentative, or provisional,

[3]"*Doxazein*" means *both* to form a belief and to hold a belief; I aim to capture both aspects by translating first in terms of belief-formation, and then in terms of holding beliefs.
[4]I am here speaking of a "subject" instead of, as in other places in the book, a "cognizer." Talk of cognizers might be confusing in the context of Stoic epistemology, where "cognition" is a central technical term.

or anything of that sort.[5] It is weak in ways that reflect the state of mind of the subject. Importantly, this means that beliefs are changeable or lacking in the kind of stability that comes with the logical relations characteristic of a body of knowledge. They are likely to be altered, reinterpreted, rearranged with respect to how they relate to other truth-claims of the subject, and so on.

Knowledge-cognition and belief-cognition (1a)

Next, consider how belief relates to cognition (*katalēpsis*). Cognitions are assents to cognitive impressions. Recall that, for the Stoics, human impressions (*phantasiai*) are *rational* impressions, that is, they are thoughts. The term 'impression' thus should not mislead us: the Stoics do not think of perception, or some other limited realm in which things 'strike' or 'impress' us. Their talk about impressions is best understood as talk about thoughts. Accordingly, there are cognitive impressions in the sensory realm (for example, *this is my computer screen*) as well as in the nonsensory realm (for example, *water is H_2O*).[6]

Cognitive impressions are 'imprinted in the soul' precisely and in every detail in accordance with what is. Noncognitive impressions are not thus imprinted (for example, blurry visions, not fully understood

---

[5]That is, belief is changeable whether or not the subject is seeking to revise her beliefs. A believer might be like Euthyphro in Plato's dialogue *Euthyphro*. When pressed to defend her beliefs, she makes ad hoc adjustments. Once it appears that she is left with an incoherent position, she might run away from the conversation, or break it off by starting a fight. Soon enough, she may lapse back into well-loved beliefs. Overall, there is a disposition for quite a few back-and-forth alterations, even if there is no willingness to revise one's beliefs in the light of new thoughts.

[6]Early research on Stoic philosophy tended to misrepresent this feature of the theory. Half a century ago, scholars often assumed that Plato and Aristotle dismissed perception as lowly and bad; when these scholars approached Stoic texts, they were struck by what appeared to be a greater appreciation of perception. In part as a consequence of this perceived contrast, and partly because there are a number of examples from the perceptual realm, they emphasized perception when reconstructing Stoic philosophy, sometimes losing sight of the fact that both thoughts and perceptions can be cognitive. Cf. Frede, "Stoic Epistemology." Baron Reed ("The Stoics' Account of the Cognitive Impression," *Oxford Studies in Ancient Philosophy* 23 [2002]: 147–79, 148), says he will assume that cognitive impressions are primarily sensory, because such cases are particularly prominent in the Stoic-skeptic debates. This seems right; however, it is only one strand of Stoic discussions.

arguments, and so on) (DL 7.46). The Stoic claim relevant to present purposes is that cognition is *stationed* in between knowledge and belief. Importantly, this does not mean that there are three kinds of doxastic attitude, belief the lowest, cognition improving upon it, and knowledge the best. Instead, it means that cognition figures in both domains: the knower assents to cognitive impressions, and so does the person who holds beliefs (though she does not do so consistently). The person who does not possess a systematic body of knowledge, that is, the nonsage or nonknower, is likely to assent to many cognitive impressions.

Consider an example of what we might call belief-cognition—a case of cognition that does not qualify as knowledge, and thus is a belief. Suppose that today I have a cognitive impression of a complicated argument: I fully understand it. This counts as cognition. Insofar as I do not possess the systematic body of knowledge that the Stoics think knowledge is, it counts as the acquisition of belief. The argument does not 'fall into place'; it does not become integrated with a theoretical framework where it would be firmly rooted. Asked to explain the argument tomorrow, I am at a loss, and I realize that I no longer understand it. Even though I assented to a cognitive impression, I only acquired belief, not knowledge.[7]

However, not all cognitions of the nonwise subject are weak in quite this way. Other cognitions might be beliefs, and weak, insofar as they lack integration into a systematic body of truth-claims (I shall consider an example of that kind below). But what about perceptual particulars? Suppose I assent to the cognitive impression that *this* (what I'm looking at while typing) is my computer screen. I am not likely to ever alter this perceptual judgment. I assented to a cognitive impression (assuming that I have full and unimpeded vision of the screen). Why then should my cognition bear any sign of weakness? The brief answer is, again, that weakness attaches to the overall *state of mind* of the nonsage assenter. All assents of the nonwise person are issued from that state of mind. For a more detailed answer, we must turn to the Stoic notion of precipitancy.

---

[7]My example reiterates the point I made above: the distinction between cognitive and noncognitive impressions cuts across the distinction between sensory and nonsensory impressions (DL 7.51). Cognitive impressions can be sensory and nonsensory.

Belief as precipitate assent (2d)

Assent to noncognitive impressions is precipitate. It is premature or rash: before the agent has carefully considered whether she has a cognitive impression, she has already accepted the impression. However, *all* belief, not just belief in which noncognitive impressions are accepted, is precipitate. This is reflected in the fact that the nonwise person is described as a precipitate person. Only the wise person is fully in control of her judgments: she never accepts anything as true that she should not accept, *and* she accepts what she should accept with the right kind of deliberative care. Cognitive impressions, the Stoics say, "almost pull us by the hair" toward assent (SE, M 7.257). Importantly, though they exert a strong pull, assent is nevertheless active and reflects the state of mind of the subject.[8] The wise person is a considerate assenter, even where assent is fully warranted. Though wise and nonwise persons may assent to the same cognitive impression, there is thus a difference that can be cashed out in terms of precipitancy. In carefully considering the impression, the wise person assents in a considered fashion. The nonwise person is likely to just buy into cognitive impressions, thus being rash. This is one reason why even assents like "this is my computer screen" count as beliefs. Not being wise, I am likely to immediately accept this impression. In a sense, I have accepted it before I even considered it.

Two kinds of beliefs (2c)

The distinction between cognitive and noncognitive impressions is crucial to Stoic philosophy. Some beliefs are assents to noncognitive impressions. Such acceptances are inherently flawed; they are in violation of the Stoic norm that one should accept only cognitive impressions (cf. DL 7.177). These beliefs are through-and-through deficient: assent is weak, *and* the object of assent is such that no assent should be given. Other beliefs are acceptances of cognitive impressions. The cognizer does something right here. She assents to a cognitive impression. Still, she assents from the overall weak state of her mind. In this condition, one's truth-claims are changeable, unstable, and precipitate. Though the subject assents to a cognitive impression, her assent is (and generates) a belief.[9]

[8]Cf. on this point Michael Frede, *A Free Will: Origins of the Notion in Ancient Thought*, A. A. Long (ed.) (Berkeley: University of California Press, 2011), 81–82; and my discussion of Frede's position in *Classical Philology* (2012): 161–68.
    [9]Cf. Constance Meinwald, "Ignorance and Opinion in Stoic Epistemology," *Phronesis* 50 (2005): 215–31; and Vogt, *Law, Reason*, chapter 3.

False assent (1c)

The claim that beliefs are weak assents (1b), discussed above, is tied to the claim that they are false assents (1c). What does this mean? It cannot mean that beliefs are generally assents to *false* impressions. For example, one might believe that water is H_2O, thereby accepting a true impression. The fact that one does not know that water is H_2O is reflected in a lack of integration of this claim with one's other truth-claims. For those of us untrained in chemistry, the claim that water is H_2O does not stand in sufficiently clear logical relations with other truth-claims to count as knowledge; for example, we might accept another impression that is in conflict with it, because we are unaware of the conflict. How, then, should we interpret the claim that beliefs are weak *and false* assents? I suggest that we read the "and" in "weak and false assents" as introducing an explanatory predicate. Beliefs, qua weak assents, are assents *falsely given*, or deficient assents: beliefs are weak-and-thereby-deficient assents.[10]

Belief as ignorance (2a)

Ignorance is defined as weak and changeable assent. Ignorance is thus identified with belief. Ignorance is *not* conceived of as a lack of any doxastic attitude to a given content. Consider someone who barely knows the word 'biomathematics.' This person is ignorant of biomathematics in the sense of having no doxastic attitudes at all to any of the subject matter of that discipline. Such a person does not have any beliefs on the issue. This kind of ignorance is the *absence* of any doxastic attitude to a given content.

---

[10]The skeptics, or at least some skeptics, take the Stoics to imply that one *should never form a belief* (cf. the Stoic-skeptic debates as depicted in Cicero's *Academica*). That is, they interpret the Stoic proposals on how to move from belief to knowledge as involving epistemic norms to the effect that one should only assent if the assent generates knowledge, and should suspend if one's assent generated belief. However, the Stoics do not formulate the norm "never form beliefs." The Stoics say that the wise person has no beliefs. Doing so, they describe an *ideal*, but the ideal does not immediately translate into an epistemic norm. If pressed, the Stoics might argue along the lines of "ought implies can": there is no point to a norm that, as they see it, cannot be adopted. Prior to being wise, one cannot live without forming beliefs. Accordingly, it is not a viable strategy to try to attain knowledge by not forming beliefs (though arguably this is a skeptic strategy). The crucial Stoic norm is "never assent to noncognitive impressions." Beliefs can be assents to cognitive impressions. Though deficient qua beliefs, such assents are a step forward qua being cognitions.

According to this notion of ignorance, belief is already 'more' than igno-rance.[11] Belief engages with some content, while ignorance does not.

The Stoics are not interested in this kind of ignorance. In claiming that the wise person is not ignorant of anything, they claim that the wise person never assents weakly. The wise person might very well have no doxastic attitude to some content, say, not holding any view on what next fall's fashion collections might bring. Ignorance, for the Stoics, is a doxastic attitude; it is weak assent to impressions. It is the same kind of assent that belief is: weak and changeable assent. The claims that the wise person has no beliefs and that she is not ignorant about anything are equivalent.

Supposition (2b)

The Stoics thus do not use 'belief' as a term that covers all truth-claims. Only truth-claims that involve weak assents are beliefs. Do they have any term that covers all truth-claims? Though this does not seem to be a cen-tral aspect of their technical terminology, it appears that 'supposition' (*hupolēpsis*) might be such a term. Apparently, one can suppose some-thing weakly, thus forming a belief, or firmly, thus acquiring a piece of knowledge. The wise person supposes nothing weakly, and therefore has no beliefs; instead, she supposes everything firmly and securely, thus ac-quiring knowledge with every assent she gives.[12] How important is the notion of 'supposition' for the Stoics? My impression is that the Stoics do not push it. Their claim is not that there is a general category, supposi-tions, with two subcategories, beliefs and knowledge. On the contrary, it appears that the term 'supposition' is used as a kind of circumlocution, at

---

[11]This kind of position might be thought of in terms of *Republic* V: Socrates argues that ignorance is not directed at anything ('set over nothing'), while belief engages with some-thing (something that participates in what is and in what is not). Accordingly, *doxa* is darker than knowledge, but brighter than ignorance. This is what the Stoics dismiss: that belief sheds any more light on things than ignorance; the opiner ('believer') is genuinely ignorant.

[12]One way in which the Stoics can refer to all cases of someone accepting an impression as true is to speak of assent (*sunkatathesis*). But assent is a "movement" of the mind (such as impression and impulse); it is not one of the attitudes discussed in normative epistemology (as we would refer to the relevant part of Stoic philosophy). Depending on a number of factors, assents—given in such and such fashion and to such and such impressions—gener-ate different cognitive attitudes.

places where it is inevitable that one looks for a term that *under*-describes what precisely is going on.

Seemings (3a)

The third text adds a puzzling idea, one that is even less attended to by interpreters than the ideas mentioned in texts 1 and 2. The fact that the wise person has no beliefs, it is said, reflects among other things that nothing seems to her (*to mē dokein autō mēden*). This is an utterly strange claim. Would it not appear that things seem to be one way or another to everyone? The wise person certainly has noncognitive impressions. It is part of her wisdom that she never assents to them. In this sense, something seems to her in a certain way, but she does not accept this impression.

'Seeming' (*dokēsis*) is explained as noncognitive belief; that is, it is explained as the kind of belief in which a noncognitive impression is accepted. The implication is that a 'seeming' or *dokēsis* actually involves acceptance, and more precisely, the acceptance of something that, noncognitively, seems to the subject to be so-and-so. For example, it seems that the tower at a distance is round. A 'seeming' is something that involves a judgment: the person thinks that the seemingly round tower is round. Apparently, the Stoics thus use a cognate of *doxa*, namely *dokēsis*, for a certain kind of appearance, namely one in which what appears noncognitively is accepted.

This point may reflect complicated discussions with skeptics. The skeptics wonder whether there is a notion of appearances that does not involve any kind of judgment component. The difficult question at issue here can be considered with the help of an example. Suppose the moon seems small to you, but you do not judge it to be small, because, in another sense, it seems large to you, because you have a vague notion of it being rather far away. The appearance of it being large might count as a *dokēsis*: you have a noncognitive impression of the moon being large, and you take it to be large. The appearance of it being small might not count as a *dokēsis*: though in a sense the moon looks small, it is not thought to be small.[13]

---

[13]Cf. Rachel Barney, "Impressions and Appearances," *Phronesis* 37.3 (1992): 283–313, who argues that appearances always involve a judgment component.

2. Knowledge as Firm Assent

Accordingly, to believe that p, and to know that p, are two modes of making a truth-claim. Knowledge does not entail belief. The Stoics define knowledge as follows:

> [The Stoics say...] Knowledge (*epistēmē*) is a cognition (*katalēpsis*) which is secure and unchangeable by reason (*hupo logou*) [4a]. It is secondly a system (*sustēma*) of such pieces of knowledge (*epistēmai*), like the one that exists in the virtuous man with respect to that which makes up the field of logic [4b]. It is thirdly a system of expert (*technikōs*) pieces of knowledge, that has by itself stability (*to bebaion*), as the virtues have [4b]. Fourthly, it is a tenor for the reception of impressions that is unchangeable by reason, and consisting, they say, in tension and power [4c]. (Stobaeus 2.73, 16–74, 3 = LS 41H = SVF 3.112, part; tr. LS with changes)

Each of these definitions is thought to explain what knowledge, understood in one sense relevant to Stoic theory, is.

Pieces of knowledge (4a)

As we saw, the wise person has no beliefs.[14] She never assents precipitately, and she never assents to noncognitive impressions. Every assent given by the wise person generates a piece of knowledge. Every assent given by a nonwise person generates a belief. Knowledge is firm assent in the sense that it is not changeable 'by reason.' That is, a subject may change her mind if given some hallucinatory drug, or if some other external force works on her.[15] But she will not change her mind because some new thought occurs to her. Insofar as the wise person accepts particular impressions, there are particular 'bits' of knowledge, or pieces of knowledge. This is an important point: though the Stoics also conceive of knowledge as a systematic body of knowledge, they hold that any particular assent—even assent to a quite mundane impression, say, "this is an apple"—can count as knowledge.

---

[14]Commentators tend to gloss this position is a way that hides its starkness. Cf., for example, a relatively old but well-known account, formulated by Michael Frede, "The Sceptic's Beliefs," 14: "They, thus, expect us to rid ourselves of all the beliefs we have acquired in ordinary ways, if these should fail to meet the rigorous criteria of reason." This is not the Stoic claim: the Stoics expect us to rid ourselves of all beliefs.

[15]Presumably, even a wise person might do so. The Stoics do not address this point. I assume they would argue that a wise person, like Socrates, does not get drunk, or, more generally, does not bring herself into states where external forces affect her cognitive powers. But if others were to drug her, then her faculties would be affected.

This position differs significantly from other ancient views, according to which knowledge is, for example, tied to a certain kind of object (say, the Forms), or to some level of generality.

Knowledge as a systematic body of knowledge (4b)

Many pieces of knowledge constitute a systematic body of knowledge. Though individual pieces of knowledge count as knowledge, it is impossible to have just one or two such pieces of knowledge. A logician, for example, only knows the particular bits of her field if she understands her field as a whole. A system of knowledge is characterized by stability. It is stable 'on its own': the individual pieces of knowledge are stabilized through the logical relations they stand in with each other and the relations they stand in with the perceptual world (in assenting to cognitive perceptual impressions, the subject accepts impressions that are 'imprinted' in her rational soul precisely as things are).[16]

Knowledge as a state of mind (4c)

In order to assent as a knower, one must already have knowledge. As in the case of the virtues, the Stoics think that the transition from being a person with beliefs to being a knower is instantaneous. After much study and hard work (and in that sense, after a long time of progression), one has gathered sufficiently many cognitions to make up a complete systematic body of knowledge. All truth-claims that formerly were beliefs come to be pieces of knowledge. That is, one already held most of the relevant views, but since there were still some false ones, or still some unclear logical relations between particular views, one's complete body of truth-claims was a body of beliefs. Once one has weeded out all falsehoods and

---

[16]I agree with Reed, "Stoics' Account," that the Stoics propose a kind of direct realism (in today's terms). I take this to be the traditional interpretation of Stoic epistemology, or very close to it, based primarily on Aetius 4.12.1–5 (= LS 39B), though of course scholars of the past did not use today's terminology (or, for that matter, were able to refer to today's theories). Reed's analysis is helpful in comparing Stoic epistemology to contemporary theories, my sole disagreement on the point of direct realism being that the talk about 'reports through branches of the soul' that Reed discusses on p. 170 is, in my view, not part of a materialist theory, but of a corporealist theory—but that is a matter about Stoic physics that does not pertain to the present issues (cf. Vogt, "Sons of the Earth: Are the Stoics Metaphysical Brutes?" *Phronesis* [2009]: 136–54.)

acceptances of noncognitive impressions, all one's truth-claims come to have the stability of knowledge. Now one will no longer change one's mind about them; they are firmly rooted.[17] From now on, this is the state of mind that issues one's future assents. Accordingly, all future assents will generate further pieces of knowledge.

As discussed in earlier chapters, these ideas have relevant ancestors in Plato. Plato's dialogues are comparatively better known, and thus it is useful to refer again to them; they help characterize the kind of position that the Stoics have in mind (though, of course, the Stoics differ in many details from any given proposal found in Plato).

In the *Meno*, Plato formulates the idea that knowledge is belief that is 'tied down by an account.' A similar idea figures in the *Theaetetus*: knowledge is belief 'with an account' (*meta logou*). These proposals are famous, not least because it seems that these are the first formulations of a conception of knowledge that has been discussed until today: that knowledge is justified true belief (JTB). There are two ways of reading Plato's proposals. First, we may think that Plato proposes that to know something is to hold a belief *plus* something else, for example, to believe that p and to have a justification for this belief.[18] This line of interpretation is in agreement with contemporary intuitions and with the JTB account of knowledge. Second, we may think that Plato proposes something quite different: when we come to know that p our earlier belief that p gradually becomes a piece of knowledge. It is key to this process that we integrate our 'holding that p' into a larger picture—a *logos* (theory, account). Though I shall not argue for an interpretation of the *Meno* or *Theaetetus* here, I take it to be important that Plato thinks of knowledge along the lines of this second interpretation.[19] In acquiring knowledge, beliefs get stabilized and thus undergo change: they become pieces of knowledge.

In the *Meno*, Plato says that understanding a matter once does not yet suffice. As beginners in a given field, we need to think through things a couple of times; otherwise our insight will be elusive. Figuratively speaking, belief does not settle down in the soul. However, when we think

[17]For detailed discussion of the wise person's body of knowledge, see chapter 4 of Vogt, *Law, Reason*.

[18]For Plato, though not for contemporary philosophers discussing these ideas, a justified truth-claim is true. The contemporary notion of justification that allows a belief to be justified, though not true, is alien to the relevant ancient discussions.

[19]For some relevant points, cf. the introduction and chapters 2 and 3.

through a problem several times, our ideas become stable, and thereby become knowledge (85c–d).[20] At the end the *Meno*, Plato proposes a related idea: beliefs 'fly around' in the soul until they are tied down by an account (97d–98a). Beliefs need to be rooted in a set of views. Otherwise we lose our grip on them. It is this set of ideas that becomes central to Stoic epistemology.[21] While a person gains knowledge, her beliefs are *replaced* by knowledge.[22] Accordingly, knowledge does not entail belief.

The predicates that attach to beliefs are thus, mostly, predicates that attach to all belief: "weak," "changeable," and "precipitate." The only differentiation between beliefs lies in whether the impression that is accepted is cognitive or noncognitive. This distinction has real significance for the Stoics. In aiming to progress toward knowledge, it is the one distinction that matters: one ought to assent only to cognitive impressions. The distinction between the cognitive and the noncognitive, however, does not map onto the distinction between the true and the false. Though all cognitive impressions, which show things precisely as they are, are true, many

---

[20]Consider some of the details of the well-known geometrical example. Socrates initially asks the slave boy whether he knows what kind of figure a square is (82b). After the slave boy's first round of responses, Socrates says to Meno that the slave boy thinks he knows the things he says, but he does not know them (82e). Socrates then asks the slave boy what seems (*dokei*) to him to be the case (83a), and the slave boy responds that, what he is saying at least seems (*dokei*) to him to be the case (83d). Now, the slave boy no longer thinks of himself as someone who has knowledge, but sees that he doesn't know the answer (84a–b). Now he wants to search what he doesn't know (84b–c). When Socrates interprets the example for Meno, he asks whether the slave boy has come up with any belief (*doxa*) that wasn't his own. These beliefs (*doxai*) were in him (85c). Right now, these beliefs are like a dream, flying around. But if the slave boy is questioned repeatedly, he will come to know these things—without being taught, he will come up with this knowledge out of himself. This is recollection (85d). The slave boy learned these beliefs prior to this life. While he is a human being, he always has these beliefs in him, and they can grow into knowledge (through questioning) (85e–86a).

[21]It is uncontroversial that the Stoics were close readers of the *Theaetetus*. It is harder to know whether the same is true for the *Meno*. However, it is clear—from a variety of sources—that the key ideas from the *Meno* were discussed extensively in the Academy, and probably also among philosophers outside of Plato's school. It seems most likely that the Stoics are well aware of the relevant ideas, whether they read them in the *Meno* or picked them up in discussion.

[22]With a view to Part III of the *Theaetetus*, we might even think that Plato suggests that our belief is replaced with an *account* (*logos*)—i.e., that there is something confused about the proposal that we need a belief plus an account, because what we have when we know that p *is* an account of p.

noncognitive impressions, which show things in less precise ways, are also true (say, a blurry vision of my friend may be true: the approaching person really is my friend; but the impression is not cognitive).

That is, the Stoics do not envisage a differentiation between two groups of beliefs, true and false beliefs. Contrary to what reformulations of the Stoic position in scholarly literature suggest, the Stoics are rather consistent in never attaching the predicates "true" or "false" to beliefs.

However, one might still wonder whether this can be the whole story. In particular, one might wonder whether, though there are no true beliefs, there could be false beliefs. Suppose that to ascribe the property "true" to something is to evaluate it positively, and suppose that this counts as a reason against describing any beliefs as true. If this was the only relevant consideration (and we saw that it is not even the dominant consideration), then it might seem that acceptances of falsehoods could be false beliefs. But a simple objection derives from bivalence: entities that can be evaluated as false must also be evaluable as true. Thus, there can be no false beliefs if there are no true beliefs.[23]

3. Statements as Bearers of Truth-Values

If beliefs are not evaluated as true and false, what is? For the Stoics, acceptance, rejection, and suspension of judgment engage with *impressions* (*phantasiai*). Human thought is described primarily on that level: we engage with impressions, accepting or rejecting them, or suspending judgment on them.[24] The truth-predicates are employed in characterizing

---

[23]The principle that, if something can be evaluated as true it must also be evaluable as false was violated by the Epicureans, who claim that all sense-perceptions are true. The Stoics go to great length in defending bivalence as a core principle of their logic, a topic that is for them connected to issues about determinism. From their point of view, the Epicurean claim must appear deeply confused: how could something be true, if it is not the kind of entity that can also be false?

[24]This is perhaps clearest in contexts that explain the fundamentals of Stoic philosophy of mind. For example, consider the claim that, according to the Stoics, there are "three movements of the rational soul": impression, impulse, and assent (Plutarch, *Against Colotes* 1122a–f = LS 69A). Reed ("Stoics' Account," 168) argues, *contra* Frede and the standard view in the literature, that assent is to (in his terms) 'propositions,' not to impressions. Reed refers to Stobaeus 2.88, 2–6 (= LS 33I). However, this passage uses a short-cut that figures in some contexts (that is, the source speaks directly of *lekta* rather than of the relevant impressions). This kind of imprecise usage occurs when the focus is elsewhere. In this particular

impressions: a true impression is an impression of which a true predication (*katēgoria*) can be made (SE, *M* 7.242–6 = LS 39G). Unfortunately,
this passage—though it contains vital information about impressions,
namely that they are only derivatively true and false—is phrased impre-
cisely in another respect: 'predication' is not the Stoics' technical term for
the bearers of truth-values.

Consider, then, what precisely it is, according to the Stoics, that
should be evaluated as true and false. Human impressions have a linguistic counterpart, so-called *lekta*, literally 'sayables' (SE, *PH* 2.80–84,
Huelser 322). *Lekta* are things that can be said (to be distinguished from
the corporeal utterance, *phōnē*). When I see the table, I have a rational
impression; rational impressions are thoughts (*noēseis*) (DL 7.51). This
means that these impressions have a linguistic counterpart, and are conceptual. I see *a table*, and I can make a statement of this impression: "this
is a table." *Lekta* can be complete or incomplete.[25] For example, "table" is
an incomplete *lekton*.

The truth-predicates attach to *axiomata*, assertions or statements.[26]
Axiomata are one kind of complete sayable; other complete sayables include questions, hypotheses, and imperativals (DL 7.65–68). *Axiomata*
are the kind of complete sayable that is true or false (DL 7.65).[27] Note

---

case, it is on a rather complex issue, namely, how to characterize assent that figures in impulse to action. The Stoics hold a view of rational motivation that differs from the more
widespread ancient view that motivation involves judging something (the action or its out-
come) to be good. Against this view (often referred to as the Guise of the Good), the Stoics
think that, in impulse to action, we assent to an impression that something is *to be done*. The
relevant *lekton* is in a certain sense incomplete (in their words, a "predicate"). The agent does
not assent to the impression that it is good for her to go for a walk now; rather, she assents to
the impression that she should go for a walk now. Cf. Vogt, *Law, Reason*, chapter 4.

[25]SE, *M* 8.70; DL 7.63. Cf. FDS 696, 699.

[26]DL 7.70.

[27]Among scholars writing on Stoic logic, it has been noted that the truth-predicates
apply, for the Stoics, only to *axiomata*—but this observation was made, for example, with
respect to the truth-predicates not applying to arguments. Cf. M. Frede on true and false
arguments (*Die stoische Logik* [Göttingen: Vandenhoeck und Ruprecht, 1974], 42); for a
recent discussion of bivalence in Stoic logic, cf. J. Barnes, *Truth, etc.: Six Lectures on Ancient
Logic* (Oxford: Oxford University Press, 2007). Though Frede explains that the truth-predicates only apply to *axiomata* when he discusses Stoic logic, he still says that epistemic
norms in Stoic philosophy are meant to steer us away from false belief ("The Sceptic's Two
Kinds of Assents and the Question of the Possibility of Knowledge," in R. Rorty, J. B. Schneewind, and Q. Skinner [eds.], *Philosophy in History* [Cambridge: Cambridge University
Press, 1984], 255–78, reprinted in Burnyeat and Frede, *The Original Sceptics*, 127–51, 137).

that, for the Stoics, bivalence is a mark of that which 'earns' being characterized by the truth predicates: that which is truth-evaluable has precisely one of the truth-values; it is true or false.[28]

One way to explain why impressions, though there are true and false impressions in a derivative sense, are not truth-evaluable in the strict sense is the following. Impressions can be true *and* false, as well as *neither* true *nor* false.[29] Though we need not fully clarify this idea for present purposes (it involves complex questions about the relationship between rational impressions and *lekta*), a brief look at the Stoic examples is helpful.[30] The impression Orestes had in his madness of Electra as a fury is said to be true and false. It is true insofar as Electra is present; it is false insofar as she is not a fury. Arguably, the impression is true and false insofar as one could make a true *and* a false assertion: "there is Electra" (true) and "Electra is a fury" (false). That is, the impression is true *and* false, but there is no single assertion that is true *and* false (whatever Orestes would state, it is true *or* false).

A certain kind of generic impression is said to be neither true nor false. "Human beings are Greeks," for example, is such a generic impression. Only

---

[28]Cf. Barnes (*Truth, etc.*, 1–2). Susanne Bobzien ("Stoic Logic," in B. Inwood [ed.], *The Cambridge Companion to the Stoics* [Cambridge: Cambridge University Press, 2003], 85–123, 87) writes: "Thus truth and falsehood are properties of assertibles, and being true or false—in a nonderivative sense—is both a necessary and a sufficient condition for something's being an assertible. [...] Assertibles resemble Fregean propositions in various respects. There are however, important differences. The most far-reaching one is that truth and falsehood are temporal properties of assertibles."

[29]SE, M 7.242–6, LS 39G. Christopher Shields begins discussion of the truth-evaluability of impressions with a shortened version of 7.242–46, as if the Stoics said that impressions can be true or false. If we report all four options (true, false, neither true nor false, true and false), we immediately see that impressions are not truth-evaluable in any standard sense. "The Truth Evaluability of Stoic *Phantasiai*: Adversus Mathematicos 7.242–46," *Journal of the History of Philosophy* 31.3 (1993): 325–47.

[30]If impressions are true and false derivatively, it might seem that they can only be true-and-false and neither-true-nor-false in the *same* derivative fashion. But that is impossible; there are no true-and-false or neither-true-nor-false *axiomata*. As Frede argues, not all aspects of an impression are captured in a corresponding *axioma*. Noncognitive impressions might be rather vague; in such cases, no particular *axioma* might correspond to them. Michael Frede, "The Stoic Doctrine of the Affections of the Soul," in M. Schofield and G. Striker (eds.), *The Norms of Nature: Studies in Hellenistic Ethics* (Cambridge: Cambridge University Press, 1986), 93–110, 103–7. For Frede, this is one of the reasons why it is important to note that we assent to an impression, not to a *lekton*. In accepting an impression, we do something different from (mentally) stating a particular *axioma*.

a compressed version of the Stoic argument survives, and it is hard to interpret. Roughly, the thought seems to be as follows. Some human beings are Greeks, some are barbarians (it is assumed that the disjunction "Greek or barbarian" is complete and exclusive). "Greek" and "barbarian" are species of the genus "human being." The particulars falling under "human being" are either Greek or barbarian; but neither "Greek" nor "barbarian" is a property of human beings qua human beings. The impression that human beings are Greeks, then, is neither true nor false, because it is a mistake to ascribe this kind of property—one that only applies to particular human beings, but not to the genus—to human beings. Accordingly, there is no assertion "human beings are Greeks." "Human beings are Greeks" is an incorrectly formed predication. The utterance "human beings are Greeks" is not truth-evaluable, because it is not a correctly formed assertoric sentence.

Axiomata are the only kind of thing that is true or false. That they are true or false is their definition: they are the kind of thing that is true or false (DL 7.65). An alternative or additional definition says that an axioma is a complete lekton that can be stated as far as itself is concerned.[31] The clause 'as far as itself is concerned' indicates that, for a lekton to be stated, two conditions must be met: it must be the kind of lekton that can be stated, and someone must have the relevant impression. An axioma is the kind of lekton that is statable as far as itself is concerned (an incomplete lekton like "table" is not statable, only sayable), but for it to be actually statable there must also be a cognizer with the relevant impression.

"True" and "false" are temporal properties of axiomata. Consider a Stoic example: "It is day" (SE, M 8.103). The axioma "it is day" is true during daytime, but false during nighttime. It belongs to the class of so-called metapiptonta: assertibles that switch their truth-value due to the passage of time (literally, metapiptonta are things that 'turn around').[32] As

---

[31]SE, PH 2.104; Gellius, Noctes Atticae XVI 8, 4; DL 7.85 says "pragma" instead of "lekton" (that is, a complete matter that can be stated, as far as itself is concerned). Cf. Huelser 874, 877, 878. I agree with Susanne Bobzien's reading of the passage in "Stoic Logic," esp. 85–89. Bobzien here modifies her own earlier view in Die stoische Modallogik (Würzburg: Königshausen und Neumann, 1986), 12 and 20. Both of her proposals reject Michael Frede's view: that statements persist in spite of what the Stoics have to say about the changes of truth-values (Die stoische Logik, 33–37). Note that we might distinguish between 'being truth-evaluable' and 'having a determinate truth-value.'

[32]On the point that metapiptonta always involve relative time-markers like "day," "night," and so on (as compared to specific dates like "09.16.2010"), cf. Frede, Die stoische Logik, 44, and Bobzien, "Stoic Logic," 21.

long as it is day, the statement "it is day" is true. At night, the statement "it is day" is false. The assertible "it is day," thus, is true or false, depending on whether it is stated during daytime *or* not. *Axiomata* have truth-values whether they are stated or not: at every given point, an assertible is either true or false, many of them having a stable truth-value (e.g., "human beings are living beings"), others switching back and forth (e.g., "it is day").[33] The Stoics do not take a diachronic perspective, according to which *metapiptonta* would be true *and* false (other than in the sense of, at one time being true and at another time being false). The claim that every *axioma* is either true *or* false views *axiomata* as stated at particular times. In this sense, the Stoics say that "*axiomata* are those things saying which we either speak true or speak false" (SE, M 8.73).[34]

In a sense, it suffices for present purposes to note that *axiomata* are the only bearers of truth-values. Even impressions, to which the Stoics do apply the truth-predicates, are merely derivatively true or false, depending on the statements that can be made of them. However, there are reasons to sketch some of the details of the Stoic theory. It helps emphasize the point that the Stoics take seriously the question of what *precisely* it is that is evaluated as true or false. They do not operate with a vague intuition, according to which one might think that, quite obviously, beliefs are the kinds of things that are true or false, simply because there is an everyday way of speaking along these lines. Rather, the Stoic conception of the bearers of truth-values is a technical one, and it involves the crucial claim that *axiomata* (and nothing else!) are true or false.[35] Where the Stoics envisage a derivative usage of the truth-predicates, namely with respect to impressions, they point this out, and they explain why the usage is merely derivative. Accordingly, it is implausible to suggest that they might recognize a derivative use of the truth-predicates for beliefs. If they were willing to do so, the sources should tell an analogous story to the one we have about impressions: the derivative usage should be mentioned and elucidated—but it is not.

[33]On timeless truths, cf. Barnes, *Truth, etc.*, 14–19.

[34]Barnes reformulates this point as follows: "Whenever it can be asserted that so-and-so, either it is true at that time that so-and-so or else it is false at that time that so-and-so" (*Truth, etc.*, 19).

[35]Barnes cites Cicero, according to whom "Chrysippus strains every sinew in order to persuade us that every assertible is either true or false" (*de fato* 10.21). Barnes emphasizes that, for the Stoics, this was not an obvious or self-evident claim. Rather, it was a claim that needed to be explored and defended (*Truth, etc.*, 1–4).

4. Truth and the True

The Stoic position, then, may appear to involve a strange separation between speech and mental states. A person may hold a belief, which, qua belief, is not characterized as true, and when uttering the belief, she makes a true statement. This seems thoroughly odd. Further, one might think that, in not characterizing beliefs as true and false, the Stoics have to make an unwelcome concession. If only *axiomata* are true, then pieces of knowledge cannot be characterized as true. Is not this a counterintuitive implication of the Stoic position, as I described it? The Stoics address these issues by drawing a distinction between truth and the true:

> The true (*to alēthes*) is said [by the Stoics] to differ from truth (*alētheia*) in three ways, in what it is (*ousia*), in its composition (*sustasis*), and in its capacity (*dunamis*). With respect to what it is, since what is true is incorporeal, for it is an *axioma* and a *lekton*; but truth is a body (for it is knowledge capable of stating everything true, and knowledge is the commanding-faculty in a certain state, just as a fist is the hand disposed in a certain way; and the commanding-faculty is a body, being a breath in their view). In composition, since what is true is something simple, e.g., "I am conversing," but truth consists of the knowledge of many truths. In its capacity, for truth belongs to knowledge, while the true does not do so at all. Hence they say that truth is only in a virtuous man, but the true is also in an inferior man; for the inferior man can say something true. (SE, PH 2.81–83 = LS 33P, tr. LS with changes)

The person without knowledge can utter a true statement. But her state of mind (or: the condition of her rational soul) is not that of the knower. The fact that her statement is true is thus, as it were, a coincidence: many of the subject's truth-claims are actually not true, though she thinks they are. In uttering any of her beliefs, she utters something that she takes to be true. Whether her statement is true or not does not, then, reflect an advantage that one state of mind would have over another state of mind. The speaker's state of mind is, in each case (whether the statement is true or false) that of a deficient truth-claim, a truth-claim in which the person takes something to be true that she does not know to be true. True statements are not the *possession* of truth. In order to 'possess' truth, one must know that what one takes to be true actually is true (and that is, any piece of knowledge must be part of a consistent body of knowledge, and in this sense firm and stable). Accordingly, only the knower possesses truth.

Truth in this sense, then, simply is a description of her state of mind: it is a description of the systematic body of knowledge that structures her mind.

Again, it is helpful to think about the Stoic position by drawing on Plato. It reflects the kind of position that figures in Plato's *Hippias Minor*. There Socrates argues that only the knower can lie. Those who hold mere beliefs, and thus are strictly speaking ignorant, cannot lie. To lie, on this account, is to utter a falsehood knowing that it is a falsehood.[36] In order to do this, one must know the truth. The upshot of this position is that only the knower can utter truths and falsehoods in an ambitious sense: for something to qualify as a truth in this sense, it must be recognized as a truth; for it to qualify as a falsehood in this sense, it must be recognized as a falsehood. Otherwise, the speaker, whether she intends to speak the truth or not, is in muddy waters: she might just as well speak the truth when she tries to lie. The Stoics aim to account for the relevant ambitious sense of truth by distinguishing between 'truths' (true assertions) on the one hand, and 'truth' on the other. Only a knower possesses truth. Someone who holds a belief, whether her corresponding statement happens to be true or not, does not possess any truth that belongs to the body of knowledge that is the truth.

The trouble with beliefs is that they are, as it were, blind. This is a Platonic expression.[37] One way to understand this claim is that beliefs are not transparent to the subject as mere beliefs. The subject makes a truth-claim, with the attitude of presumed knowledge. An unqualified truth-claim (that is, a truth-claim that is not bracketed by some clause like "as far as I can see," or "I'm assuming this," etc.) arguably implies that the person takes herself to be in the position to make this claim. In the terms of the ancient debates, this means that she takes herself to be a knower of the relevant claim. Many attitudes that we, today, might classify as beliefs (thereby using the notion in a wide sense), thus are not described as

---

[36]Barnes (*Truth, etc.*, 7–8) mentions that the relevant verbs, *alētheuein* and *pseudesthai*, literally mean 'to true-say' and 'to false-say.'

[37]In Book VI of the *Republic*, Socrates is asked for his beliefs about the good. He responds by asking Adeimantus whether he has not realized that beliefs without knowledge (*aneu epistēmēs doxai*) are ugly (*aischra*), shameful (*tuphla*), and crooked (*skolia*), and that even the best of them are blind (*tuphlon*) (506c). The expression "beliefs without knowledge," which I discussed in chapter 2, is alien to the Stoic framework: for the Stoics, there could be no beliefs with knowledge, and the notion of beliefs without knowledge also makes no sense.

beliefs. Any claim, for example, that comes with even a mild proviso—a qualifier that indicates that the subject merely assumes that this is how things are, or considers it possible to revise her view in the light of further evidence, and so on—does not count as a belief. Instead, it would count as an assumption, or a hypothesis, or something of that kind. In belief, the subject does not take herself to hold 'merely' a belief. According to her self-perception, she is in a position to make an unqualified truth-claim. Thus beliefs are blind in the sense that they are instances of self-deception. They are ignorance in a Socratic sense: presumed knowledge. All beliefs are, from the point of view of the cognizer, true: they are truth-claims. The subject would not believe what she believes if she did not consider it true. From the point of view of the subject, then, it is impossible to hold a false belief. To believe something and at the same time believe that it is false is incoherent; arguably, this is simply not something one can do. That is, from the point of view of the subject, beliefs are non-transparent with regard to their truth and falsity; only the knower is in a position to claim that what she asserts as true actually is true.

But what about the problem that, though the knower knows her assertions to be true, knowledge itself is not adequately characterized as true? The Stoic position could be rephrased in Parmenidean terms: truth and knowledge *belong together*. That is, to have knowledge is to be in possession of truth.[38] But since knowledge is unerring (as Plato rephrases the Parmenidean point in the *Theaetetus*), knowledge is indeed not adequately *evaluated* as true. Knowledge is, qua knowledge, *of* the truth. But pieces of knowledge are not bearers of a truth-value. For that to be the case, there would have to be false pieces of knowledge, and there are not. Something can only be a bearer of a truth-value if it can be true *or* false. Accordingly, it is plausible that knowledge cannot be evaluated as true.

5. An Application: Emotions Are Beliefs

Now, someone might object that my reinterpretation of Stoic epistemology amounts to no more than a kind of 'policing' of the language. Why not say, in some loose sense, that Stoic beliefs are true or false? In order to show that this is not an adequate response, I shall briefly sketch how

---

[38]Cf. chapter 3 on the *Theaetetus*.

drastically one must reinterpret Stoic theory of the emotions if one agrees with my claims about Stoic beliefs.

As is well known, the Stoics claim that the wise (knowledgeable, virtuous) person has no emotions (*pathē*). Instead, she has rational feelings (*eupatheia*) (DL 7.116).[39] This idea has received much attention, even outside of the circles of ancient philosophy scholarship. Its discovery in the 1990s coincided with a contemporary interest in the view that emotions are (or crucially involve) judgments; the Stoics were cast as early proponents of a view of that kind. The accounts of Stoic theory that figure in these discussions, however, are seriously misleading. They are misleading because the fundamental point that, for the Stoics, there are no false beliefs, was not recognized. Martha Nussbaum's discussions were particularly influential, and they can serve as an example: Nussbaum says that the Stoic wise person has no emotions insofar she has no *false beliefs*.[40] However, the Stoic wise person has no emotions insofar she has no *beliefs*. Consider two passages that contain core ideas.

In the case of all the soul's emotions, when they [the Stoics] call them beliefs (*doxai*), 'belief' is used in the sense of (*anti*) 'weak supposition,' and 'fresh' in the sense of 'the stimulus of an irrational contraction or swelling.' (Stobaeus 2.88,22–89,3 = LS 65C = SVF 3.378, part; tr. LS with changes)

Pain is an irrational contraction, or a fresh belief (*doxa prosphatos*) that something bad is present, at which people think it right to be contracted [i.e. depressed]. Fear is an irrational aversion, or avoidance of an expected danger. Appetite is an irrational desire, or pursuit of an expected good. Pleasure is an irrational swelling, or a fresh belief that something good is present, at which people think it right to be swollen [i.e. elated]. (Andronicus, *De passionibus* I = LS 65B = SVF 3.391, part; tr. LS with changes)

---

[39]Emotions are defined as excessive impulses, that is, as impulses that lead up to irrational actions (Stobaeus 2.88, 8–22 = LS 65A = SVF 3.378). There are two ways in which one can explain why the wise person has no emotions: because emotions are beliefs, and because emotions are excessive impulses.

[40]Martha Nussbaum, "Extirpation of the Passions," 366: "Among the most notorious and paradoxical theses in the history of philosophy is Chrysippus' thesis that the passions are forms of *false* judgment or *false* belief" (my emphasis). I present a detailed version of my interpretation in Vogt, "Die stoische Theorie der Emotionen," in Barbara Guckes (ed.), *Zur Ethik der älteren Stoa* (Göttingen: Vandenhoeck & Ruprecht, 2004), 69–93.

Emotions, then, are said to be beliefs, not false beliefs. They are beliefs in the sense that they are *weak suppositions*. As we saw, *all* beliefs are weak assents. That is, though many emotions are likely to be assents to false and to noncognitive impressions, emotions can also be assents to true and to cognitive impressions. Consider as an example an emotion that traditional interpretations cannot explain. Suppose I am grieving because I realize that I am not virtuous. For a moment, I see things clearly: virtue is the only good; I am not virtuous; this is misery. These impressions are *true*, and since I see things clearly, *cognitive*. However, they throw me into an irrational, emotional state. I am in grief about my misery. The assents I give to these true and cognitive impressions are beliefs. Not being wise, I cannot assent with the stability and firmness of the knower.[41]

This becomes evident when, a week later, I recover from my grief. Not being wise, I tend to default to the typical views of a fool: health, wealth, and so on, seem good to me; I forget the momentary insight that virtue is the only good. Last week's judgments were merely beliefs, and as such they are not stable. However, I do not recover from my grief at the very moment I recall my old views, according to which I'm quite well off because I'm healthy, have a job, and so on. Emotions have—because judgments are movements of the mind—a kind of physiological inertia. I shall not instantly feel better. Last week's beliefs were, in the technical terms of the Stoics, *fresh* beliefs. At the moment of judgment, the mind was stirred up. Such a state of mind cannot be wiped out in an instant. The Stoics explain this through the image of someone who runs.[42] If the runner were to think "now I'll stop," she would still need to make a couple of steps— she cannot come to a halt instantaneously. This is how emotions work:

---

[41]My claim that an emotion could be assent to the cognitive impression that something good is lacking, implies that emotions and their rational replacements do not engage exclusively with preferred and dispreferred indifferents (wealth, health, etc.), but also with the good and bad. The misleading reconstruction, according to which emotions always involve acceptance of a false impression, may imply that, in every emotion, something that is not genuinely good or bad is judged to be good or bad (cf. Nussbaum, "Extirpation of the Passions," 399). Though many examples are of this kind (say, money is judged to be good), not all are (cf. Andronikos, *De passionibus* 6.1–4 = SVF 3.432). In a sense, it is clear that another set of examples is crucial to Stoic theory. The wise person's rational feelings must engage with the good (say, in well-wishing, the wise person certainly hopes for something that is genuinely good for others). If there is to be progression toward wisdom, the emotions of progressors must also engage with the genuinely good and bad.

[42]Galen, *On Hippocrates' and Plato's doctrines* 4.2.10–18 = SVF 3.462, part = LS 65J.

though one might have changed one's mind, they still need some time to 'fade out.'

The Stoics also consider the opposite phenomenon: suppose someone grieves for the death of her child. This person is not likely to change her mind any time soon. The premature death of her child seems terrible to her. And yet the grief eventually wears off, or comes to have a less acutely painful quality.[43] Again, this is because emotions are *fresh* beliefs. The pain is generated at the moment when the belief is formed. While the belief persists, the movement in the agent's mind comes from the *formation* of the belief, not from the fact that the belief persists; accordingly, the emotion eventually loses intensity.

Emotions, then, are weak assents and fresh beliefs. That is, insofar as they are a particular kind of belief, this reflects a *temporal gap* between beliefs-revision and alteration of emotions. But in no way is it suggested that emotions are false beliefs. Otherwise, there could be no grief in seeing how bad it is not to be virtuous. Though many emotions involve assents to false and noncognitive impressions, this is not a necessary feature of emotion. In particular, the kind of back and forth I sketched, between the realization of the importance of virtue, and lapsing back into one's old ways, is integral to how the Stoics imagine the path toward virtue. Certainly, their theory should be able to account for it.[44]

6. Conclusion

The Stoics are quite unambiguous about the claim that beliefs are not bearers of truth-values. As I tried to show, getting clear about this aspect of Stoic philosophy affects how we reconstruct other Stoic theories. Most immediately, however, it helps us understand that Stoic philosophy

---

[43]Chrysippus discusses the case where one's judgment is not altered, but the pain still wears off, in his second book *On the emotions*: "On the lessening of pain, the question might be asked as to how it occurs, whether because a particular belief is altered, or with them all persisting". Chrysippus favors the second answer: "I think that this kind of belief does persist—that what is actually present is something bad—but as it grows older the contraction [. . .] lessen(s)." (Galen, *De plac. Hippocr. et Plat.* 4.7.12–17 = LS 65O).

[44]For example, one might think that many of Seneca's *Letters* exemplify the emotional struggle of someone who tries to make progress toward virtue, but constantly falls back into old ways, concerning herself with money, reputation, health, and so on.

contains a conception of belief that is rather different from our conception of belief. Though this conception might initially appear alien, it is not clear to me that, in the end, it is implausible. The Stoics' division of labor between logic and philosophy of language on the one hand—the fields that analyze the bearers of truth-values—and normative epistemology on the other hand—the field that formulates norms for engaging with impressions—seems compelling. The claim that beliefs are not bearers of truth-values reflects the equally basic point that pieces of knowledge are not bearers of truth-values. If knowledge is 'unerring,' it is *associated* with truth. It is misleading to evaluate particular bits of knowledge as true. This would suggest that knowledge could also be false. The truth-values, it seems, are quite adequately assigned to something else, namely the Stoic cousin of today's propositions: *axiomata*.

8

Concluding Remarks: Skepticism and Relativism

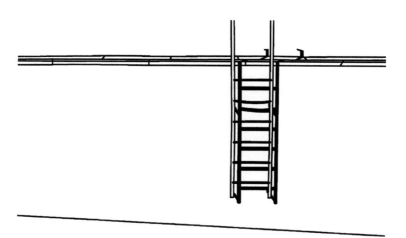

I began this book by saying that the skepticism I'm interested in is not one that asks whether I know you are not a zombie. It is a skepticism that, if you were a zombie, would ask you how things look to you. It is a skepticism that considers it quite likely that the world looks different to zombies and that is unwilling to say that zombies, if there were any, would be in a better or worse position than human cognizers to say how things are.

Indeed, the thought experiment that there might be zombies could just be added to the many options that the Ten Tropes of Aenesidemus envisage. Just as the skeptic does not privilege waking over sleeping, being healthy over being deranged, humans over pigs, or gods over humans, the existence of zombies with their viewpoint—whatever that might be— would be yet another reason for the skeptic to hold back from judging that the world is as it looks to her.

This kind of skepticism has metaphysical and epistemological roots. It inherits concerns from a long-standing metaphysical tradition in Greek thought, where questions are raised about the status of appearances, the world of change, and perceptual properties. It inherits another set of questions from the Sophists and Socrates: it is difficult and yet greatly important to get clear about questions that matter to the way one leads one's life. Skepticism aims to avoid beliefs because beliefs fall short of knowledge. In holding a belief, one holds something to be true without knowing that it is true, and thus one holds something to be true that, for all one knows, might be false. Beliefs, accordingly, do not reach the truth in the sense that is relevant for the cognizer: in holding beliefs, the cognizer is not in possession of truths. And this raises the normative question of whether one should hold beliefs at all—if not, a cognizer might be left with nothing but how things appear to her. This is how I see the ancestry and motivation of Pyrrhonian skepticism, the kind of skepticism I aimed to explore (and that, for short, I largely just referred to as skepticism). It combines metaphysical concerns about conflicting appearances and Socratic concerns about belief, knowledge, and truth. It is a philosophy that can be arrived at by reading and thinking about Plato.

The chapters in this book have mapped out core ingredients of the mix of philosophical ideas relevant to Pyrrhonism: a Socratic emphasis on the importance of questions concerning the leading of one's life (chapter 1); a Platonic discussion of the metaphysical domain of belief as envisaged in the *Republic* (chapter 2); a Socratic-Stoic reading of the *Theaetetus*, according to which beliefs do not reach the truth (chapter 3); an analysis of skeptical responses to the relativism of the *Theaetetus* (chapter 4); discussion of how skeptical investigation aims at the truth (chapter 5); a defense of the skeptic's ability to think without thereby forming beliefs (chapter 6); and a reconstruction of the Stoic view that beliefs are never true (chapter 7).

On the proposed reading, Pyrrhonian skepticism is a cousin of relativism as construed in Plato's *Theaetetus*. It reflects not just on whether one of several interlocutors gets the answer to a given question right. It also reflects on the unsettling fact that interlocutors seem to speak from the point of view of the people they are: healthy or sick people, Egyptians or Greeks, and so on. And it reflects on philosophical worries about whether there is such a thing as 'how things are'—whether, say, perceptual or evaluative properties are real features of the world. Sextus's skeptics hold back from responding to these questions. They are not going to say that one cannot find out how things are because there is no such thing as how things are. That there is no such thing as how things are appears to them to be yet another contestable claim.

Plato's dialogues are an inspiration for skeptics of that sort. For indeed, it might seem as if Plato wanted—at least at times, or in certain contexts—to grant something to the relativist. In the *Apology*, Socrates insists on a human perspective, invoking the idea that, qua humans, we shall think *human thoughts*. This is a weighty insight and it calls for a rather complicated response. One should recognize that ours is one particular perspective. To aim to say things that, from within this perspective, are inherently inaccessible—say, the question of what death is—is philosophically wrongheaded. The recognition that one inhabits a perspective that comes with such limitations may provide some reason to aim to supersede it. A number of famous passages in Plato—say, the ascent from the cave in the *Republic*—speak to the idea that one should turn one's soul away from those things with which human beings tend to be concerned and turn instead toward intelligible entities. And yet in dialogues as late as the *Philebus*, there is also the idea that, when we ask questions about the good, we want to know about the human good. It is genuinely worthwhile to find out how *we*, within the confines of our kind of life, can lead a good life. Socrates' exemplary human wisdom stands for the aim of inhabiting a human perspective in a self-conscious way.

Compare this to Protagoras's claim, discussed in the *Theaetetus*, that "man is the measure." 'Man' can be taken to have various scopes. It can refer to human beings as opposed to other kinds of beings, groups of human beings such as cultures, and individual human beings, as well as individual beings in given states, locations, conditions, and so on. Aenesidemus's tropes mirror these distinctions. They begin with a mode of argument that considers human beings and their access to the world in comparison to other animals. The question of how a dog might engage with the world is pursued in some detail, presumably because dogs are considered worthless—and still, or so it is argued, one cannot show that the way things appear to humans is more credible than the way they appear to dogs (PH 1.63–78). The rest of the Ten Modes continue to develop similar lines of thought. As a human cognizer, one inhabits a whole range of perspectives: that of a human being, of a member of a given society, of an individual person, and of a person in a given state at a given time.

Moreover, there are not only differences within and between cognizers. There might also be change or indeterminacy in that which appears. There are, thus, three modes of argument that, in the most general way, sum up the approach of Aenesidemus's skeptic: modes of argument that are based on *who judges* things, on *what is judged*, and on a *combination* of both (PH 1.38). Accordingly, one should be aware of a multitude of ways the world might appear. What seems to be the case to others, or to herself in other states and conditions, carries weight with the skeptic, so much so that she distances herself from what would otherwise be her judgment of what is, but is, in Sextus's vocabulary, merely 'what appears to her now' (PH 1.4).

Against this line of thought, one might insist that conflicting appearances, as they figure in the lives of agents in particular contexts, conditions, and so on, are not on a par. One might argue that things appear in a more trustworthy way, say, when one is healthy rather than sick, or awake rather than asleep, or when certain viewing conditions are in place, and so on. Accordingly, it might seem that one should aim to be in what are, presumably, better conditions. Protagoras, as resurrected by Socrates in the *Theaetetus*, pursues this line of thought. He defends his Measure Doctrine against the charge that it calls into question the profession of teaching. If all appearances are on a par, why would anyone need a teacher, and what would it be that a teacher can offer? Protagoras bites the bullet: as a doctor produces a change through drugs, so does the Sophist through words; this does *not* involve that he brings anyone who holds false beliefs to hold true beliefs (167a4–7). It involves bringing people to hold 'better' beliefs. It is not possible for a given cognizer to believe differently from how things are for her (167a7–b1). Things appear to a cognizer in a way that reflects the condition she is in; thus this *condition* is what a Protagorean teacher addresses.

Part of this point, I take it, is a Platonic insight about belief: if a cognizer is going to form a belief, she will hold something to be true that seems to her to be the case. This is what it is to form a belief. For example, I cannot form the belief that what I'm looking at on my computer screen while I'm adjusting the colors of an image has a magenta tint when in fact it looks bluish to me. I can withhold judgment on whether there *is* too much magenta, using some of the skeptic's modes of argument; but I cannot judge it to be otherwise than it seems to me to be.

Suppose now that I want to improve my situation. Suppose I take great care to color-calibrate the screen and learn everything I can about color management. Suppose I remove any artificial light sources that alter my perception of the color temperature of the screen. I draw the blinds so that the sun doesn't distract me or affect my vision while I'm looking at the image. Do I do all this to find out what the image *really* looks like? A skeptic would push back and say it only amounts to norms relative to a contingent standard: for example, I want the print generated from the digital file to look a certain way to human cognizers in viewing conditions that are typical for images that are displayed on walls. Suppose I am aiming at a photographic print that draws much of its impact from subtle color shades, with some areas that I want to be displayed in neutral grey, areas that I think would look garish if they had a color tint.

Admittedly, this is a complicated example, involving screens, printers, and so on. But it helps to highlight the skeptic's instinct: it is very well possible to consider certain viewing conditions 'better'—but only relative to a contingent standard that reflects my given aims. In the example, the point is not to aim for neutral grey as if there were a 'real' grey; this is similar to the way in which there is no point in aiming to settle whether the dog or the pig sees colors as they *really* are.

Contrary to the skeptic, a certain kind of relativist buys into Protagoras's idea that there are better conditions to be in. She might expect that, with the blinds down, and so on, she has better viewing conditions. And she might expect that then things will strike her in an improved way. When she now forms the belief that things are as they seem to her, she takes herself to have the 'better' belief. Recall Protagoras's analogy between doctor and teacher. The doctor does not aim to change how things taste to the sick person; rather, he aims to cure her, and as a consequence, things shall no longer taste bitter (166e–167d). A teacher's task is similar. In another comparison, a teacher is like a gardener who waters plants (167b–c). He can put the students in a condition in which he expects they will flourish. The students, in a changed condition, will come to think different thoughts. Things will now appear to them in another way. Protagoras proposes that there are harmful and beneficial conditions to be in, which come with views that are akin to them (167b). Thus there are better and worse ways for things to appear, and there are wiser and less wise people, but no one ever has a false belief (167d). The skeptic, I take it, does not buy into this suggestion. Who is to judge which condition is better? And what does it mean that some beliefs are better than others without this translating into a claim about some beliefs being false and others true?

Both parties to the dispute could point to features of Plato's dialogues. The relativist might point out that Plato seems to take quite seriously the idea that 'souls' must be brought into improved conditions—with the right affective attitudes and so on—for people to acquire the views that Plato thinks they should acquire.[1] The skeptic might point to the very structure of the dialogues, where different responses to philosophical questions are under scrutiny. In the terms of the skeptics, there is disagreement. To some extent, suspension of judgment follows because we cannot decide between the arguments for one position and against different positions. But more than that, arguments are not laid out simply as arguments; they are put forward as the arguments of particular people who occupy particular points of view.

As a skeptic reader might put this, in engaging with the arguments for and against philosophical proposals in Plato's dialogues, one engages with how things appear to particular thinkers. Arguments are formulated by interlocutors who come from Elea or Athens, who have studied with particular teachers, have allegiances and loyalties, and so on. The very way in which people tend to say things reflects who they are and what they love. As in the *Sophist*, some may be 'friends of the Forms' and some 'sons of the earth'—some love to think about lofty entities and some love to think about physical 'stuff.' In responding to their conversations, the skeptic is prone to note that things appear differently to different people, depending on their constitutions, likes and dislikes, and so on.

These kinds of phenomena give pause to the skeptic. She finds it hard to privilege someone's perspective over someone else's, even if one of these perspectives may appear *prima facie* absurd to her. Consider the case of Ion from Plato's *Ion*. He thinks that the world revolves around Homer and that, qua expert reciter of Homer, he is going to have some-

---

[1] In the *Republic*, for example, education is envisaged as a turning around of the soul, and as an instilling of affective dispositions. In a short and simplified fashion, one might say that, for a cognizer to come to see things as she should, she must love the good. Cf. Burnyeat's influential discussions in his "Culture and Society" and "Why Mathematics Is Good."

thing to say on everything, chariots and wars and so on. If Ion were to recommend one military strategy, and a general were to recommend another strategy, any person in her right mind would prefer the general's advice. At least, this is what Protagoras would argue, as would Plato: there are better positions to be in for judging things.

The skeptic, by contrast, would recognize that people tend to make certain statements, given who they are and how they think of themselves. The skeptic is not going to adopt a presumably obvious criterion, according to which Ion is an unqualified rhapsode, while generals know about wars. Instead, the skeptic is unsettled by the ways in which perspectives (self-images, professions, locations, etc.) shape what people say. Accordingly, she will wonder whether someone who thought very seriously about Homer's *Iliad* and *Odyssey*—the pretexts for wars, the trauma of battle, the difficulty of returning to life at home—might actually be better at deciding whether one should go to war than a general. That is, just as for Ion everything is contained in Homer, so for generals everything might call for a warlike response. And thus it is not impossible that what appears to an expert in Homeric poetry is to be set against what appears to the general, in such a way that it becomes an open question who is right.

The Pyrrhonian skeptics hold back from forming beliefs due to Socratic caution, *and* they appreciate phenomena of disagreement as unsettling. With these two lines of thought combined, full-blown relativism appears greatly unreasonable. How can anyone who appreciates Socratic worries simply hold on to a truth-claim when others have conflicting views? Socratic caution is inspired by the recognition that our beliefs inform our actions. It is important to us not to mess up our lives, and therefore it must be important to us to think carefully about questions that are relevant to the leading of one's life. The relativist simply assumes that what appears to her is true. From the point of view of Socratic epistemology, this appears crazy: why risk being committed to beliefs that will lead one into misery? The Socratic side of skepticism saves skepticism from relativism.

Relativism assumes that, when we disagree, we hold on to our views— and that appears, to the skeptic, irrational. One should be unsettled if one sees that others disagree. If one does not want to be like Euthyphro, one is going to allow for the possibility that one might be wrong, and one will find it reasonable to rethink one's views in the face of opposition from other cognizers. And yet relativism seems to get something right.

Thoughts are thoughts of particular cognizers, not just thoughts 'simpliciter.' The relativist saves the skeptic from being narrowly concerned with epistemic matters. Relativism, as conceived in Plato's *Theaetetus* and ascribed to Protagoras, engages with a wide range of questions about what the world must be like to accommodate conflicting appearances. Pyrrhonian skepticism, while not—or not in Sextus's incarnation—itself a metaphysical enterprise, is informed by the subtleties of these discussions.

There is no conclusion for a book on these matters. As in the investigations of the Pyrrhonian skeptic, or indeed, as in Plato's dialogues, the next puzzle is sure to be around the corner. More questions will arise and more arguments will need to be explored. I hope to have made the case, however, that belief is a risky endeavor, because belief's relationship to truth is problematic. The skeptics might be right, therefore, in suggesting that any careful cognizer would opt instead for investigative attitudes that fall short of truth-claims.[2]

---

[2]My concluding remarks began with a drawing by Jens Haas that is also on the cover, of an empty swimming pool in the sun. During much of the time that I worked on the manuscript, I knew that I wanted to use the drawing: though there is no water, and thus presumably no way in which things could look different from what they are—no bent sticks submerged in water and so on—the very fact that the pool is empty, thus being in a condition that one may find surprising, makes for a perplexing impression. The shadows add to the effect. This is the kind of example that Aenesidemus might have proudly included in his Ten Tropes, had he had the drawing. I am grateful for Jens's willingness to let me use it.

Bibliography

Abbreviations are used throughout to cite the following works:

DK   H. Diehls and W. Kranz, *Die Fragmente der Vorsokratiker*
DL   Diogenes Laertius, *Lives of the Eminent Philosophers*
FDS   Karlheinz Hülser. *Die Fragmente zur Dialektik der Stoiker: Neue Sammlung der Texte mit Übersetzung und Kommentar*
LS   A. A. Long and D. N. Sedley, *The Hellenistic Philosophers*
SE, M   Sextus Empiricus, *Against the Mathematicians*
SE, PH   Sextus Empiricus, *Outlines of Scepticism*
SVF   Johannes von Arnim, *Stoicorum Veterum Fragmenta*

Primary Sources

Aristotle. *The Complete Works of Aristotle*. Ed. Jonathan Barnes. 2 vols. Princeton, N.J.: Princeton University Press, 1984.

———. *Nicomachean Ethics*. Translation with historical introduction by Christopher Rowe. Philosophical introduction and commentary by Sarah Broadie. Oxford: Oxford University Press, 2002.

———. *The Works of Aristotle*. Ed. Sir David Ross. The Oxford Aristotle. 12 vols. Oxford: Oxford University Press, 1908–52.

Cicero. *On Academic Scepticism*. Translated with introduction and notes by Charles Brittain. Indianapolis: Hackett, 2006.

———. *Tusculan Disputations*. With an English translation by G. E. King. Cambridge, Mass.: Harvard University Press, 1945.

Diogenes Laertius. *Lives of the Eminent Philosophers*. Translated by R. D. Hicks. Vols. 1 and 2. Loeb Classical Library. Cambridge, Mass.: Harvard University Press, 1991 [DL].

Herodotus. *Histories*. Translated by Aubrey de Sélincourt. Revised with introductory matter and notes by John Marincola. London: Penguin, 1996.

Homer. *Odyssey*. Translated with an introduction by Richard Lattimore. New York: HarperCollins, 1999.

Hume, David. *Enquiry concerning Human Understanding*. Oxford: Oxford University Press, 1999.

Plato. *Apology*. With an introduction, translation, and commentary by Michael C. Stokes. Warminster: Aris & Phillips, 1997.

——. *Complete Works*. Ed. John M. Cooper. Indianapolis: Hackett, 1997.

——. *Meno and Phaedo*. Edited with introduction and translation by David Sedley and Alex Long. Cambridge: Cambridge University Press, 2011.

——. *Philebos. Platon Werke*. Vol. 3.2. Translation and commentary by Dorothea Frede. Göttingen: Vandenhoeck und Ruprecht, 1997.

——. *Plato's Republic*. Edited by Lewis Campbell and Benjamin Jowett. Vol. 3. New York: Garland, 1987.

——. *Republic*. Translation and commentary by Desmond Lee. New York: Penguin, 1974.

——. *Republic*. Translation by G. M. A. Grube. Revision by C. D. C. Reeve. Indianapolis: Hackett, 1992.

——. *The Republic of Plato*. Translated with introduction and notes by Francis MacDonald Cornford. London: Oxford University Press, 1945.

——. *Theaetetus*. Translated with notes by John McDowell. Oxford: Clarendon Press, 1973.

——. *The Theaetetus of Plato*. Introduction and revision of M. J. Levett's translation by Myles F. Burnyeat. Indianapolis: Hackett, 1990.

——. *Werke in Acht Bänden, Griechisch und Deutsch*. Vol. 6: *Theaitetos, Der Sophist, Der Staatsmann*. German translation by Friedrich Schleiermacher. Revised by Peter Staudacher. Darmstadt: Wissenschaftliche Buchgesellschaft, 1990.

Seneca. *Selected Philosophical Letters*. Translated with an introduction and commentary by Brad Inwood. New York: Oxford University Press, 2007.

Sextus Empiricus. *Sextus Empiricus*. Translated by R. G. Bury [SE]. Vol. 1 [PH 1–3] (1933); vol. 2 [M 7, 8] (1935); vol. 3 [M 9–11] (1936); vol. 4 [M 1–6] (1949). Loeb Classical Library. Cambridge, Mass.: Harvard University Press, 1933–49.

——. *Grundriss der pyrrhonischen Skepsis*. Introduction and translation by M. Hossenfelder. Frankfurt am Main: Suhrkamp, 1985.

——. *Against the Ethicists*. Translated with an introduction by Richard Bett. Oxford: Clarendon Press, 2000. First published 1997. Citations are to the 2000 edition.

——. *Outlines of Scepticism*. Translated by Julia Annas and Jonathan Barnes. Cambridge: Cambridge University Press, 1994.

——. *The Sceptic Way: Sextus Empiricus's Outlines of Pyrrhonism*. Translated with introduction and commentary by Benson Mates. New York: Oxford University Press, 1996.

Stobaeus. *Ioannis Stobaei Anthologii*. Books 1 and 2. Edited by C. Wachsmuth. Berlin: Weidmann, 1884. Books 3 and 4. Edited by O Hense. Berlin: Weidmann, 1894–1909.

Collections of Fragments

Diehls, H., and W. Kranz. *Die Fragmente der Vorsokratiker.* Zurich: Weidmann, 1952 [DK].

Hülser, Karlheinz. *Die Fragmente zur Dialektik der Stoiker: Neue Sammlung der Texte mit Übersetzung und Kommentar.* Vols. 1–3 (1987); vol. 4 (1988). Stuttgart: Metzler, 1987–88 [FDS].

Long, A. A., and D. N. Sedley. *The Hellenistic Philosophers.* Vol. 1. *Translations of the Principal Sources, with a Philosophical Commentary.* Vol. 2. *Greek and Latin Texts with Notes and Bibliography.* Cambridge: Cambridge University Press, 1992 [LS].

Kirk, G. S., J. E. Raven, and M. Schofield. *Presocratic Philosophers: A Critical History with a Selection of Texts.* Cambridge: Cambridge University Press, 1983.

von Arnim, Johannes. *Stoicorum Veterum Fragmenta.* Vols. 1–4. Leipzig: Teubner, 1903–24 [SVF].

Secondary Literature

Adalier, Gokhan. "The Case of 'Theaetetus.'" *Phronesis* 46 (2001): 1–37.

Algra, K., J. Barnes, J. Mansfeld, and M. Schofield (eds.). *The Cambridge History of Hellenistic Philosophy.* Cambridge: Cambridge University Press, 1999.

Alesse, Francesca. *La Stoa e la Tradizione Socratica.* Naples: Bibliopolis, 2000.

Annas, Julia. *An Introduction to Plato's Republic.* Oxford: Clarendon, 1981.

———. *The Morality of Happiness.* New York: Oxford University Press, 1993.

———. "Plato the Skeptic." In Paul A. Vander Waerdt (ed.), *The Socratic Movement,* 309–40. Ithaca: Cornell University Press, 1994.

Annas, Julia, and Jonathan Barnes. *The Modes of Scepticism.* Cambridge: Cambridge University Press, 1985.

Barnes, Jonathan. "The Beliefs of a Pyrrhonist." *Proceedings of the Cambridge Philological Society* 28 (1982): 1–29. Reprinted in Myles Burnyeat and Michael Frede (eds.), *The Original Sceptics: A Controversy,* 58–91. Indianapolis: Hackett, 1997.

———. *The Toils of Scepticism.* Cambridge: Cambridge University Press, 1990.

———. *Truth, etc.: Six Lectures on Ancient Logic.* Oxford: Oxford University Press, 2007.

Barney, Rachel. "Impressions and Appearances." *Phronesis* 37 (1992): 283–313.

———. "Plato on the Desire for the Good." In Sergio Tenenbaum (ed.), *Desire, Good, and Practical Reason,* 34–64. Oxford: Oxford University Press, 2010.

———. "The Sophistic Movement." In Marie Louise Gill and Pierre Pellegrin (eds.), *A Companion to Ancient Philosophy,* 77–100. Malden, Mass.: Blackwell, 2006.

Benson, Hugh H. "Socratic Method." In Donald Morrison (ed.), *Cambridge Companion to Socrates,* 179–200. Cambridge: Cambridge University Press, 2011.

194   Bibliography

Benson, Hugh H. *Socratic Wisdom. The Model of Knowledge in Plato's Early Dialogues.* Oxford: Oxford University Press, 2000.

Berryman, Sylvia. "Democritus." First published 2004, substantive revision 2010.
In Edward N. Zalta (ed.), *Stanford Encyclopedia of Philosophy.* http://plato.
stanford.edu/entries/democritus/.

Bett, Richard. "The Sophists and Relativism." *Phronesis* 34.1 (1989): 139–69.

——. "Is There a Sophistic Ethics?" *Ancient Philosophy* 22 (2002): 235–62.

——. *Pyrrho, His Antecedents, and His Legacy.* Oxford: Oxford University Press,
2000.

——. "Scepticism and Ethics." In Richard Bett (ed.), *The Cambridge Companion
to Ancient Scepticism,* 181–94. Cambridge: Cambridge University Press,
2010.

——. "Socratic Ignorance." In Donald Morrison, *Cambridge Companion to Socrates,* 215–36. Cambridge: Cambridge University Press, 2011.

Bobzien, Susanne. "Stoic Logic." In Brad Inwood (ed.), *The Cambridge Companion
to the Stoics,* 85–123. Cambridge: Cambridge University Press, 2003

——. *Die stoische Modallogik.* Würzburg: Königshausen und Neumann, 1986.

Brickhouse, Thomas C., and Nicholas D. Smith. *The Philosophy of Socrates.* Boulder, Colo.: Westview Press, 2000.

——. *Plato's Socrates.* Oxford: Oxford University Press, 1994.

——. *Socrates on Trial.* Oxford: Oxford University Press, 1990.

——. *Socratic Moral Psychology.* Cambridge: Cambridge University Press, 2010.

Brunschwig, Jacques. "La formule *hoson epi tō logō* chez Sextus Empiricus." In
Brunschwig, *Études sur les philosophies Hellénistiques,* 321–41. Paris: Presses
Universitaires de France, 1995.

——. "Sextus Empiricus on the κριτήριον: The Sceptic as Conceptual Legatee." In
Brunschwig, *Papers in Hellenistic Philosophy,* translated by Janet Lloyd, 230–
43. Cambridge: Cambridge University Press, 1994.

——. "The Stoic Theory of the Supreme Genus and Platonic Ontology." In
Brunschwig, *Papers in Hellenistic Philosophy,* translated by Janet Lloyd,
92–157. Cambridge: Cambridge University Press, 1994. Originally published
as "La théorie stoicienne du genre supreme et l'ontologie platonicienne." In
Jonathan Barnes and M. Mignucci (eds.), *Matter and Metaphysics: Fourth
Symposium Hellenisticum,* 19–127. Napoli: Bibliopolis, 1988.

Burnyeat, Myles. "Culture and Society in Plato's Republic." *The Tanner Lectures on
Human Values* 20. Salt Lake City: University of Utah Press, 1999.

——. "The Impiety of Socrates." *Ancient Philosophy* 17 (1997): 1–12.

——. "Plato on Why Mathematics Is Good for the Soul." In Timothy Smiley (ed.),
Mathematics and Necessity. Essays in the History of Philosophy, 1–81. Oxford:
Oxford University Press, published for The British Academy, 2000.

——. "Socratic Midwifery, Platonic Inspiration." *Bulletin of the Institute of Classical Studies* 24 (1977): 7–16.

Burnyeat, Myles F., and Jonathan Barnes. "Socrates and the Jury: Paradoxes in Plato's Distinction between Knowledge and True Belief." *Proceedings of the Aristotelian Society*, supplementary volume 54 (1980): 173–91 and 193–206.

Burnyeat, Myles, and Michael Frede (eds.). *The Original Sceptics: A Controversy*. Indianapolis: Hackett, 1997.

Castagnoli, Luca. "Self-Bracketing Pyrrhonism." *Oxford Studies in Ancient Philosophy* 18 (2000): 263–328.

Cooper, John M. "Arcesilaus: Socratic and Sceptic." In V. Karasmanis (ed.), *Year of Socrates 2001—Proceedings*, 81–103. Athens: European Cultural Center of Delphi, 2004. Reprinted in Cooper, *Knowledge, Nature, and the Good: Essays on Ancient Philosophy*. Princeton, N.J.: Princeton University Press, 2004.

Cornford, Francis M. *Plato's Theory of Knowledge*. London: K. Paul, Trench, Trubner, 1933.

Corti, Lorenzo. *Scepticisme et Langage*. Paris: Vrin, 2009.

Couissin, P. "Le stoicisme de la nouvelle Académie." *Revue d'histoire de la Philosophie* 3 (1929) : 241–76. Translation and reprint in Myles Burnyeat (ed.), *The Sceptical Tradition*, 31–63. Berkeley: University of California Press, 1983.

Davidson, J. E., and C. L. Downing. "Contemporary Models of Intelligence." In R. J. Sternberg, *Handbook of Intelligence*, 34–49. New York: Cambridge University Press, 2000.

Dillon, John. *The Heirs of Plato: A Study of the Old Academy (347–274 BC)*. Oxford: Oxford University Press, 2003.

Doyle, James. "The Socratic Elenchus: No Problem." In Jonathan Lear and Alex Oliver (eds.), *The Force of Argument: Essays in Honour of Timothy Smiley*, 68–81. New York: Routledge, 2010.

———. "Socratic Methods." Forthcoming in *Oxford Studies in Ancient Philosophy*.

Ebert, Theodor. *Meinung und Wissen in der Philosophie Platons*. Berlin: Walter de Gruyter, 1974.

Engel, Pascal. "Truth and the Aim of Belief." In D. Gillies (ed.), *Laws and Models in Science*, 77–79. London: King's College, 2005.

Fine, Gail. "Does Socrates Claim to Know That He Knows Nothing?" *Oxford Studies in Ancient Philosophy* 35 (2008): 49–88.

———. "False Belief in the *Theaetetus*." *Phronesis* 24 (1979): 70–80.

———. "Knowledge and Belief in Republic V." *Archiv für Geschichte der Philosophie* 1978, 121–39.

———. "Knowledge and Belief in Republic V–VII." In Stephen Everson (ed.), *Epistemology*, 85–115. Companions to Ancient Thought 1. Cambridge: Cambridge University Press, 1990. Reprinted in Fine (ed.), *Plato*, vol. 1, *Metaphysics and Epistemology*, 215–46. Oxford: Oxford University Press, 1999.

———. "Knowledge and True Belief in the *Meno*." *Oxford Studies in Ancient Philosophy* 27 (2004): 41–81.

Fine, Gail. "Nozick's Socrates." *Phronesis* 41 (1996): 233–44.

———. *Plato on Knowledge and Forms: Selected Essays.* Oxford: Oxford University Press, 2003.

———. "Sceptical Enquiry." In D. Charles (ed.), *Definition in Greek Philosophy*, 342–77. Oxford: Clarendon Press, 2010.

———. "Sextus and External World Scepticism." *Oxford Studies in Ancient Philosophy* 23 (2003): 341–85.

Frede, Dorothea. "Rumpelstiltskin's Pleasures: True and False Pleasures in Plato's *Philebus*." *Phronesis* 30 (1985): 151–80.

Frede, Michael. "An Empiricist View of Knowledge: Memorism." In Stephen Everson (ed.), *Epistemology*, 225–50. Companions to Ancient Thought 1. Cambridge: Cambridge University Press, 1990.

———. *A Free Will: Origins of the Notion in Ancient Thought.* Berkeley: University of California Press, 2011.

———. Introduction to Michael Frede and Gisela Striker, *Rationality in Greek Thought*, 1–28. Oxford: Oxford University Press, 1996.

———. "The Literary Form of the Sophist." In Christopher Gill and Mary Margaret McCabe (eds.), *Form and Argument in Late Plato*, 135–52. Oxford: Oxford University Press, 1996.

———. "Observations on Perception in Plato's Later Dialogues." In Gail Fine (ed.), *Plato*, vol. 1, *Metaphysics and Epistemology*, 377–83. Oxford: Oxford University Press, 1999

———. "Plato's Arguments and the Dialogue Form." *Oxford Studies in Ancient Philosophy*, sup. vol. (1992): 201–19.

———. "The Sceptic's Two Kinds of Assent and the Question of the Possibility of Knowledge." In R. Rorty, J. B. Schneewind, and Q. Skinner (eds.), *Philosophy in History*, 255–78. Cambridge: Cambridge University Press, 1984. Reprinted in Myles Burnyeat and Michael Frede (eds.), *The Original Sceptics: A Controversy*, 127–51. Indianapolis: Hackett, 1997.

———. "Des Skeptikers Meinungen." *Neue Hefte für Philosophie* 15–16 (1979): 102–29. Reprinted as "The Sceptic's Beliefs." In Myles Burnyeat and Michael Frede (eds.), *The Original Sceptics: A Controversy*, 1–24. Indianapolis: Hackett, 1997.

———. "The Stoic Conception of Reason." In K. J. Boudouris (ed.), *Hellenistic Philosophy*, vol. 2, 50–61. Athens: International Center for Greek Philosophy, 1994.

———. "The Stoic Doctrine of the Affections of the Soul." In Malcolm Schofield and Gisela Striker (eds.), *The Norms of Nature: Studies in Hellenistic Ethics*, 93–110. Cambridge: Cambridge University Press, 1986.

———. "Stoic Epistemology." In K. Algra, J. Barnes, J. Mansfeld, and M. Schofield (eds.), *The Cambridge History of Hellenistic Philosophy*, 295–322. Cambridge: Cambridge University Press, 1999.

———. "Stoics and Sceptics on Clear and Distinct Impressions." In Myles Burnyeat (ed.), *The Sceptical Tradition*, 65–94. Berkeley: University of California Press, 1983.

———. *Die stoische Logik.* Göttingen: Vandenhoeck und Ruprecht, 1974.

Gonzalez, F. G. "Propositions or Objects? A Critique of Gail Fine on Knowledge and Belief in Republic V." *Phronesis* 41 (1996): 245–75.

Gosling, J. C. B. "Doxa and dunamis in Plato's Republic." *Phronesis* 13 (1968): 119–30.

———. "Republic V: *ta polla kalla* etc." *Phronesis* 5 (1960): 116–28.

Grgic, Filip. "Sextus Empiricus on the Possibility of Inquiry." *Pacific Philosophical Quarterly* 89 (2008): 436–59.

Hankinson, R. J. *The Sceptics.* London: Routledge, 1995.

Haidt, Jonathan, Fredrik Bjorklund, and Scott Murphy. "Moral Dumbfounding: When Intuitions Find No Reasons." 2000. http://faculty.virginia.edu/haidtlab/articles/manuscripts/haidt.bjorklund.working-paper.when%20intuition%20finds%20no%20reason.pub603.doc.

Holton, Richard. "Partial Belief, Partial Intention." *Mind* 117 (2008): 27–58.

Horwich, Paul. "The Value of Truth." *Nous* 40 (2006): 347–60.

Inwood, Brad (ed). *The Cambridge Companion to the Stoics.* Cambridge: Cambridge University Press, 2003.

Ioppolo, Anna Maria. *Opinione e Scienza: Il dibattito tra Stoizi e Academici nel III e nel II a. C.* Naples: Bibliopolis, 1986.

———. "Presentation and Assent: A Physical and Cognitive Problem in Early Stoicism." *Classical Quarterly* 40 (1990): 433–49.

Irwin, Terence. *Plato's Moral Theory.* Oxford: Clarendon Press, 1977.

Janaçek, Karl. *Prolegomena to Sextus Empiricus.* Olomouc: N.p., 1948.

———. "Skeptische Zweitropenlehre und Sextus Empiricus." *Eirene* 8 (1970): 47–55.

Kahn, Charles H. "The Greek Verb 'Be' and the Concept of Being." *Foundations of Language* 2 (1966): 245–65.

———. *Plato and the Socratic Dialogue: The Philosophical Use of a Literary Form.* Cambridge: Cambridge University Press, 1996.

———. "The Presentation of the Forms." In Kahn, *Plato and the Socratic Dialogue. The Philosophical Use of a Literary Form*, 329–70. Cambridge: Cambridge University Press, 1996.

———. "Some Philosophical Uses of "to be" in Plato." *Phronesis* 26 (1981): 105–35.

Kasser, Jeff, and Shah, Nishi. "The Metaethics of Belief: An Expressivist Reading of 'The Will to Believe.'" *Social Epistemology* 20.1 (2006): 1–17.

Inwood, Brad. "Moral Judgement in Seneca." In Inwood, *Reading Seneca: Stoic Philosophy in Rome*, 201–23. Oxford: Oxford University Press, 2005.

Lear, Jonathan. *A Case for Irony.* Cambridge, Mass.: Harvard University Press, 2011.

Lee, Mi-Kyoung. "Antecedents in Early Greek Philosophy." In Richard Bett (ed.), *Cambridge Companion to Ancient Scepticism*, 13–35. Cambridge: Cambridge University Press, 2010.

——. *Epistemology after Protagoras: Responses to Relativism in Plato, Aristotle, and Democritus*. Oxford: Oxford University Press, 2005.

Levi, Isaac. "Knowledge as True Belief." In Eric J. Olsson and Sebastian Enqvist (eds.), *Belief Revision Meets Philosophy of Science*, 269–302. Dordrecht: Springer, 2011.

Long, Alex. *Conversation and Self-Sufficiency in Plato*. Forthcoming from Oxford University Press.

Long, A. A. "How Does Socrates' Divine Sign Communicate with Him?" In S. Ahbel-Rappe and R. Kamtekar (eds.), *Blackwell Companion to Socrates*, 63–74. Oxford: Oxford University Press, 2006.

——. "Zeno's Epistemology and Plato's *Theaetetus*." In Long, *From Epicurus to Epictetus: Studies in Hellenistic and Roman Philosophy*, 223–35. Oxford: Oxford University Press, 2006.

MacFarlane, John. "Relativism and Disagreement." *Philosophical Studies* 132 (2007): 17–31.

Matthew, Gareth. "Socratic Ignorance." In Hugh H. Benson (ed.), *A Companion to Plato*, 103–18. Malden, Mass.: Blackwell, 2006.

——. *Socratic Perplexity*. Oxford: Oxford University Press, 1999.

McCabe, Mary Margaret. "Form and the Platonic Dialogues." In Hugh H. Benson, *A Companion to Plato*, 39–54. Malden, Mass.: Blackwell, 2006.

McDowell, John. "Identity Mistakes: Plato and the Logical Atomists." *Proceedings of the Aristotelian Society* 70 (1970): 181–96.

McPherran, M. "Ataraxia and Eudaimonia in Ancient Pyrrhonism: Is the Sceptic Really Happy?" *Proceedings of the Boston Area Colloquium in Ancient Philosophy* 5 (1989): 135–71.

——. "Socrates and the Duty to Philosophize." *Southern Journal of Philosophy* 24 (1986): 283–309.

Meinwald, Constance. "Ignorance and Opinion in Stoic Epistemology." *Phronesis* 50 (2005): 215–31.

Morris, T. F. "Plato's *Ion* and What Poetry Is About." *Ancient Philosophy* 13 (1993): 265–72.

Morrison, Donald. *Cambridge Companion to Socrates*. Cambridge: Cambridge University Press, 2011.

Nagel, Thomas. *The View from Nowhere*. New York: Oxford University Press, 1986.

Nehamas, Alexander. "Socratic Intellectualism." In John J. Cleary (ed.), *Proceedings of the Greater Boston Area Ancient Philosophy Colloquium*, vol. 2, 275–316. Washington, D.C.: University Press of America, 1986.

Nozick, Robert. "Socratic Puzzles." *Phronesis* 40 (1995): 143–55.

Nussbaum, Martha. "Skeptic Purgatives: Disturbance and the Life Without Belief." In Nussbaum, *The Therapy of Desire: Theory and Practice in Hellenistic Ethics*, 280–315. Princeton, N.J.: Princeton University Press, 1994.

Palmer, J. "Skeptical Investigation." *Ancient Philosophy* 20 (2000): 351–73.

Pappas, Nickolas. "Plato's 'Ion': The Problem of the Author." *Philosophy* 64 (1989): 381–89.

Peacocke, Christopher. *The Realm of Reason*. Oxford: Oxford University Press, 2006.

Perin, Casey. "Pyrrhonian Scepticism and the Search for Truth." *Oxford Studies in Ancient Philosophy* 30 (2006): 337–60.

Reed, Baron. "The Stoics' Account of the Cognitive Impression." *Oxford Studies in Ancient Philosophy* 23 (2002): 147–79.

Reeve, C. D. C. *Socrates in the Apology: An Essay on Plato's Apology of Socrates*. Hackett: Indianapolis, 1989.

Romm, James S. *The Edges of the Earth in Ancient Thought: Geography, Exploration, and Fiction*. Princeton, N.J.: Princeton University Press, 1992.

Rowe, Christopher. "Interpreting Plato." In Hugh H. Benson (ed.), *A Companion to Plato*, 13–24. Malden, Mass.: Blackwell, 2006.

Schofield, Malcolm. "Aenesidemus: Pyrrhonist and Heraclitean." In A. M. Ioppolo and D. Sedley (eds.), *Pyrrhonists, Patricians, Platonizers: Hellenistic Philosophy in the Period 155–86 BC*, 269–338. Naples: Bibliopolis, 2007.

Schwitzgebel, Eric. "Acting Contrary to Our Professed Beliefs, or The Gulf between Occurrent Judgments and Dispositional Belief." *Pacific Philosophical Quarterly* 91 (2010): 531–53.

———. "Self-Ignorance." In JeeLoo Liu and John Perry (eds.), *Consciousness and the Self: New Essays*, 184–97. Cambridge: Cambridge University Press, 2011.

Scott, Dominic. *Plato's Meno*. Cambridge: Cambridge University Press, 2006.

———. *Recollection and Experience: Plato's Theory of Learning and Its Successors*. Cambridge: Cambridge University Press, 1995.

Sedley, David. "The Collapse of Language? *Theaetetus* 179c–183c." *Plato* 3 (2003). http://gramata.univ-paris1.fr/Plato/article38.html.

———. *The Midwife of Platonism: Text and Subtext in Plato's Theaetetus*. Oxford: Oxford University Press, 2004.

———. "Three Ancient Interpretations of the *Theaetetus*." In Christopher Gill and Mary Margaret McCabe (eds.), *Form and Argument in Late Plato*, 79–104. Oxford: Oxford University Press, 1996.

Shah, Nishi. "How Truth Governs Belief." *Philosophical Review* 112 (2003): 447–82.

Shah, Nishi, and David Velleman. "Doxastic Deliberation." *Philosophical Review* 114 (2005): 497–534.

Sherman, Nancy. *Stoic Warriors: The Ancient Philosophy behind Military Minds*. Oxford: Oxford University Press, 2005.

Shields, Christopher. "The Truth Evaluability of Stoic Phantasiai: Adversus Mathematicos 7.242–46." *Journal of the History of Philosophy* 31.3 (1993): 325–47

Sosa, Ernest. "Value Matters in Epistemology." *Journal of Philosophy* 107.4 (2010): 167–90.

———. *A Virtue Epistemology: Apt Belief and Reflective Knowledge*. New York: Oxford University Press, 2007.

Sprute, Jürgen. "Der Begriff der DOXA in der platonischen Philosophie." *Hypomnemata. Untersuchungen zur Antike und ihrem Nachleben*. Vol. 2. Göttingen: Vandenhoeck und Ruprecht, 1962.

Stern-Gillet, Suzanne. "On (Mis)interpreting Plato's 'Ion.'" *Phronesis* 49 (2004): 169–201.

Stokes, Michael. "Plato and the Sightlovers of the Republic." *Apeiron* 25 (1992): 103–32.

Striker, Gisela. "κριτηριον της αληθειας." *Nachrichten der Akademie der Wissenschaften in Göttingen, Phil.-hist. Kl.* 1974, 47–110.

———. "Plato's Socrates and the Stoics." In Paul Vander Waerdt (ed.), *The Socratic Movement*, 241–71. Ithaca: Cornell University Press, 1994.

———. "Sceptical Strategies." In Malcolm Schofield, Myles Burnyeat, and Jonathan Barnes (eds.), *Doubt and Dogmatism: Studies in Hellenistic Epistemology*, 54–83. Oxford: Oxford University Press, 1980. Reprinted in Striker, *Essays on Hellenistic Epistemology and Ethics*, 92–115. Cambridge: Cambridge University Press, 1996.

———. "Scepticism as a Kind of Philosophy." *Archiv für Geschichte der Philosophie* 83 (2001): 113–29.

Stroud, Sarah. "Epistemic Partiality in Friendship." *Ethics* 116 (2006): 498–524.

Szaif, Jan. *Platons Begriff der Wahrheit*. Freiburg: Alber, 1996.

Tarrant, Harold. "Socratic Method and Socratic Truth." In S. Ahbel-Rappe and R. Kamtekar (eds.), *Blackwell Companion to Socrates*, 254–72. Oxford: Oxford University Press, 2006.

Taylor, Shelley E., and Jonathan D. Brown. "Illusion and Well-Being: A Social-Psychological Perspective on Mental Health." *Psychological Bulletin* 103 (1988): 193–210.

Vander Waerdt, Paul. *The Socratic Movement*. Ithaca: Cornell University Press, 1994.

Van Eck, Job. "Fine's Plato." *Oxford Studies in Ancient Philosophy* 28 (2005): 303–26.

Van Fraasen, Bas C. "Belief and the Will." *Journal of Philosophy* 81 (1984): 235–56.

Velleman, David. "On the Aim of Belief." In Velleman, *The Possibility of Practical Reason*, 244–81. Oxford: Oxford University Press, 2000.

Vlastos, Gregory. *Platonic Studies*. Princeton, N.J.: Princeton University Press, 1973.

———. "Socrates' Disavowal of Knowledge." *Philosophical Quarterly* 35 (1985): 1–31.

———. *Socrates, Ironist and Moral Philosopher.* Ithaca: Cornell University Press, 1991.

Vogt, Katja Maria. "Academic Scepticism." In Frisbee Sheffield and James Warren (eds.), *Routledge Companion to Ancient Philosophy.* Forthcoming from Routledge.

———. "Appearances and Assent: Skeptical Belief Reconsidered." Forthcoming from *Classical Quarterly.*

———. "Plato on Madness and the Good Life." In William Harris (ed.), *Mental Disorders in Antiquity.* Forthcoming.

———. Review of Michael Frede, *A Free Will. Classical Philology* 107 (2012): 161–68.

———. "The Aims of Sceptical Investigation." In Diego Machuca (ed.), *Pyrrhonism in Ancient, Modern, and Contemporary Philosophy*, 33–50. Dordrecht: Springer, 2011.

———. "Ancient Skepticism." In Edward N. Zalta (ed.), *Stanford Encyclopedia of Philosophy* (Spring 2010 edition). http://plato.stanford.edu/entries/skepticism-ancient/.

———. "Scepticism and Action." In Richard Bett (ed.), *The Cambridge Companion to Ancient Greek Scepticism*, 165–80. Cambridge: Cambridge University Press, 2010.

———. "Why Pleasure Gains Fifth Rank: Against the Anti-hedonist Interpretation of the *Philebus.*" In John Dillon and Luc Brisson (eds.), *Plato's Philebus*, 250–55. St. Augustin: Akademia Verlag, 2010.

———. "Belief and Investigation in Plato's Republic." *Plato* 9 (2009): 1–24.

———. "Sons of the Earth: Are the Stoics Metaphysical Brutes?" *Phronesis* 54 (2009): 136–54.

———. "The Good Is Benefit: On the Stoic Definition of the Good." In *Proceedings of the Boston Area Colloquium in Ancient Philosophy*, 155–74. Leiden: Brill, 2008.

———. *Law, Reason, and the Cosmic City: Political Philosophy in the Early Stoa.* New York: Oxford University Press, 2008.

———. "Skeptische Untersuchung und das Verstehen von Begriffen." In Ch. Rapp and T. Wagner (eds.), *Wissen und Bildung in der antiken Philosophie*, 325–39. Stuttgart: Metzler, 2006.

———. "Die stoische Theorie der Emotionen." In Barbara Guckes (ed.), *Zur Ethik der älteren Stoa*, 69–93. Göttingen: Vandenhoeck und Ruprecht, 2004.

———. *Skepsis und Lebenspraxis: Das pyrrhonische Leben ohne Meinungen.* Freiburg: Alber, 1998.

Wedgwood, Ralph. "The Aim of Belief." *Philosophical Perspectives* 16 (2002): 267–97.

Wildberg, Christian. "Socrates and Euripides." In S. Ahbel-Rappe and R. Kamtekar (eds.), *Blackwell Companion to Socrates*, 21–35. Oxford: Oxford University Press, 2006.

Williams, Bernard. "Deciding to Believe." In Williams, *Problems of the Self: Philosophical Papers 1956–72*, 136–37. Cambridge: Cambridge University Press, 1974.

———. "Relativism, History, and the Existence of Values." In Jay Wallace (ed.), *Joseph Raz: The Practice of Value*, 16–20. Oxford: Oxford University Press, 2005.

Williamson, Timothy. *Knowledge and Its Limits*. Oxford: Oxford University Press, 2000.

———. "The Truth in Relativism." *Proceedings of the Aristotelian Society* 75 (1974–75): 215–28.

Wolfsdorf, David. "Socrates' Avowals of Knowledge." *Phronesis* 49 (2004): 75–142.

Woodruff, Paul. "The Skeptical Side of Plato's Method." *Revue Internationale de Philosophie* 156–57 (1986): 22–37.

———. "Expert Knowledge in the Apology and the Laches: What a General Needs to Know." *Proceedings of the Boston Area Colloquium in Ancient Philosophy* 3 (1987): 79–115.

———. "Plato's early theory of knowledge." In Stephen Everson, *Epistemology*, 60–84. Companions to Ancient Thought 1. Cambridge: Cambridge University Press. Reprinted in Hugh H. Benson (ed.), *Essays on Socrates*. Oxford: Oxford University Press, 1992.

Woodruff, Paul, and Nicholas D. Smith (eds.). *Reason and Religion in Socratic Philosophy*. Oxford: Oxford University Press, 2000.

Woolf, Raphael. "Misology and Truth." In John J. Cleary and Gary M. Gurtler (eds.), *Proceedings of the Boston Area Colloquium in Ancient Philosophy* 23 (2007): 1–16.

———. "Socratic Authority." *Archiv für Geschichte der Philosophie* 90 (2008): 1–38.

———. "Truth as a Value in Plato's Republic." *Phronesis* 54 (2009): 9–39.

Wright, Crispin. "Intuitionism, Realism, Relativism, and Rhubarb." In P. Greenough and M. P. Lynch (eds.), *Truth and Realism*, 77–99. Oxford: Oxford University Press, 2006.

Index

CPSIA information can be obtained at www.ICGtesting.com
Printed in the USA
LVOW06s0202280715

447794LV00006B/9/P

9 780190 277192